SCHOLASTIC

100 ENGLISH LESSONS

Terms and conditions

IMPORTANT – PERMITTED USE AND WARNINGS – READ CAREFULLY BEFORE USING

Recommended system requirements:

- Windows: XP (Service Pack 3), Vista (Service Pack 2), Windows 7 or Windows 8 with 2.33GHz processor
- Mac: OS 10.6 to 10.8 with Intel Core™ Duo processor
- 1GB RAM (recommended)
- 1024 x 768 Screen resolution
- CD-ROM drive (24x speed recommended)
- 16-bit sound card
- Adobe Reader (version 9 recommended for Mac users)
- Broadband internet connections (for installation and updates)

For all technical support queries, please phone Scholastic Customer Services on 0845 6039091.

SCHOLASTIC

Book End, Range Road, Witney, Oxfordshire, OX29 0YD
www.scholastic.co.uk

© 2014, Scholastic Ltd

2 3 4 5 6 7 8 9   4 5 6 7 8 9 0 1 2 3

British Library Cataloguing-in-Publication Data
A catalogue record for this book is available from the
British Library.

ISBN 978-1407-12759-0
Printed by Bell & Bain Ltd, Glasgow

Due to the nature of the web we cannot guarantee the
content or links of any site mentioned. We strongly
recommend that teachers check websites before using
them in the classroom.

Extracts from *The National Curriculum in English, English
Programme of Study* © Crown Copyright. Reproduced
under the terms of the Open Government Licence
(OGL). http://www.nationalarchives.gov.uk/doc/open-
government-licence/open-government-licence.htm

Author
Jean Evans

Editorial team
Rachel Morgan, Melissa Somers, Suzanne Adams,
Marion Archer

Cover Design
Andrea Lewis

Design Team
Sarah Garbett, Shelley Best and Andrea Lewis

CD-ROM development
Hannah Barnett, Phil Crothers, MWA Technologies
Private Ltd

Typesetting
Brian Melville

Illustrations
Cathy Hughes

Acknowledgements
The publishers gratefully acknowledge permission
to reproduce the following copyright material:

James Carter for the use of the poem 'A tree' by
James Carter first published in *Time-Travelling
Underpants* by James Carter. Poem © 2007, James
Carter (2007, Macmillan Children's Books).
Scholastic Inc for the use of the poem 'Raindrop' by
Helen H Moore, first published in *A Poem a Day* by
Helen H Moore. Poem © 1997, Helen H Moore (1997,
Scholastic Ltd).
Scholastic Inc for the use of the poem 'Water' by
Meish Goldish first published in *101 Science Poems
and Songs for Young Learners* by Meish Goldish.
Poem © 1996, Meish Goldish (1996, Scholastic Inc).
Spike Milligan Productions for the use of 'On the
Ning Nang Nong' by Spike Milligan from *Silly verse
for kids* by Spike Milligan. Poem © 1968, Spike
Milligan (1968, Puffin).
Walker Books Ltd for the use of an extract and
illustrations from *Handa's Surprise* by Eileen
Browne. Text and illustrations © 1994, Eileen
Browne (1994, Walker Books Ltd).

Every effort has been made to trace copyright
holders for the works reproduced in this book,
and the publishers apologise for any inadvertent
omissions.

The author wishes to thank her daughter, Charlotte
Spiers, Phonics Screening Check Administrator and
Year 1 Classroom Teacher at The Rydal Academy,
Darlington, for her helpful practical suggestions,
and the children of Class 6 for their positive and
constructive comments when trialling some of the
activities.

Contents

Introduction

About the series

The *100 English Lessons* series is designed to meet the requirements of the 2014 Curriculum, English Programmes of Study. There are six books in the series, Years 1–6, and each book contains lesson plans, resources and ideas matched to the new curriculum. It can be a complex task to ensure that a progressive and appropriate curriculum is followed in all year groups; this series has been carefully structured to ensure that a progressive and appropriate curriculum is followed throughout.

About the new curriculum

The curriculum documentation for English provides a single-year programme of study for Year 1 and Year 2, but joint programmes of study for Years 3–4 and Years 5–6.

There is a much greater focus on the technical aspects of language – including grammar, punctuation, spelling, handwriting and phonics. These are the building blocks to help children to read and write. It has been perceived that these aspects have to be taught discretely, however the approach encouraged in this series is to embed these elements into existing learning. For example, using a focus text to identify the use of punctuation and using that as a springboard to practise it.

There is a spoken language Programme of Study which outlines statutory requirements across Years 1–6. Within the English curriculum there are also attainment targets that involve 'discussion', 'talking', 'participating' and 'listening'. The aims of speaking and listening are below:

> The National Curriculum for English reflects the importance of spoken language in children's development across the whole curriculum – cognitively, socially and linguistically. The quality and variety of language that children hear and speak are vital for developing their vocabulary, grammar and their understanding for reading and writing. Teachers should therefore ensure the continual development of children's confidence and competence in spoken language. Children should develop a capacity to explain their understanding of books and other reading, and to prepare their ideas before they write. They must be assisted in making their thinking clear to themselves as well as to others and teachers should ensure that children build secure foundations by using discussion to probe and remedy their misconceptions. Children should also be taught to understand and use the conventions for discussion and debate.
>
> Statutory requirements which underpin all aspects of speaking and listening across the six years of primary education form part of the National Curriculum. These are contextualised within the reading and writing domains which follow.

Terminology

The curriculum terminology has changed; the main terms used are:

- **Domains:** The area of the subject, for English the domains are 'Reading' and 'Writing'.
- **Sub-domains:** The next level down to the domains. In English, Reading's sub-domains are 'Word reading' and 'Comprehension' and Writing's sub-domains are 'Transcription' and 'Composition'.
- **Curriculum objectives:** These are the statutory programme of study statements or objectives.
- **Appendix:** Any reference to an appendix refers to an appendix of the National Curriculum for English document. There are two appendices – one for spelling (Appendix 1) and one for vocabulary, grammar and punctuation (Appendix 2).

About the book

This book is divided into six chapters; each chapter contains a half-term's work and is based around a topic or theme. Each chapter follows the same structure:

Chapter introduction

At the start of each chapter there is a summary of what is covered. This includes:

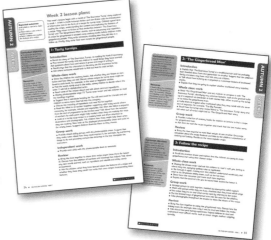

- **Introduction:** A description of what is covered in the chapter.
- **Expected prior learning:** What the children are expected to know before starting the work in the chapter.
- **Overview of progression:** A brief explanation of how the children progress through the chapter.
- **Creative context:** How the chapter could link to other curriculum areas.
- **Preparation:** Any resources required for the teaching of the chapter, including things that need to be sourced or prepared and the content that can be located on the CD-ROM.
- **Chapter at a glance:** This is a table that summarises the content of each lesson, including: the curriculum objectives (using a code system, please see pages 8–10), a summary of the activities and the outcome.
- **Background knowledge:** A section explaining grammatical terms and suchlike to enhance your subject knowledge, where required.

Lessons

Each chapter contains six weeks' of lessons, each week contains five lessons. At the start of each week there is an introduction about what is covered and the expected outcomes. The lesson plans then include the relevant combination of headings from below.

- **Curriculum objectives:** A list of the relevant objectives from the Programme of Study.
- **Resources:** What you require to teach the lesson.
- **Introduction:** A short and engaging activity to begin the lesson.
- **Whole-class work:** Working together as a class.
- **Group/Paired/Independent work:** Children working independently of the teacher in pairs, groups or alone.
- **Differentiation:** Ideas for how to support children who are struggling with a concept or how to extend those children who understand a concept without taking them onto new work.
- **Review:** A chance to review the children's learning and ensure the outcomes of the lesson have been achieved.

Assess and review

At the end of each chapter are activities for assessing and reviewing the children's understanding. These can be conducted during the course of the chapter's work or saved until the end of the chapter or done at a later date. There are four focuses for assess and review activities in each chapter:

- Grammar and punctuation
- Spelling
- Reading
- Writing

Elements of speaking and listening will be included where relevant within these four areas.

All four focuses follow the same format:

- **Curriculum objectives:** These are the areas of focus for the assess and review activity. There may be one focus or more than one depending on the activity.
- **Resources:** What you require to conduct the activities.
- **Revise:** A series of short activities or one longer activity to revise and consolidate the children's learning and ensure they understand the concept(s).
- **Assess:** An assessment activity to provide a chance for the children to demonstrate their understanding and for you to check this.
- **Further practice:** Ideas for further practice on the focus, whether children are insecure in their learning or you want to provide extra practice or challenge.

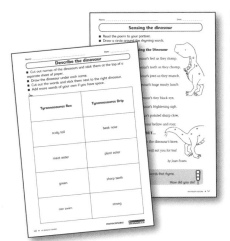

Photocopiable pages

At the end of each chapter are some photocopiable pages that will have been referred to in the lesson plans. These sheets are for the children to use; there is generally a title, an instruction, an activity and an 'I can' statement at the bottom. These sheets are also provided on the CD-ROM alongside additional pages as referenced in the lessons (see page 7 About the CD-ROM). The children should be encouraged to complete the 'I can' statements by colouring in the traffic lights to say how they think they have done (red – not very well, amber – ok, green – very well).

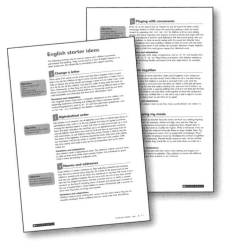

English starter activities

At the beginning of the book there is a bank of English starter activities (pages 11–14). These are games and activities that will help children familiarise and consolidate their knowledge of grammar, punctuation and spelling. The use of these will be suggested throughout the chapters, but they are also flexible and therefore could be used at any time.

SCHOLASTIC

About the CD-ROM

The CD-ROM contains:
- Printable versions of the photocopiable sheets from the book and additional photocopiable sheets as referenced in the lesson plans.
- Interactive activities for children to complete or to use on the whiteboard.
- Media resources to display.
- Printable versions of the lesson plans.
- Digital versions of the lesson plans with the relevant resources linked to them.

Getting started
- Put the CD-ROM into your CD-ROM drive.
  - For Windows users, the install wizard should autorun, if it fails to do so then navigate to your CD-ROM drive. Then follow the installation process.
  - For Mac users, copy the disk image file to your hard drive. After it has finished copying double-click it to mount the disk image. Navigate to the mounted disk image and run the installer. After installation the disk image can be unmounted and the DMG can be deleted from the hard drive.
- To complete the installation of the program you need to open the program and click 'Update' in the pop-up. Please note – this CD-ROM is web-enabled and the content will be downloaded from the internet to your hard-drive to populate the CD-ROM with the relevant resources. This only needs to be done on first use, after this you will be able to use the CD-ROM without an internet connection. If at any point any content is updated you will receive another pop-up upon start up with an internet connection.

Navigating the CD-ROM
There are two options to navigate the CD-ROM either as a Child or as a Teacher.

Child
- Click on the 'Child' button on the first menu screen.
- In the second menu click on the relevant class (please note only the books installed on the machine or network will be accessible. You can also rename year groups to match your school's naming conventions via the Teacher > Settings > Rename books area).
- A list of interactive activities will be displayed, children need to locate the correct one and click 'Go' to launch it.
- There is the opportunity to print or save a PDF of the activity at the end.

Teacher
- Click on the Teacher button on the first menu screen and you will be taken to a screen showing which of the *100 English* books you have purchased. From here, you can also access information about getting started and the credits.
- To enter the product click 'Next' in the bottom right.
- You then need to enter a password (the password is: login).
- On first use:
  - Enter as a Guest by clicking on the 'Guest' button.
  - If desired, create a profile for yourself by adding your name to the list of users. Profiles allow you to save favourites and to specify which year group(s) you wish to be able to view.
  - Go to 'Settings' to create a profile for yourself – click 'Add user' and enter your name. Then choose the year groups you wish to have access to (you can return to this screen to change this at any time). Click on 'Login' at the top of the screen to re-enter the disk under your new profile.
- On subsequent uses you can choose your name from the drop-down list. The 'Guest' option will always be available if you, or a colleague, wish to use this.
- You can search the CD-ROM using the tools or save favourites.

For more information about how to use the CD-ROM, please refer to the help file which can be found in the teacher area of the CD-ROM. It is a red button with a question mark on it on the right-hand side of the screen just underneath the 'Settings' tab.

Curriculum grid

This grid shows the full curriculum objectives for Year 1. The codes are referenced in the chapter introductions. Additional information is provided in italics, this includes the statutory information from the appendices.

Domain	Code	Curriculum objective
Reading: Word reading	RWR1	To apply phonic knowledge and skills as the route to decode words.
	RWR2	To respond speedily with the correct sound to graphemes (letters or groups of letters) for all 40+ phonemes, including, where applicable, alternative sounds for graphemes.
	RWR3	To read accurately by blending sounds in unfamiliar words containing GPCs that have been taught.
	RWR4	To read common exception words, noting unusual correspondences between spelling and sound and where these occur in the word.
	RWR5	To read words containing taught GPCs and '-s', '-es', '-ing', '-ed', '-er' and '-est' endings.
	RWR6	To read other words of more than one syllable that contain taught GPCs.
	RWR7	To read words with contractions and understand that the apostrophe represents the omitted letter(s).
	RWR8	To read aloud accurately books that are consistent with their developing phonic knowledge and that do not require them to use other strategies to work out words.
	RWR9	To re-read these books to build up their fluency and confidence in word reading.
Reading: Comprehension	RC1	To develop pleasure in reading, motivation to read, vocabulary and understanding by listening to and discussing a wide range of poems, stories and non-fiction at a level beyond that at which they can read independently.
	RC2	To develop pleasure in reading, motivation to read, vocabulary and understanding by being encouraged to link what they read or hear read to their own experiences.
	RC3	To develop pleasure in reading, motivation to read, vocabulary and understanding by becoming very familiar with key stories, fairy stories and traditional tales, retelling them and considering their particular characteristics.
	RC4	To develop pleasure in reading, motivation to read, vocabulary and understanding by recognising and joining in with predictable phrases.
	RC5	To develop pleasure in reading, motivation to read, vocabulary and understanding by learning to appreciate rhymes and poems, and to recite some by heart.
	RC6	To develop pleasure in reading, motivation to read, vocabulary and understanding by discussing word meanings, linking new meanings to those already known.
	RC7	To understand books read and listened to by drawing on what they already know or on background information and vocabulary provided by the teacher.
	RC8	To understand books read and listened to by checking that the text makes sense to them as they read and correcting inaccurate reading.
	RC9	To understand books read and listened to by discussing the significance of the title and events.
	RC10	To understand books read and listened to by making inferences on the basis of what is being said and done.

Domain	Code	Curriculum objective
Reading: Comprehension	RC11	To understand books read and listened to by predicting what might happen on the basis of what has been read so far.
	RC12	To participate in discussion about what is read to them, taking turns and listening to what others say.
	RC13	To explain clearly their understanding of what is read to them.
Writing: Transcription	WT1	To spell words containing each of the 40+ phonemes already taught.
	WT2	To spell common exception words.
	WT3	To spell days of the week.
	WT4	To name the letters of the alphabet in order.
	WT5	To name the letters of the alphabet using letter names to distinguish between alternative spellings of the same sound.
	WT6	To add prefixes and suffixes using the spelling rule for adding '-s' or '-es' as the plural marker for nouns and the third person singular marker for verbs.
	WT7	To add prefixes and suffixes using the prefix 'un-'.
	WT8	To add prefixes and suffixes using '-ing', '-ed', '-er' and '-est' where no change is needed in the spelling of root words.
	WT9	To apply simple spelling rules and guidelines, as listed in English Appendix 1. *Including:* ● */f/, /l/, /s/, /z/ and /k/ spelled 'ff', 'll', 'ss' and 'ck'.* ● *The 'ng' sound spelled 'n' before 'k'.* ● *Division of words into syllables.* ● *'-tch', 'wh', 'ph', 'k' for /k/, /v/ sound at the end of words.* ● *New vowel representations including digraphs and trigraphs.* ● *Words ending in '-y'.* ● *Compound words.* ● *Common exception words.*
	WT10	To write from memory simple sentences dictated by the teacher that include words using the GPCs and common exception words taught so far.
	WT11	To sit correctly at a table, holding a pencil comfortably and correctly.
	WT12	To begin to form lower-case letters in the correct direction, starting and finishing in the right place.
	WT13	To form capital letters.
	WT14	To form digits 0-9.
	WT15	To understand which letters belong to which handwriting 'families' and to practise these.

Domain	Code	Curriculum objective
Writing: Composition	WC1	To write sentences by saying out loud what they are going to write about.
	WC2	To write sentences by composing a sentence orally before writing it.
	WC3	To write sentences by sequencing sentences to form short narratives.
	WC4	To write sentences by re-reading what they have written to check that it makes sense.
	WC5	To discuss what they have written with the teacher or other children.
	WC6	To read aloud their writing clearly enough to be heard by their peers and the teacher.
	WC7	To develop their understanding of the concepts set out in English Appendix 2 by leaving spaces between words.
	WC8	To develop their understanding of the concepts set out in English Appendix 2 by joining words and joining sentences using *and*.
	WC9	To develop their understanding of the concepts set out in English Appendix 2 by beginning to punctuate sentences using a capital letter and a full stop, question mark or exclamation mark.
	WC10	To develop their understanding of the concepts set out in English Appendix 2 by using a capital letter for names of people, places, the days of the week, and the personal pronoun *I*.
	WC11	To develop their understanding of the concepts set out in English Appendix 2 by learning the grammar for Year 1 in English Appendix 2. *Concepts for Year 1:* ● *Plural noun suffixes, including the effects of these suffixes on the meaning of the noun.* ● *Suffixes that can be added to verbs where no change in needed in the spelling of root words.* ● *How the prefix 'un-' changes the meaning of verbs and adjectives.*
	WC12	To use the grammatical terminology in English Appendix 2 in discussing their writing. *Terminology for Year 1: letter, capital letter, word, singular, plural, sentence, punctuation, full stop, question mark, explanation mark.*

English starter ideas

The following activities can be used to support your children's grammar, punctuation and spelling. They can be used as a part of English lessons or at other points over the school day to consolidate and support learning.

1 Change a letter

Objectives
- To spell regular CVC words.
- To apply phonic knowledge and skills as the route to decode words.

Write some CVC words on the board and read them together. Point to each letter and ask the children to say its name and the sound that it makes. Ask a child to choose one of the words and change a letter in it to make a new word, as in *fit, bit, bin*. At first children may find this easier if they write the word on their whiteboards so that they can see the letters and try different ones in their places. Go around the class asking children to change the word by one letter until possibilities are exhausted and then start with another word.

Variations and adaptations
Use magnetic letters if you have a magnetic whiteboard so that children can physically experience removing and adding the letters. Introduce double-consonant graphemes, such as 'sh', 'ch', and then alternative graphemes, such as 'oa', 'ow', 'o-e', according to the children's reading levels.

2 Alphabetical order

Objectives
- To name the letters of the alphabet in order.

Ask children to sit around a set of alphabet cards that are placed face down, in alphabetical order, with 'a' at the top. Explain that they are going to practise naming the alphabet letters in order. Ask them to take turns to pick up a card, name the letter and place the card face up, in an alphabetical line. Continue until all children have had a turn and all cards are face up (you may have to add more letters, or ask children more than once). Choose a child to say the first letter of the alphabet. Continue around the circle, with each child saying the next letter until the last letter is reached. Now start with another child, this time asking each child to pick up the corresponding card to the letter called out.

Variations and adaptations
Give children cards in alphabetical order. Tap alternate children and ask them to hold up their cards while others remain hidden. Ask individuals to guess hidden letters by looking at adjacent cards.

3 Names and addresses

Objectives
- To use a capital letter for the names of people, places and the personal pronoun *I*.

Invite children to write a sentence on their individual whiteboards including their full name and the place they live. Sit in front of the board and put the children's whiteboards on the floor. Ask individuals to say their full name in turn and clap the syllables together. Do the same with the rest of the class. Decide who has the longest first name, shortest surname and so on. Write a sample sentence on the board including names of people and places and comment on the use of capital letters. Invite children to swap whiteboards with a partner to check that they have correctly used capitals.

Variations and adaptations
Children could practise writing their names and the place where they live on recycled envelopes. More confident learners could write their full address.

4 Playing with consonants

Objectives
● To apply phonic knowledge and skills as the route to decode words.
● To respond speedily with the correct sound to graphemes for all 40+ phonemes, including, where applicable, alternative sounds for graphemes.

Write 'sh' on the board and ask children to say the sound the letters make. Encourage children to think about the sound by creating a chant to stamp around to, repeating /sh/, /sh/, /sh/, /sh/. Sit children in three same-ability groups. Ask those requiring more support to think of words that begin with this sound, and allocate a word to each individual. Ask the second group, who are more confident, to think of words ending with this sound and allocate these words. Challenge the most confident children to think of words with this letter combination somewhere in the middle, for example, *fisherman*. Invent rhythmic chants with a child from each group saying their allocated word.

Variations and adaptations
Do the same with other letter combinations, such as 'ch', 'th', and double-letter endings, 'ff', 'ss', 'll', 'zz', 'ck'. Play linking card games, with children making up words by combining double-consonant cards and single letters, for example, *b-i-ll, ch-a-t*.

5 Join together

Objectives
● To apply phonic knowledge and skills as the route to decode words.
● To read compound words by reading each component word separately.

Create two sets of word cards that, when paired together, form compound words (*sea* and *shore*, *bed* and *room*). Invite children to sit in two lines facing each other. Give the children in one line a card each from a set. Give the children opposite a card each from the other set. Select a child and ask them to stand facing the two lines before reading their own card and holding it up. The child who can make a word by adding their card to it can then join the first child and both children can hold their cards together to show the compound word. If children are satisfied this is a real word, ring a bell to signal a correct match. If not, hoot a horn to ask them to try again.

Variations and adaptations
Play this game using a timer to see how many words children can make in a given time.

6 Clapping my meals

Objectives
● To read words of more than one syllable.
● To recognise and join in with repeated phrases.

Encourage children to describe favourite meals and have fun creating rhyming strings with them, for example, *chicken and chips, curry and rice*. Clap the syllables or use percussion instruments to emphasise them. Repeat them in unison, changing the words to modify the rhythm. Write a restaurant menu on the board to include the children's favourite dishes as they mention them. Try to introduce some compound words, such as *peppermint, cheeseburger*. Read the final menu together breaking it down by identifying the number of syllables and tackling them separately. Present simple menus to read, ask the children to identify which dishes they would like to try and write down an order for a class feast.

Variations and adaptations
Clap children's names and read their name cards. Identify the longest and shortest name and count the syllables. Clap syllables to words with different themes, for example, farm animals or sea creatures.

7 More than one?

Objectives
● To read words containing taught GPCs and '-s', '-es', '-ing', '-ed', '-er' and '-est' endings.
● To use the spelling rule for adding '-s' or '-es' as the plural marker for nouns and the third-person singular marker for verbs.

Arrange children in two lines. Invite the child at the end of one line to call the name of an object to the child opposite, who responds by saying the word in plural. Continue to the end of the line and then swap over so that the opposite side name objects first. Remind children of the spelling rule for adding '-s' or '-es' as the plural marker for nouns. Name an object, or show a picture, and ask children to write the word on their whiteboards. Now ask them to write the same word in plural. Ensure that you provide some examples of nouns with '-es' plural endings, such as *bus, branch, dress*. Write each word on the board so that children can check spelling.

Variations and adaptations
Invite children to work in pairs, with one writing a word for their partner to write in plural, and then reverse this.

8 Make me different

Objectives
● To read words containing taught GPCs and '-s', '-es', '-ing', '-ed', '-er' and '-est' endings.

Remind children of any previous work on changing word endings and recall examples. Make a set of cards showing adjectives and verbs to which endings could be added, such as *fresh, quick, grand, hunt, buzz, jump*. Also make a set of cards displaying endings in large letters, for example '-s', '-es', '-ing', '-ed', '-er' and '-est'. Make several cards for each ending. Put the endings in separate piles on the floor in the middle of the children. Read the endings and give examples where they are used, such as *higher, highest, helped, helping, helper.* Explain that you are going to give a child a word to hold in the centre of the circle. Invite another child to choose one of the endings and link on to the first child to make a new word. If the result is a real word, ask the class to clap. Repeat with different endings and new words.

Variations and adaptations
Provide a selection of objects or images that could be compared, perhaps small-world animals of increasing size, or images of runners finishing a race. Make labels with comparison adjectives, such as *large, larger, largest* and *fast, faster, fastest* and ask children to match them to the objects or images.

9 Add my prefix

Objectives
● To use the prefix 'un-'.
● To spell words containing each of the phonemes already taught.

Create sets of word cards to which the prefix 'un-' could be added, such as *kind, happy, lock, fair*. Make another set of cards with 'un' written in large letters. Provide same-ability groups with a set of word cards and a prefix card. Ask the children to take turns to pick a word and read it to the others. Compose a story sentence together using the word, for example, *Once there was a kind witch who loved children.* Now ask them to put the prefix card in front of the word card to create the opposite word. Compose another sentence using this word, for example, *I am an unkind troll who eats children!* Continue in the same way with the remaining word cards. Support those who struggle with reading the words. Challenge confident children to write their sentences down to read to the class.

10 Join us together

Objectives
● To respond speedily with the correct sound to graphemes for all 40+ phonemes, including, where applicable, alternative sounds for graphemes.
● To read compound words by breaking them down into separate units.

Make individual word cards that can be paired to make longer words, for example *foot* and *ball*, *white* and *board*, *sea* and *shore*. Sort these into two piles so that they can be matched. Hold up some example cards and read them together, encouraging children to respond to graphemes already taught. Draw attention to words with alternative graphemes, for example *board* and *shore*. Sit in two rows, one row holding one set of words and the other the remaining set. Tap a child and ask them to show the word to the children opposite. If anyone has a word that can be joined to this word to make a longer word, they should walk over and take the first child into the centre. They then hold up their cards to make a compound word.

Variations and adaptations
Devise a flag system, holding up a green flag to verify a match and a red one to indicate no match.

11 Exception to the rule

Objectives
● To read exception words, noting unusual correspondences between spelling and sound and where these occur in the word.

Recall spelling rules already taught. Discuss what is meant by 'the exception to the rule'. Make cards depicting common exception words and write them on the board. Ask children which ones they recognise and try reading those they find difficult. Hide the display and play a game to see how quickly children recognise these words as you hold them up. Set a timer for a given time and display the words one by one. When children say the correct word, lower the card and lift up another. Continue until the buzzer goes to signal the end. Count how many words have been recognised and record this. Continue to do this regularly to see how well the children's recognition skills develop.

Variations and adaptations
Encourage children to play the game in threes, with one holding the cards up, one calling the words and the other timing and recording.

12 Bank or bin

Objectives
● To respond speedily with the correct sound to graphemes for all 40+ phonemes, including, where applicable, alternative sounds for graphemes.
● To apply phonic knowledge and skills as the route to decode words.

Write four sets of word cards containing already taught phonemes, including some with alternative graphemes, and the same number of nonsense words that can be plausibly decoded. Put the sets in separate buckets. Divide the class into four teams. Arrange four bins and four 'bank deposits' (boxes) at one end of the hall and the buckets midway. Blow a whistle to start the game. One child from each team must run to the team bucket, pull out a card, read it and drop it into the bin or bank deposit according to whether it is a real or nonsense word. They then run back and touch the next team member who does the same. Once all cards are placed, analyse the results. The first team to finish with all cards correctly placed is the winner.

Variations and adaptations
Use this idea to revise specific phonemes, digraph and trigraph combinations.

13 Captions and combinations

Objectives
● To join words and join sentences using *and*.
● To read aloud writing clearly enough to be heard by their peers and the teacher.

Create some three-word captions relating to food combinations with *and* joining the two nouns, such as *fish and chips*, *pie and peas*. Read one of the captions together, 'sound talking' each word if necessary. Do this with a few captions and ask the children to tell you what they have in common (food). Invite children to write a caption on their whiteboards showing two things they like to eat, using the word *and* to join the food words. Encourage them to read their captions aloud clearly so that the rest of the class can hear them.

Variations and adaptations

Have some pictures of different foods ready and ask children to choose suitable ones to pair and write a caption for, such as *soup and bread*, *sausage and chips*. Write captions for displays and sentences about favourite meals, joining distinct ideas with *and*, for example, describing the first and second courses.

14 Yes or no?

Objectives
● To respond speedily with the correct sound to graphemes for all 40+ phonemes, including, where applicable, alternative sounds for graphemes.
● To apply phonic knowledge and skills as the route to decode words.

Write a series of questions on cards to match the reading levels of the children so that they can decode words without difficulty. The questions could relate to a current topic you are covering in class. Make a separate set of cards with *Yes* on one side and *No* on the other. Ask children to work in same-ability pairs and provide *Yes/No* cards to indicate responses. Write a question on the board, or show a card, and allow time for pairs to read it and agree their response. Invite all children to hold up their cards and choose someone to read the sentence. Discuss any variations in the children's responses and re-read the question if necessary to provide the opportunity for children to realise errors and change decisions. Repeat with further questions.

Variations and adaptations

Invite confident pairs to compile questions for another pair to answer. Write theme- or book-related questions to revise new vocabulary and encourage understanding.

Dinosaurs

The dinosaur theme of this half-term is designed to engage children and provides opportunities to work as a class, in groups and pairs, and individually. After exploring popular dinosaur stories they move on to create a large classroom display, appreciate dinosaur poems and write both class and individual dinosaur stories. Prior learning is embedded and new learning opportunities are introduced.

Expected prior learning
- Can listen and respond.
- Can recite the alphabet and understand alphabetical order.
- Can recognise capital and lower-case letters.
- Know what a sentence is.
- Can recognise rhyme.
- Know that a story has characters, a setting and a plot.

Overview of progression
- Children develop their understanding of the terms *plot, character* and *setting* by exploring a dinosaur story. They consider the differences between fiction and non-fiction by searching reference books for dinosaur facts. They learn to create labels and captions, use correct sentence terminology and work with letters of the alphabet and alphabetical order by creating a classroom display.
- Poetry appreciation is developed as children read dinosaur poems and find rhyming words. Adding percussion helps them to identify the syllabic rhythm of the words.
- Writing a class dinosaur story introduces children to planning with storyboards and story maps, and provides opportunities to revisit plot, characters and setting. Finally, children write their own stories and read them to others, creating opportunities to revise sentence structure and punctuation.

Creative context
- Children are encouraged to express their ideas creatively, for example, using paint and collage to create a display, and use drama, role play, and small-world equipment to re-enact stories.
- Exploring dinosaurs through non-fiction books and models links with classification and habitats (science).
- Aspects of order and sequence (maths) are included in activities involving alphabetical order and ordering of story events.

Preparation
The text suggested for this chapter is *Tyrannosaurus Drip* by Julia Donaldson, this title also ties in with a later chapter focussed on the work of Julia Donaldson. However, you could use an alternative dinosaur story if you prefer.

You will also need:
Tyrannosaurus Drip by Julia Donaldson; draw string bag; selection of model dinosaurs and other animals; sticky notes; materials to create a swamp area; large sheets of paper; coloured pens; materials to make stick puppets; large bags; fiction and non-fiction books about dinosaurs; items for book shop role-play area; small-world farmyard equipment; dinosaur display materials; alphabet letter cards; book of dinosaur poems; percussion instruments; examples of comic strips.

On the CD-ROM you will find:
Media resource '*Tyrannosaurus Drip* book cover'; interactive activity 'Missing punctuation'; photocopiable pages: 'Extract from *Tyrannosaurus Drip*', 'Stick puppets'

Chapter at a glance

An overview of the chapter. For curriculum objective codes, please see pages 8–10.

Week	Lesson	Curriculum objectives	Summary of activities	Outcomes
1	1	RWR: 1, 3 RC: 6, 11	Compare features of dinosaurs and other creatures. Explore book cover for clues in making predictions as to content.	• Can make predictions based on pictorial and contextual clues and prior reading. • Can use phonic knowledge to read words.
	2	RC: 4 RC: 13	Enjoy class chanting of repeated phrases. Make verbal and written comparisons between the story characters.	• Can join in with predictable phrases. • Can comment on differences between two characters described in the book.
	3	RC: 1, 10	Listen to *Tyrannosaurus Drip*. Use this as an influence for imaginative role play. Modify direction of play based on actions of others.	• Can discuss a story. • Can confidently change ideas in the light of interaction during play.
	4	RC: 9, 13	Re-enact *Tyrannosaurus Drip* using story plans. Watch other re-enactments and comment on accuracy.	• Can re-enact a story showing understanding of the significance of title and key events. • Can comment on accuracy of re-enactments.
	5	RC: 3, 4	Retell *Tyrannosaurus Drip* using props and story plans, emphasising repeated phrases. Make stick puppets. Watch others and comment constructively.	• Can retell a story using props. • Can comment on interpretations, and accuracy and order of events.
2	1	WT: 11, 12	Establishing differences between fiction and non-fiction. Sort books into those categories. Focus on correct letter formation and posture.	• Can use good handwriting posture and use correct lower-case letter formation. • Can recognise the difference between fiction and non-fiction.
	2	WT: 1, 10 WC: 1	Write a dictated sentence. Create a role-play dinosaur area in a book shop. Write sentence captions about the books.	• Can write a dictated sentence with correct letter formation and punctuation. • Can plan and explain a sentence before writing.
	3	WT: 4, 15	Revise knowledge of handwriting 'families' by 'air' writing. Write name labels for dinosaurs. Arrange themselves in alphabetical order.	• Can understand handwriting 'families'. • Can arrange letters or initial letters in words in alphabetical order.
	4	WC: 9, 12	Write sentence signs and labels for a dinosaur park. Focus on punctuation. Discuss writing with teacher and peers.	• Can write, with correct punctuation, signs and captions describing dinosaurs. • Can discuss effectiveness of signs.
	5	WT: 11 WC: 7	Create a dinosaur mini-display using skills taught this week. Write signs and captions, or complete a photocopiable sheet.	• Can adopt correct writing posture. • Can write sentences with spaces between words.
3	1	WT: 11, 12 WC: 5	Decide what makes a good display. Create display plans in groups. Hold class discussion before deciding on final display content.	• Can sit correctly and form letters accurately when designing plans. • Can describe group plans and explain reasoning to teacher and class.
	2	WT: 11 WC: 5	Create display background, using some of the skills associated with good handwriting. Talk about plans and describe creations.	• Can explain their plans clearly to others and talk about their finished work. • Can handle tools with growing skill.
	3	WT: 13 WC: 2, 9	Write information signs, labels and captions for the display. Complete the photocopiable sheet involving composing sentences.	• Can compose a simple sentence with correct punctuation. • Can form capital letters correctly.
	4	WT: 4, 12	Form an interactive table display by writing alphabetical card lists of dinosaurs and informative signs for model dinosaurs.	• Can name the alphabet letters and arrange them in order.
	5	WC: 5, 7	Fill in 'Dinosaur display review' page. Focus on writing sentences and leaving spaces between words. Share reviews with others.	• Can leave spaces between words when writing sentences. • Can share written opinions.
4	1	RWR: 2 WT: 1	Explore *Tyrannosaurs Drip* extract. Identify rhymes with same/alternate GPCs. Group performances of extract for class review.	• Can read words with taught phonemes in rhyming words. • Can identify words with same/alternate GPCs.
	2	RC: 1, 5	Recall and recite poems. Enhance poems with sound using percussion and everyday objects. Perform poems with these effects.	• Can listen to and discuss a range of poems on a theme and recite some by heart. • Can enhance performance with sound.
	3	RWR: 2 WT: 5	Read dinosaur words involving same/alternative spellings of same sound. Match rhyming cards depicting these words.	• Can distinguish between alternative spellings of same sound on displayed words and use letter names to describe these differences.
	4	RWR: 2 WT: 5	Read a poem and discuss spelling of rhyming words. Complete 'Sensing the dinosaur' page, reading aloud and identifying rhyming words.	• Can read correct sound for taught graphemes, including alternative spellings. • Can use letter names to distinguish alternative spellings.
	5	RC: 1, 5	Recall poems explored during the week. Write a dinosaur poem. Share and comment on finished poetry.	• Can extend appreciation of rhymes and poems and recite some poems by heart. • Can listen to and discuss a range of poems.

Chapter at a glance

Week	Lesson	Curriculum objectives	Summary of activities	Outcomes
5	1	RC: 9, 13	Recall *Tyrannosaurus Drip* explorations. Discuss the significance of title and events. Analyse the beginning, middle and end of the story.	• Can understand the significance of title and events. • Can talk about how a story has a beginning, middle and end.
	2	RC: 9 WT: 13	Create a class plan for a story. Write ideas on a board under headings main character, setting, events. Group work to choose best points. Class discussion to arrive at final plan.	• Can plan a simple story considering main character, setting and events.
	3	RC: 13 WC: 9	Start planning own stories. Draw a picture of the setting and write a sentence about it. Read to the class for comment.	• Can decide the setting for a story as part of the plan. • Can write a sentence to reinforce punctuation skills.
	4	WT: 13 WC: 10	Discuss initial capitals for dinosaur names. Invent and write dinosaur names for children and the main characters in their stories.	• Can use capital letter for invented names. • Can form capital letters correctly when writing these names.
	5	WC: 7, 9	Create a story map of *Tyrannosaurus Drip*. Draw own story maps and complete 'Dinosaur story map' page involving writing sentences.	• Can read questions and write sentence answers, remembering capital letters and full stops. • Can leave spaces between words.
6	1	WT: 12, 13	Explore comic strips to introduce storyboards. Create a class storyboard for a favourite story. Create group storyboards and discuss.	• Can create class storyboards, remembering to use correct upper- and lower-case letter formation.
	2	WT: 12, 13 WC: 7	Explore storybook illustrations, and those created on storyboards, to depict a character's changing feelings. Create own storyboards and discuss.	• Can create individual storyboards, remembering to use correct upper- and lower-case letter formation and leave spaces between words.
	3	WC: 3, 9	Sort jumbled story sentences. Write three sentences to tell a story. Reinforce story structures.	• Can sort sentences into story sequence. • Can write three sentences for story using correct punctuation.
	4	WC: 6, 10	Begin to work on first draft. Pairs to share drafts and make constructive comments before class review of drafting process.	• Can write first draft of their story, with correct punctuation and use of capitals.
	5	WC: 3, 6	Write final version of stories. Discuss changes from first draft. Work in groups, reading stories aloud and asking about them.	• Can write sentences in the correct sequence to form a short narrative. • Can read final story clearly to others.

Background knowledge

Digraph: A type of grapheme where two letters represent one phoneme.

Grapheme-phoneme correspondences (GPC): The links between letters, or combinations of letters, and the speech sounds that they represent.

Grapheme: A letter, or combination of letters, that corresponds to a single phoneme within a word.

Phoneme: The smallest unit of sound that signals a distinct contrasting meaning. There are around 44 phonemes in English.

Split digraph: When two letters representing a phoneme are not next to one another.

Syllable: Sounds like a beat in a word. Syllables consist of at least one vowel and possibly one or more consonants.

Week 1 lesson plans

The lessons for this week introduce the theme 'Dinosaurs' by engaging children's initial interest with a popular contemporary dinosaur story. Children are encouraged to predict the story content using clues apparent from exploration of the cover. They then listen to the story and discuss their reactions. Subsequent lessons extend their enjoyment through a more detailed analysis of plot, character and setting before moving on to their own interpretations of these through role play. The final lesson embeds overall learning with the opportunity to retell the story to peers.

1: *Tyrannosaurus Drip*

Introduction

● Ask the class to sit in a circle and pass around a bag containing model creatures. Motivate initial discussion by inviting individuals to pull one out and describe it before standing it in the middle of the circle.
● Make comparisons between the dinosaurs and the other creatures. Do the dinosaurs share any common features?
● Encourage children to share their knowledge of the names of the dinosaurs and any interesting facts about them.

Whole-class work

● Open media resource '*Tyrannosaurus Drip* book cover' on the CD-ROM and ask the children to read this with you and discuss whether this is a familiar dinosaur. Introduce the word *Rex*, usually linked to Tyrannosaurus, and compare this with the word *Drip*. Ask if children think *Tyrannosaurus Drip* might be the main character and what this name might tell us about this character.
● Reveal the name of the author and encourage children to think of other books by Julia Donaldson (see Spring 2). Ask what they enjoyed about them.
● If possible, display the front and back covers together as you explain that David Roberts is the illustrator. Invite comments about the style of the illustration. Does it give us any clues about the story?
● Focus on the back cover and read the quotes to the children, encouraging them to join in where they can and explaining any new vocabulary, such as *rollicks, comic, engrossingly, dynamic*. Consider what the words tell us about the style of the book, for example, that it is amusing and fast paced.

Paired work

● Invite children to discuss the words and images on the cover in pairs, using this information to predict together what they think might happen in the story.

> **Differentiation**
> ● Explore covers of other books so that children become familiar with this approach to support prediction of content. If children are struggling with understanding the cover blurb, join pairs together, encouraging them to draw upon their existing phonic knowledge and skills to decode words.
> ● More confident learners could write down their predictions.

Review

● Bring the children together and ask pairs to tell the class what they think will happen in the story. Suggest that one child talks about the images while the other talks about the words to ensure equal participation. As they talk, write their predictions on sticky notes and attach them to the board image.
● Use this evidence to assess children's ability to make predictions based on pictorial and contextual clues on the cover. Refer to them during subsequent readings so that children can check the accuracy of their predictions.
● Note how they use their phonic knowledge and skills when reading quotes.

Expected outcomes

● All children enjoy listening to and discussing a contemporary story.
● Most children are able to make predictions about what comes next and story content.
● Some children can apply their phonic knowledge and skills to decode words, for example, *found, thick, grisly.*

Curriculum objectives

● To predict what might happen on the basis of what has been read so far.
● To apply phonic knowledge and skills as the route to decode words.
● To read accurately by blending sounds in unfamiliar words containing GPCs that have been taught.
● To discuss word meanings, linking new meanings to those already known.

Resources

Tyrannosaurus Drip by Julia Donaldson; media resource '*Tyrannosaurus Drip* book cover' on the CD-ROM; drawstring bag; selection of model dinosaurs and other creatures (such as dog, fish, giraffe); sticky notes

Curriculum objectives
• To recognise and join in with predictable phrases.
• To explain clearly their understanding of what is read to them.

Resources
Tyrannosaurus Drip by Julia Donaldson; photocopiable page 40 'Describe the dinosaur'

2: Contrasting characters

Introduction
• Read *Tyrannosaurus Drip* together and enjoy the exciting rhythms of Julia Donaldson's words through class participation, for example clapping or stamping repeated phrases such as *Up with rivers! Up with reeds!*
• Divide the class into two with one half repeating loud Tyrannosaurus chants, while the other repeats soft duckbill chants.

Whole-class work
• Discuss why the main character is called Tyrannosaurus Drip when he is really a duckbill dinosaur. Decide whether he is gentle or fierce, using words and images as evidence, for example the gentle duckbill dinosaur hooting *Down with hunting! Down with war!* while the fierce Tyrannosaurus Rex shouts *Up with hunting! Up with war!*
• Divide a whiteboard into columns headed *Tyrannosaurus Rex* and *Tyrannosaurus Drip*. Ask children to suggest adjectives to describe the different types of Tyrannosaurus, and write down their suggestions.

Paired work
• Divide children into mixed-ability pairs and provide each child with photocopiable page 40 'Describe the dinosaur'. Read through the instructions with them *and* suggest that they discuss the features of the dinosaurs before completing the sheet.

Review
• Arrange the pairs in groups to compare their work. Read the adjectives written together and invite further additions based on children's paired work. Have they been able to extend their character descriptions?

Curriculum objectives
• To make inferences on the basis of what is being said and done.
• To listen to and discuss a wide range of poems, stories and non-fiction at a level beyond that at which they can read independently.

Resources
Tyrannosaurus Drip by Julia Donaldson; long lengths of green, blue and grey fabric; green tissue or crepe paper; large cushions; small stones; clay bones; eggs; dry twigs; red and green tabards; additional resources suggested by the children

3: Green swamp, grey rock

Introduction
• Spread a length of blue fabric on the ground to represent a river and drape the grey fabric on one side and the green fabric on the other to represent the contrasting dinosaur habitats. Use large cushions under the fabric to create undulating landscape.
• Invite the children to sit along the river bank on the side of their choosing.
• Sit beside them and read *Tyrannosaurus Drip.*

Whole-class work
• Explain that the fabric represents the book setting and explore the book images that show this. Invite ideas for additional resources to enhance the scene, for example, green tissue fronds suspended from above, green cushions scattered on green fabric or rocks, clay bones and twigs. Aim to make one side comfortable and the other harsh.
• Show the children the tabards for dressing-up and the 'dinosaur' eggs. Suggest that they set up the environment so they can enjoy being dinosaurs.

Group work
• Allocate time for groups to use the area. Allow them the freedom to follow the story or invent their own scenarios.

Review
• Bring the children together after they have all spent time in the area and ask groups to talk about what they enjoyed about being there. Discuss the influence of the book in deciding on play, and whether they changed direction in the light of what was said and done during play.

4: Down by the river

Curriculum objectives
● To explain clearly their understanding of what is read to them.
● To discuss the significance of the title and events.

Resources
Tyrannosaurus Drip by Julia Donaldson; role-play setting as for lesson 3; large sheets of paper; coloured pens

Introduction
● Recall the previous lesson and ask children what they enjoyed most about it.
● Explain that they are going to return to the role-play area in groups, but this time to act out the story rather than play freely. Talk about key events that should be included in this and ask how the main character might act, given that the title is *Tyrannosaurus Drip*.
● Demonstrate how to make a rough story plan by dividing the board into three columns headed *Beginning*, *Middle* and *End*. Ask the children for suggestions about what they might write in each box based on their knowledge of the story.
● Write these suggestions in the columns, modifying and extending until the children are satisfied.

Group work
● Divide the children into groups to begin creating a story plan.
● Ask the groups to take turns to take the plan into the role-play area and work on their re-enactments.

Review
● Bring the class together to watch some re-enactments. Invite comments on how well groups have understood and represented the key events in the story and consider omissions.
● Discuss whether the main character acts in the way that the title suggests.

5: Retell the story

Curriculum objectives
● To become very familiar with key stories, fairy stories and traditional tales, retelling them and considering their particular characteristics.
● To recognise and join in with predictable phrases.

Resources
Tyrannosaurus Drip by Julia Donaldson; photocopiable page 'Stick puppets' from the CD-ROM; sheets of thick card; glue; scissors; small sticks or canes; colouring pens; large boxes; green, blue and grey paper and fabric; small-world dinosaurs; large bags; children's written plans from lesson 4

Introduction
● Read *Tyrannosaurus Drip* again and recall lessons 3 and 4 involving role play and re-enactment. Encourage children to join in with phrases that are becoming increasingly familiar.
● Explain that you think the children are ready to retell the story to others and talk about props that could be used to enhance this retelling, for example, small-world characters, a story bag or puppets.

Group work
● Divide the children into groups and supply a class bank of resources.
● Suggest that they choose either small-world dinosaurs in a 'story bag' or make stick puppets as their props (see photocopiable page 'Stick puppets' from the CD-ROM).
● Show them how boxes can be used as puppet theatres, or small-world landscapes, when suitably embellished with fabrics and paper.
● Ask them to plan their retelling and decide how they are going to use their props. Draw attention to the children's written plans from the previous lesson and encourage them to use them for guidance as to the order of events.

> **Differentiation**
> ● Support those making puppets with reading the photocopiable sheet and following instructions, where necessary.
> ● Extend learning by asking more confident groups to design their story retelling for a younger class.

Review
● Invite groups of children to retell the story to the class using their chosen props. Encourage comments on the different interpretations and the accuracy and order of events. Talk about what made performances enjoyable, for example, chanting and repetition, characterisation and use of props.

Week 2 lesson plans

The lessons for this week form part of a two-week block culminating in the creation of a class interactive dinosaur display. The focus for the week is to support children in their understanding of non-fiction, sentence and alphabetical order before they create the display next week. Initially children recall their previous explorations of *Tyrannosaurus Drip* and identify the difference between fiction and non-fiction books about dinosaurs. Subsequent lessons involve writing labels to define fiction and non-fiction books and composing informative sentences about content. Other activities involve making dinosaur labels to carry in alphabetical order in a 'dinosaur parade' before writing sentences about a class table display using dinosaur models.

1: Discovering dinosaurs

Introduction
● Display the books on a table so that the covers can be seen. Ask the children if they can tell what they are about by looking at the style of these covers.
● Hold up *Tyrannosaurus Drip* and recall the previous lessons about it. Decide together whether the illustrations are accurate representations of dinosaurs. Comment on how these dinosaurs can chant and speak like humans. Introduce the word *imagination* and talk about the difference between true stories and made-up ones. Establish that imaginary stories are known as *fiction*.

Whole-class work
● Choose a non-fiction book and ask the children about whether the cover shows real or storybook dinosaurs. Discuss the content. Explain that, as it is not fiction, it is known as a *non-fiction* book. Ask which type of book would help us to discover more dinosaur facts and why.
● Write *fiction* and *non-fiction* as large headings on the board, emphasising correct letter formation to support children in writing their own labels. Comment on direction and starting and finishing points while moving a finger along each letter. Draw the letters in the air together and then read the words.
● Invite children's examples of fiction and non-fiction books that they may have read or had read to them, and write these titles under the appropriate headings. Leave the headings on the board for later reference.

Group work
● Ask groups to take turns to go through the dinosaur books and decide whether each one is fiction or non-fiction. Encourage them to discuss their decisions with others in the group to see if they agree.
● Provide card and black pens so that each group can make two labels, *fiction* and *non-fiction,* and stand each one on their table, arranging their books next to the appropriate one. Remind them to refer to the board for correct spelling and letter formation.
● Suggest that they count the number of books in each category and write this on the card labels before returning the books to the table for the next group. Retain the cards for class review.
● Provide reinforcing activities for groups to do while one group completes the main activity above. For example, arranging a selection of library books into categories, such as *Books about animals, Stories about pirates.*

Review
● Bring the class together with their card labels. Ask each group to write the number of books counted under the matching whiteboard heading. These numbers should correspond if children have sorted the books accurately. Discuss discrepancies and consider why some books are difficult to define, for example, because of realistic illustrations of fictional characters. Ask whether the children now have a better idea where to look for a story or factual book.

Curriculum objectives
- To write from memory simple sentences dictated by the teacher that include words using the GPCs and common exception words taught so far.
- To spell words containing each of the 40+ phonemes already taught.
- To write sentences by saying out loud what they are going to write about.

Resources
Fiction and non-fiction dinosaur book selection as used in previous lesson; card rectangles; small chairs; table; book shop items chosen by children, for example, till, money and bags

2: Bookseller's choice

Introduction
- Discuss how booksellers and librarians leave captions alongside books to capture the interest of buyers and readers.
- Write a sentence about a dinosaur book, including the word *fiction* or *non-fiction*, and ask the class what it tells them about the book.

Independent work
- Dictate one sentence reviewing a book for the children to write, stressing sounds and reminding them about punctuation.

Paired work
- Invite pairs of children to imagine they are booksellers in the dinosaur section of a book shop.
- Supply card for children to write their own sentences to attract buyers to the books. Encourage children to discuss with their partners what they plan to write. Retain the cards for review later.

Differentiation
- Support those struggling to write their own sentences by providing an incomplete caption for them to finish.

Review
- As a class, discuss the writing of your dictated sentence. Ask about aspects children found easy/tricky and whether this experience helped when writing their own sentences.
- Invite the booksellers to read some captions to the class. Comment on the influence of captions in book purchase.

Curriculum objectives
- To name the letters of the alphabet in alphabetical order.
- To understand which letters belong to which handwriting 'families' and to practise these.

Resources
Non-fiction books about dinosaurs

3: Dinosaur parade

Introduction
- Use starter activity 2 'Alphabetical order' to introduce the task.
- Remind children of the handwriting families.
- Write large examples of letters that involve strokes that go down and off in another direction, for example, 'j', 'l', 't'.
- Draw these letters in the air together, inventing chants such as *all the way down and off and across* ('t').
- Repeat with letters that go down and retrace upwards ('r', 'b', 'h'), go anticlockwise round ('c', 'g', 's'), and zigzag ('w', 'z', 'v').
- Write popular dinosaur names on the board (all lower-case letters).

Independent work
- Ask children to choose a dinosaur from the board or a book and write the name on paper, recalling handwriting families to support formation.

Whole-class work
- Write a lower-case alphabet in order, helped by the children.
- Invite a child to call out each letter in order while others who have chosen a dinosaur starting with that letter form a line in order.
- When all dinosaurs have lined up, ask them to take turns to call their names, stamp the syllables and hold up their written labels.

Review
- Discuss how drawing 'air' letters helps handwriting. March around chanting *Dinosaurs, dinosaurs, all in order* before considering how an exciting dinosaur parade helped learning.

Curriculum objectives
• To begin to punctuate sentences using a capital letter and a full stop.
• To use the grammatical terminology in Appendix 2 in discussing their writing.

Resources
Small-world farmyard equipment such as fences and food racks; green fabric; small boxes; rocks; model dinosaurs; card rectangles

4: Dinosaur park

Introduction
• Talk about when you visited a zoo. Explain that enclosures were labelled to indicate the creatures living there and information was displayed as captions.
• Encourage children to share their experiences of discovering information at such venues.

Whole-class work
• Draw attention to the designated activity space and ask if children think it could become a dinosaur park using given resources.
• Discuss how information about resident dinosaurs could be communicated.

Group work
• Divide into groups to write name labels and sentence cards explaining key dinosaur features. Remind children of the need for correct punctuation, including capital letters and full stops.

> **Differentiation**
> • Collect images of signs and captions found at a zoo. Share these with children who struggle with this concept and help them to create a simple sentence caption.

Review
• Discuss which signs and captions provide the most information and which ones are most effective. Check for correct sentence formation and punctuation. Encourage children to use grammatical terminology, such as word, sentence and letter, when discussing their work.

Curriculum objectives
• To sit correctly at a table, holding a pencil comfortably and correctly.
• To leave spaces between words.

Resources
Model dinosaurs; non-fiction books about dinosaurs; green fabric; rocks; small plants; card; photocopiable page 42 'Dinosaur facts'

5: Mini display

Introduction
• Explain that next week the children will be creating an interactive classroom display and that this week's lessons will help with this.
• Discuss how children revised alphabetical order, and learned where to find dinosaur facts and communicate them to others through writing.
• Invite them to make a dinosaur table mini-display using these skills.

Whole-class work
• Decide what could be included in this display, such as model dinosaurs in alphabetical order with captions. Make a list and choose the most popular.
• Divide these into separate headings and allocate group tasks.

Group work
• Allow time for groups to complete their task, for example, writing signs and captions for dinosaurs, or arranging books and writing sentences about them.
• Reinforce correct posture and pencil position as children write. Remind them of the importance of leaving spaces between words to make their writing clear.
• Arrange children's contributions as the mini-display.

> **Differentiation**
> • Invite less confident children to complete photocopiable page 42 'Dinosaur facts'. These can then be incorporated into the display to ensure equal contribution.

Review
• Discuss whether or not creating written materials for a display is an enjoyable way of developing handwriting skills. Decide which aspects of the display work well enough to be incorporated into a larger display next week.

Week 3 lesson plans

This week, lessons draw upon the learning and experiences of last week in order to create an interactive classroom display about dinosaurs. Initially children are involved in creating visual plans of their proposed display before building it up during the remaining lessons. They concentrate on preparing the wall board to reflect the environment in the dinosaur era, with groups working creatively on different aspects, such as background, vegetation, dinosaur community and border. Written work ensures that the display abounds with facts, labels and alphabetical lists. The interactive aspect includes a table display for exploration of dinosaurs and opportunities to add to alphabetical lists. Finally, children write reviews of their completed display for discussion.

1: Dinosaur display

Introduction
● Show the children the wall board and explain to them that they are going to use this to create the dinosaur display they discussed last week.
● Have a 'shout out' session to gather ideas and initiate planning.

Whole-class work
● Remind the children of work they completed last week and show examples. Suggest that they might incorporate some of these ideas into their display.
● Talk about what makes a good display and introduce the words *attractive, enjoyable* and *informative*. Establish who will be looking at the display. Consider how to make it enjoyable to look at and full of interesting facts.
● Ask the children for suggestions about things that make the display bright and colourful, for example, they might say that the artwork does this. Write a heading *Attractive* and note their comments here. Do the same with things that children enjoy about the display, such as flaps to lift, under the heading *Enjoyable*. Finally, ask for things that they think help them to learn something, for example, labels and captions, using the heading *Informative*.
● Discuss why it helps learning to be able to do things with a display rather than simply look at it. Introduce the word *interactive*. Discuss how the display could be created so that items can be touched or added to, such as providing lists to extend, flaps to lift, and a table to place models on to explore.

Group work
● Divide the class into mixed-ability groups and invite them to draw a plan of the wall display, discussing suitable materials as they do so and using appropriate colours. For example, shading a green and brown background to represent landscape. Challenge those who are more confident to add their own simple labels indicating materials used, and support less confident learners by writing down their ideas for them to copy onto labels.
● While engaging with each group, comment positively on individuals who are sitting correctly and forming letters well, to inspire others to do the same. Recall that it is important to sit in the proper writing position.

> **Differentiation**
> ● Encourage any children who seem to find it difficult to link an actual plan to an abstract notion, by pointing to the plan and commenting, for example, *I see a cave here. Do you think dinosaurs might like caves? Shall we put one inside it?*

Review
● Bring the class together to explain their plans to others. Talk about whether the children enjoyed this activity. Encourage constructive comments and decide which aspects could be incorporated into your wall display. Make a list of these on the whiteboard and draw a rough plan including as many of these aspects as the class think will be effective. Retain this work for the next lesson.

Expected outcomes
● All children can say out loud what they plan to do towards their classroom project.
● Most children can name the letters of the alphabet and arrange things in alphabetical order.
● Some children can compose sentences and punctuate accurately, using capital letters and full stops.

Curriculum objectives
● To begin to form lower-case letters in the correct direction, starting and finishing in the right place.
● To sit correctly at a table, holding a pencil comfortably and correctly.
● To discuss what they have written with the teacher or other children.

Resources
Large display board; examples of work retained from last week, such as labels and captions; large sheets of white paper; black and coloured pens

Curriculum objectives
● To discuss what they have written/created with the teacher or other children.
● To sit correctly at a table, holding a pencil comfortably and correctly.

Resources
Backing paper in natural colours; newspaper; paint; dinosaur printing items such as sponge shapes, stencils and rubber stamps; border roll; collage materials; card; whiteboard displaying plan from previous lesson; glue; staples and stapler

2: Dinosaur landscape

Introduction
● Recall the plan created in the previous lesson and discuss the content.

Whole-class work
● Make a class list of tasks involved in the proposed display creation, for example, putting up background, painting dinosaurs, making trees.
● Allocate tasks to groups and ask them to talk about what they might do.

Group work
● Work with the group creating the background. Spread paper on the floor and lightly blob/sponge/daub paint on it together. Attach it to the display board, adding texture with screwed up newspaper pushed beneath the paper.
● Encourage other groups to prepare vegetation and dinosaurs, perhaps painting along a border roll. Demonstrate techniques, such as use of fabric scraps for a rough dinosaur skin, or stippled painting for mottled effects.
● Stick the finished items in place on the background.

Differentiation
● Support the development of the fine motor skills by ensuring that hand-held tools are the correct size, and that children adopt a good posture when using them. Be aware of left-handed children requiring additional input.

Review
● Consider the process of display creation. Talk about the usefulness of creating a plan in the previous lesson and consider how much it was followed.

Curriculum objectives
● To compose a sentence orally before writing it.
● To form capital letters.
● To begin to punctuate sentences using a capital letter and a full stop, question mark or exclamation mark.

Resources
Coloured paper; coloured pens; card; scissors; non-fiction books about dinosaurs (particularly those with an alphabetical index); photocopiable page 43 'Dinosaur information'

3: Bubbles, lists and labels

Introduction
● Explore the display so far and consider whether it is attractive, enjoyable and informative. Invite children to suggest ways of adding information.

Group work
● Divide children into the same groups as in the previous lesson.
● Provide books for children to source information to add to the creative display, for example types of dinosaur and environmental features.
● Ask children to use this information to create labels, signs and captions in attractive colours and shapes. Emphasise the need to check spelling and remember capital letters and full stops. Introduce the notion of writing questions, or indicating startling facts with an exclamation mark.

Independent work
● Invite individuals to use the books to help them complete photocopiable page 43 'Dinosaur information' when they finish their group work.

Whole-class work
● Ask groups and individuals to bring their finished work to the display and to indicate where to position it. Pin it in place temporarily.

Differentiation
● Encourage less confident learners to compose a simpler sentence based on previously taught GPCs, for example, *This tree is tall and green.*

Review
● Observe the display together and discuss positioning. Staple the most effective contributions into place. Discuss the benefits of the completed display.

Curriculum objectives
● To name the letters of the alphabet in order.
● To begin to form lower-case letters in the correct direction, starting and finishing in the right place.

Resources
Two tables; green fabric; model dinosaurs; children's work retained from previous week, such as information cards, book captions and dinosaur labels; card; 26 A4 cards depicting lower-case letters of the alphabet at the top with space for a list below

4: Display extension

Introduction
● Recall the notion of making the display interactive.
● Suggest that aspects of the mini-display and dinosaur park previously created could be incorporated into a table display.

Whole-class work
● Share ideas for using a table to add attraction, enjoyment and information, for example, a captioned book section, labelled dinosaur models and alphabetical dinosaur lists.
● Choose the most popular ideas and allocate tasks to mixed-ability groups.

Group work
● Work with the group arranging the dinosaurs initially, draping the tables with green fabric. Allocate one end of the table for the model dinosaurs and leave children working on this.
● Ask another group to arrange books at the other end. Suggest utilising captions from the resource bank built up last week or creating new ones.
● Divide the letter cards (see Resources) between three groups and ask them to write names of dinosaurs under appropriate letters, referring to books for examples. Display the cards alphabetically in a pile for children to search through when adding a dinosaur name.

Differentiation
● Support alphabetical order with a paper strip of letters. Demonstrate correct letter formation by moving a finger over plastic letters. Encourage children to follow.

Review
● Explore the finished table together for successful aspects. Discuss whether the alphabetical order tasks reinforce previous knowledge.

Curriculum objectives
● To leave spaces between words.
● To discuss what they have written with the teacher or other children.

Resources
The completed display; photocopiable page 44 'Dinosaur display review'

5: Review and revise

Introduction
● Ask children to comment on what they like best about the finished display.
● Consider aspects that could be more effective and how children might change them.

Whole-class work
● Explain the meaning of *review* and consider why we might read reviews, for example, about books, films, toys, recipes. Discuss how reviews can help us, such as when deciding whether to try a recipe or buy a particular toy.
● Explain that the children are going to write a review, and display photocopiable page 44 'Dinosaur display review'. Ask the children to read the questions with you and discuss suggestions for responses. Write some of these as examples, reminding them of the need to finish the sentences with full stops.

Independent work
● Supply each child with the photocopiable sheet to complete. Ask them to attempt tricky words and leave spaces between words.

Review
● Invite individuals to share their reviews and ask the class whether they will reconsider their own responses in the light of them. Discuss the value of completing the review, for example, in changing aspects of future displays and practising sentence writing. Take photographs of the display and save them.

Expected outcomes
● All children learn to appreciate rhymes and poems, and to recite some by heart.
● Most children respond speedily with the correct sound to graphemes for all 40+ phonemes.
● Some children use letter names to distinguish between alternative spellings of the same sound.

Curriculum objectives
● To respond speedily with the correct sound to graphemes (letters or groups of letters) for all 40+ phonemes, including, where applicable, alternative sounds for graphemes.
● To spell words containing each of the 40+ phonemes already taught.

Resources
Photocopiable page 'Extract from *Tyrannosaurus Drip*' from the CD-ROM

Week 4 lesson plans

This week's lessons focus on recognising rhyme and enjoying poems about dinosaurs. Children explore an extract from *Tyrannosaurus Drip* in depth to identify rhymes and phrase repetition. Awareness of rhythm is encouraged by accompanying rhyme reading with percussion and body sounds to stress syllables and beat. A fun 'swamp' of green scrap paper invites children to find card leaves to hang on a large stegosaurus. These leaves depict words that rhyme with the word on each bony plate of the dinosaur. Children are introduced to a new poem about a meat-eating dinosaur and recite it aloud, identifying any rhyming words. Finally, children choose dinosaur poems to perform with added sound accompaniment of their choice.

1: Exploring an extract

Introduction
● Recall the story of *Tyrannosaurus Drip* and display photocopiable page 'Extract from *Tyrannosaurus Drip*' from the CD-ROM.
● Read it to the class and ask them to describe what is happening.
● Talk about what happened at the beginning of the story, before the dinosaur eggs hatched, and what happens after.

Whole-class work
● Ask the children to clap in time as you read the extract. Discuss how the extract is like a poem as it has a good rhythm. Substitute words for alternate rhymes, for example, *Four* instead of *Three*, *thin* instead of *weak*, and discuss whether the sound is as satisfying when the rhyme element is removed.
● Identify the rhyming words, *be* and *Three*, *weak* and *beak*, and ask individuals to highlight them. Discuss the positioning of these words, at the end of alternate lines, creating a pattern.
● Explain that repeated phrases often help with the rhythm of a poem and ask children to find and underline the repeated three-word phrase, *And she grumbled*. Discuss whether this improves the rhyme-like quality of the extract. Consider how the 'd' at the end of the word *grumble* changes sound and tense.
● Question other aspects, for example, why *Babies One, Two and Three* and *Mother T* have capital letters and what the 'T' stands for in *Mother T*. Recall the use of capitals at the start of names.
● Write the rhyming words on the whiteboard and discuss spelling. What is similar about the /e/ sound in *weak* and *beak*? What is different about the /e/ sound in *be* and *Three*? Invite volunteers to write down three different spellings of the sound /e/ in these words ('e', 'ee', 'ea').

Group work
● Explain that you would like the children to try choral reading/speaking to see if this makes poetry sound more exciting. To demonstrate this, choose a rousing well-known rhyme or chorus, such as 'The Grand Old Duke of York'. March around in groups, feeling the rhythm of the words through strong stamps and claps.
● Provide children with the photocopiable sheet and suggest they act out the scene, allocating the parts of baby dinosaurs and the mother to individuals.
● Ask the rest of the group to chant the text while the babies clap in time, pausing to let the mother say her lines.

Review
● Display the extract. Discuss any words children found tricky to read at first and talk about how the lesson's activities helped with this. Ask the class to sit in a circle while each group performs their re-enactment in the centre. Comment constructively on whether the performances emphasise the rhyme and rhythm of the extract.

Curriculum objectives
• To learn to appreciate rhymes and poems, and to recite some by heart.
• To listen to and discuss a wide range of poems at a level beyond that at which they can read independently.

Resources
Books of dinosaur poems, such as *Bumpus Jumpus Dinosaurumpus* by Tony Mitton and Guy Parker-Rees; a range of percussion instruments, such as claves, rainsticks, drums and cymbals; everyday objects, such as stones, sticks, trays, pans, spoons and thin boards

2: Fun with sound

Introduction
• Choose one of the poetry books together and read some rhymes from it.
• Recall how children created bodily sound effects, to accompany rhyme in the previous lesson. Invite suggestions for other ways of adding sound.

Whole-class work
• Ask individuals to choose a percussion instrument to play in turn while you read a rhyme.
• Listen to the results and decide which instruments make the most effective dinosaur sounds, such as rainsticks for dinosaurs moving through grass, or drums for plodding feet.
• Invite children to suggest ways of using everyday objects for sound effects, for example tapping two stones together to represent dinosaur teeth clacking.
• Demonstrate how to make a thunderous sound by wobbling a thin board.

Group work
• Invite groups to explore instruments and everyday objects before finding a rhyme to read, accompanied by chosen sounds. Encourage lots of exploration.

> **Differentiation**
> • Support those whose level of reading is below that required by composing a short four-line poem for them to read using already taught GPCs.

Review
• Invite groups to explain to the class the process of arriving at their choice of rhymes and sound makers, before they perform their rhymes.
• Discuss which sounds are most appropriate and why. Decide upon the most effective performance.

Curriculum objectives
• To name the letters of the alphabet using letter names to distinguish between alternative spellings of the same sound.
• To respond speedily with the correct sound to graphemes (letters or groups of letters) for all 40+ phonemes, including, where applicable, alternative sounds for graphemes.

Resources
Large sheet of green paper; cards; sand tray; shredded and torn green and brown paper; model dinosaurs; green collage scraps; hooks; string

3: Rhyme detectives

Introduction
• Create a paper stegosaurus with rhyming words on each bony plate. Decorate the stegosaurus together, creating texture with green collage materials, such as fabric scraps, cellophane and tissue.
• Make sure the rhyming words on the bony plates are visible and attach a hook underneath each word.
• Invite children to create a dinosaur swamp in the tray using the resources.
• Prepare leaf-shape cards containing words to rhyme with the words on the bony plates. Hide the leaf cards in the swamp.
• Read the words on the stegosaurus together. Explain that there are rhyming words hidden in the swamp to hang on the hooks under the corresponding rhyming word.

Paired work
• Invite pairs to find cards and hang them up. Emphasise the need to say the correct letter names when discussing alternative graphemes for phonemes.

Group work
• While pairs are at the swamp, ask groups to list rhyming words from the dinosaur poems. Encourage them to come up with new rhyming words to add to the list.

Review
• Ask children to consider how working with others can help reading and identifying rhyming words, especially those with different graphemes.

Curriculum objectives
● To respond speedily with the correct sound to graphemes (letters or groups of letters) for all 40+ phonemes, including, where applicable, alternative sounds for graphemes.
● To name the letters of the alphabet using letter names to distinguish between alternative spellings of the same sound.

Resources
Photocopiable page 41 'Sensing the dinosaur'

4: Sensing the dinosaur

Introduction
● Display photocopiable page 41 'Sensing the dinosaur' and read it together.
● Discuss how the poet has included the five senses so that we can imagine not only how the dinosaur looks, but also how it smells, sounds and feels. Why does the poet describe the taste of a dinosaur lunch rather than the taste of the dinosaur?

Whole-class work
● Invite individuals to come and highlight the pairs of rhyming words.
● Talk about which words have the same grapheme(s) to make the phoneme(s), for example, the 'o' in *stomp* and *chomp*, the 'u' in *lunch* and *munch*. Underline these words.
● Using the correct letter names, discuss which words have alternative graphemes to create the same phoneme, for example, in *claw* and *roar*, *eye* and *sigh*, *knee* and *tea*. Highlight these words in a different colour. Children may need support with the word *eye* as it is a common exception word.

Paired work
● Provide pairs of children with the photocopiable sheet and ask them to follow the instructions, reading the poem to one another first.

Review
● Bring children together to discuss the poem and their explorations of it. Recall the expected learning outcomes, (exploring words with same/alternative graphemes, using correct letter names) and ask how discussions about GPCs in the rhyming words supported their achievement of them.

Curriculum objectives
● To learn to appreciate rhymes and poems, and to recite some by heart.
● To listen to and discuss a wide range of poems at a level beyond that at which they can read independently.

Resources
Photocopiable page 41 'Sensing the dinosaur'; completed 'Sensing the dinosaur' sheets from previous lesson; dinosaur poetry books; writing materials

5: Perfect performances

Introduction
● Recall poems the children have read/recited over the week and suggest that they use ideas from these to write their own poems.

Whole-class work
● Display photocopiable page 41 'Sensing the dinosaur' and recall how the poet mentions the five senses. Invite the children to think of ways they might describe a dinosaur through a particular sense, asking questions, such as *How might a dinosaur's breath smell?*
● Encourage the children to think of rhyming words for each description. For example, *lumpy* and *bumpy* skin, *pointed* and *jointed* claws and bones.

Independent work
● Invite children to write their own dinosaur poems.
● Display the photocopiable page 41 'Sensing the dinosaur', poetry books and the list of words compiled together, to help with rhymes. Emphasise that these resources provide ideas for writing poems, and that children should try and come up with their own, new ideas.

> **Differentiation**
> ● Support those who struggle by introducing rhyming words with familiar GPCs, for example, *small* and *tall*, *bump* and *lump*.

Review
● Ask the class to share their poems and comment constructively on what works well.

Week 5 lesson plans

The final two weeks of lessons involve children in planning and writing their own dinosaur story. This week the focus is on what makes a good story, referring initially to previous explorations of *Tyrannosaurus Drip*. Children take part in activities focusing on the main character and setting of the story, and decide why the plot is so effective. They use these experiences to decide upon their own main characters and where the story will be set. A plan is created by the end of the first week, ready to begin writing the actual story in the final week. Sentence structure, punctuation skills and letter formation are reinforced.

Expected outcomes
● All children talk about and identify character, setting and events in stories.
● Most children can plan a simple story with a beginning, middle and end.
● Some children can plan a story with a complex plot.

Curriculum objectives
● To discuss the significance of the title and events.
● To explain clearly their understanding of what is read to them.

Resources
Green, blue and grey lengths of fabric; *Tyrannosaurus Drip* by Julia Donaldson

1: What makes a good story?

Introduction
● Recreate the setting using lengths of fabric as in your reading of *Tyrannosaurus Drip* in lesson 3, week 1, page 20.
● Invite the children to sit there with you while you read and recall the story.

Whole-class work
● Explain that, over the next two weeks, the children are going to write their own story about a dinosaur. Talk about how reading story books might help with this by allowing children to consider how main characters, settings and events are created and used in stories.
● Recall your discussions about the main character, setting and events in *Tyrannosaurus Drip* in week 1.
● Encourage children to say what they like about Tyrannosaurus Drip as a main character. Explore text and images and think of how these help to build up a picture of his character. He looks endearing and seems to be gentle yet brave. Notice how his feelings change as the story progresses.
● Discuss the importance of the setting to the story, for example, the way the author and illustrator create contrasting calm habitats for the gentle plant-eating dinosaurs and harsh habitats for the fierce meat-eating dinosaurs.
● Consider whether having the name of the main character as the title is a good idea. What else might the book be called?
● Talk about how a story always has a beginning, middle and end. Some may have a more complex 'middle' section, but all follow this pattern.

Group work
● Divide into groups to discuss how the plot for *Tyrannosaurus Drip* has a definite beginning, middle and end.
● Hand out prepared A4 sheets titled *Tyrannosaurus Drip*, with the headings *beginning, middle* and *end*, and invite children to make notes on their discussion.
● Explain how to explore the start of the story and note this in the first section, followed by events in the middle, and finally how the story ends.

> **Differentiation**
> ● If some children struggle with coping with writing notes covering the whole story, encourage them to look at images from the beginning, middle and end of the story and draw a sequence of three separate pictures. Help with captions underneath by writing partial sentences and asking children to finish them, for example: *1.Tyrannosaurus Drip lives in a _____ ; 2. Tyrannosaurus Drip does not look like the other _____ in the nest; 3. Tyrannosaurus Drip is _____ to be home.*

Review
● Bring the class together to share ideas and decide key features of a good plot. Ask questions to support children's thinking on this, for example: *Did the beginning of this story make you want to read more? Did you find the events in the middle of the story exciting? What happened to the main character in this section? Was the ending of the story happy or sad? Did it make you feel satisfied?*

Curriculum objectives
● To discuss the significance of the title and events.
● To form capital letters.

Resources
An A4 sheet of paper divided into three sections for each group

2: Class story plan

Introduction
● Recall the previous lesson and talk about exploring *Tyrannosaurus Drip*. Remind children of the terms *main character*, *setting* and *events*.
● Discuss what they wrote about events at the beginning, middle and end of the story.

Whole-class work
● Suggest that you work together to create a plan for a class story.
● Divide the board into three sections headed *Main character*, *Setting*, *Events*.
● Discuss each heading in turn, writing suggestions in the appropriate sections. Draw attention to correct capital-letter formation while writing, commenting on correct starting and finishing points and direction.

Group work
● Divide into mixed-ability groups and supply each group with a sheet of A4 paper divided into three sections.
● Ask the children to copy the headings from the board and read through the sections before making final choices about what they think should be included in the class story. Ask them to write these on their paper.
● Encourage the groups to invent a title for their story.

Review
● Discuss the group decisions and then arrive at an overall class decision about what to delete from the main board, leaving an agreed plan.

Curriculum objectives
● To explain clearly their understanding of what is read to them.
● To begin to punctuate sentences using a capital letter and a full stop.

Resources
Coloured paper and card; mark-making tools such as pencils, pastels, pens, crayons, chalk; small collage materials such as paper curls, fabric, buttons; PVA glue

3: Setting the scene

Introduction
● Recall the class story planning in the previous lesson and explain that it is time to start thinking of the children's own stories.
● Remind them of the terms *character*, *setting* and *events*, and suggest that they start by setting the scene.

Whole-class work
● Remind children that the story is about a dinosaur and invite suggestions for settings they could use for such a story. Ask questions to support thinking, for example: *What would you expect to see if your dinosaur character is a plant eater? Where do you think a meat-eating dinosaur might live?*
● Invite them to think about where the story might be happening within this larger setting. Ask: *What does the dinosaur do in the story? Is the dinosaur at home/out playing with friends/at school?*

Independent work
● Encourage the children to make a picture of their chosen setting and write a sentence describing it.
● Provide individuals with the above resources to create their picture.
● Emphasise the benefit of writing a complete sentence to describe the picture, and remind children to pay close attention to punctuation.
● Suggest that they write the sentence on a strip of white paper and glue it to the picture as a caption.

Review
● Invite individuals to show their pictures to the class and read their sentences. Encourage positive comments on effective ideas and praise correct punctuation.

Curriculum objectives
● To use a capital letter for names of people, places, the days of the week, and the personal pronoun *I*.
● To form capital letters.

Resources
Lists of dinosaur names made as alphabetical lists in Week 3; non-fiction dinosaur books

4: What's in a name?

Introduction

● Invite children to write some dinosaur names on the board. Ask what they notice about the initial letters. Recall other words that start with a capital.

Whole-class work

● Ask children if they know any storybook names for dinosaurs and write *Tyrannosaurus Drip* on the board. Comment on the two capital letters.
● Talk about how many dinosaur names end in *saurus* which means *lizard*. Explain that *Tyrannosaurus* means *terrible lizard* and *Stegosaurus* means *covered lizard*, because of the bony plates.
● Point out that some dinosaur names have different endings, for example, *Triceratops* means *three-horned face*, *Pterodactyl* means *winged finger*.
● Discuss how some amusing dinosaur names can be made by combining first names with dinosaur endings, such as *Hettiesaurus* or *Adamtops*.

Paired work

● Invite pairs to make up suitable dinosaur names for each other. Ask children to draw a picture of their partner and write the chosen name underneath, remembering capital letters. Pairs can then discuss names for the main dinosaur character(s) in the stories they are each planning.

Independent work

● Ask individuals to draw a picture of their main story character and write the chosen name underneath. Provide support with spelling where needed.

Review

● Discuss the pictures children have drawn. Share positive comments on choices, and praise correct use and formation of capital letters.

Curriculum objectives
● To leave spaces between words.
● To begin to punctuate sentences using a capital letter and a full stop, question mark or exclamation mark.

Resources
Tyrannosaurus Drip by Julia Donaldson; large sheets of paper; selection of writing tools, such as pencils, coloured pencils, pens; photocopiable page 45 'Dinosaur story map'

5: Story map

Introduction

● Recall the week's lessons. Explain that children should now have a main character and setting for their story. Tell them they need to decide what happens to this character within this setting. Introduce the words *plot* and *events*. Suggest that a story is like a journey and can be represented on a map.

Whole-class work

● Demonstrate how to create a story map, using *Tyrannosaurus Drip*. Draw a wavy path on the board, marking the beginning and end.
● Ask volunteers to indicate on the map, using words and drawings, what happened at the beginning of the story.
● Continue along the path, marking significant story events in the same way.

Independent work

● Encourage children to develop their ideas of what is going to happen in their own stories and to write events at the appropriate points on their story maps.
● Once complete, provide photocopiable page 45 'Dinosaur story map'.

> **Differentiation**
> ● Draw a simple map for those needing support, with a numbered beginning, middle and end point. Help them to use the map rather than complete the photocopiable sheet.

Review

● Bring the class together to share story maps and written sheets. Talk about the value of story maps in helping to clarify the sequence of events.

Week 6 lesson plans

In this final week of lessons focusing on dinosaurs, children draw upon their experiences of the previous five weeks as they produce their own dinosaur stories. They use their explorations of character, setting and events, and the creation of story maps from last week to support them in planning storyboards based on a comic strip. This is followed by a more detailed look at illustration – in particular, how a character's feelings are portrayed at different points in the story. Activities involving using connecting words and sequencing sentences from well-known stories support awareness of story structure. Finally, children write and illustrate their stories and share them with peers.

1: Creating a storyboard

Introduction
● Display a page from a comic on the board. Talk about the content.
● Share experiences of similar pages children have looked at.

Whole-class work
● Ask questions to establish what children can find out from the comic pictures, for example: *Do you think these pictures tell a story? What do we know about the characters? What is the setting for the story? What is happening?*
● Draw attention to how the text is presented, such as speech bubbles, caption boxes. Read the words in one of the pictures together.
● Recall the story map the children created and explain that some writers and illustrators plan their stories on a storyboard like the page they are exploring.
● Remove the comic image and draw three squares on the board. Ask the children to choose a favourite story, perhaps one you have shared as a class, and suggest making a simple storyboard for it.
● Label the squares Beginning, Middle and End and ask what the children might draw in the first square to show what happens at the beginning of the story. Invite someone to draw the chosen image.
● Discuss words that could be added to the square, and how this could be done, such as a speech bubble from the character, or a caption underneath the drawing. Ask another child to add this in the chosen way.
● Complete the squares labelled Middle and End in the same way.
● Explain that one square for each main event is ideal.

Group work
● In groups and ask them to create a storyboard about another story of their choice.
● Supply paper and a pile of smaller squares, as well as coloured pens. Emphasise that, when writing words in the squares, they should remember to form the letters in the right direction, starting and finishing in the right place.
● Once squares are completed, ask groups to arrange them on the table or floor and discuss whether they tell the story in order. They can move or add squares until they are happy with the positioning and content.
● The squares can then be stuck on to the sheet in the correct order.

> **Differentiation**
> ● Prepare three simple drawings that tell a story. Support those who struggle with storyboards to write a short sentence at the bottom of each drawing and arrange them in order, for example: *The cat runs away. The cat is stuck in the tree. The boy lifts the cat down.*

Review
● Invite the class to share their storyboards. Discuss what worked well, and whether this is a good way to plan a story. Comment on how correct letter formation makes the storyboards easy to read.

Curriculum objectives
● To begin to form lower-case letters in the correct direction, starting and finishing in the right place.
● To form capital letters.
● To leave spaces between words.

Resources
Display of group storyboards created in previous lesson; selection of dinosaur stories; small squares of white paper; larger sheets of white paper; glue; scissors; coloured and black pens

2: Dinosaur storyboards

Introduction
● Recall the group creation of storyboards in the previous lesson.
● Suggest that children use this method to plan their dinosaur stories.

Whole-class work
● Choose a popular dinosaur story the children have enjoyed from your selection and explore how the feelings of the characters are depicted.
● Ask children to talk about different feelings they experience and write these on the board, for example, *happy, angry, surprised, worried, frightened*.
● Invite children to take turns to act one of these emotions to the rest of the class while the others try to guess which one it is.
● Discuss the character drawings the children included in their storyboards. How well did they show the characters' feelings?

Independent work
● Invite the children to create their storyboards. Remind them to show changes in the feelings of their characters as the story progresses.
● Stress that it is important to remember the need for correct letter and word formation when they include writing.

Review
● Gather the class to share and display their storyboards. Encourage reflection on those that give good detail about character, setting and events.

Curriculum objectives
● To begin to punctuate sentences using a capital letter and a full stop, question mark or exclamation mark.
● To sequence sentences to form short narratives.

Resources
Photocopiable page 46 'The sad little dinosaur'

3: Connections and sequences

Introduction
● Recall how creating storyboards involved putting story events in the correct order, and introduce the word *sequence*.

Whole-class work
● Identify the sequence of events in a well-known story and write these on the board. For example: *Jack climbed the beanstalk. He met a giant. The giant chased him down the beanstalk.*
● Display photocopiable page 46 'The sad little dinosaur', and read through the sentences, asking the children to decide which sentence starts the story. Number this sentence '1'.
● Continue through the story, numbering the sentences in the children's suggested order. Agree the final sentence order and read the complete story.
● Talk about how words, such as, *Once upon a time, Next, Then, In the end*, are used to connect the story events, and highlight these.

Group work
● Invite groups of three to compose three sentences to tell a simple story, taking turns to act as scribe. Display the photocopiable sheet to prompt them with suitable connecting words and phrases. Encourage them to follow the sequence, *beginning, middle, end*.

Independent work
● Provide each child with the photocopiable sheet to complete independently.

Review
● Invite the children to read their sentences aloud and comment on language used. Talk about whether connective words helped with sequencing 'The sad little dinosaur'. Encourage positive comments about correct use of punctuation.

Curriculum objectives
● To use a capital letter for names of people, places, the days of the week, and the personal pronoun *I*.
● To read their writing aloud, clearly enough to be heard by their peers and the teacher.

Resources
Children's work from previous lessons relating to their individual stories, such as story maps and storyboards, setting pictures, completed photocopiable sheets

4: Drafting the story

Introduction
● Introduce the word *draft* and explain the meaning. Talk about how writers might write several drafts of their stories before they are happy with them.

Whole-class work
● Recall previous lessons when children decided on titles, characters, settings and events for their stories and created different kinds of plan.
● From these recollections, compile a class list of things to include in the first story draft. For example: *events, character* and *setting, connecting words* and *title*. Leave these displayed on the board for reference during draft writing.
● Remind children that all characters' names should begin with a capital letter.
● Discuss whether the children think they are ready to write their first drafts.

Independent work
● Encourage children to have their previous written work to hand so that they can ensure that their stories follow their planned sequence of events.
● Ask children to write their individual drafts.

Paired work
● Once the individual drafts are written, invite children of similar abilities to read their stories to each other. Support, if necessary, with checking punctuation, constructive discussion about what they like, and positive comments about things that could be changed or added.

Review
● Bring the class together to share their experiences of writing a first draft. Ask how previous lessons have helped with this.

Curriculum objectives
● To read aloud their writing clearly enough to be heard by their peers and the teacher.
● To sequence sentences to form short narratives.

Resources
The same resources used in the previous lesson; children's first drafts of their stories

5: Final story

Introduction
● Recall the creation of first drafts and invite comments on the experience.

Whole-class work
● Establish that the children feel ready to produce the final versions of their stories, and encourage those who answer negatively with extra support.
● Talk about ways to make the story attractive, for example, using paper of different shapes and colours, and including illustrations. Some children may like to work on squares as they did for the storyboard and stick these onto coloured pages in a book. Others may want to write the story on an A4 sheet of paper and stick this on larger coloured paper so that they can add illustrations around it. Encourage them to be as innovative as they like.

Paired work
● Invite children to find their partners from the previous lesson to discuss how they plan to set out their story and any changes they propose.

Independent work
● Allocate the main lesson time to children's independent work involving writing and illustrating their stories.

Review
● Ask individuals to read their stories to small groups and to answer questions about them. Encourage some children to choose a story other than their own to read and talk about.
● Hold a whole-class discussion about the success of this writing project.

Curriculum objectives
● To write from memory simple sentences dictated by the teacher that include words using the GPCs and common exception words taught so far.
● To begin to punctuate sentences using a capital letter and a full stop.
● To leave spaces between words.
● To use the grammatical terminology in Appendix 2 in discussing their writing.

Resources
Interactive activity 'Missing punctuation' on the CD-ROM

Grammar and punctuation: Punctuating sentences

Revise
● Display the opening screen of interactive activity 'Missing punctuation' on the CD-ROM. Read the instructions with the class and identify the task.
● Decide together what is missing in the first sentence and invite one child to drag and drop the label into the box to identify this.
● Continue in the same way through all five sentences.
● Complete the activity by choosing an appropriate face to reflect the overall score and type in a comment about how well they managed the activity.
● Recall previous lessons involving sentence writing, using correct grammatical terminology when discussing capital letters, full stops and word spaces.

Assess
● Dictate a simple sentence to the children, making sure that words used are from a bank of those already taught so that the main focus will be on punctuation. Ask them to write the sentence down, paying attention to the above aspects.

Further practice
● Simplify or extend the words used in the sentence to reflect the levels of those involved.
● Challenge children to follow your sentence with another sentence of their own to say what might happen next, for example: *The boy went out in the rain. He got very wet.*

Curriculum objectives
● To respond speedily with the correct sound for all 40+ phonemes, including, where applicable, alternative sounds for graphemes.
● To read accurately by blending sounds in unfamiliar words containing GPCs that have been taught.

Resources
A set of cards showing words that contain taught graphemes; objects to link with the cards (for example, soap, chair, tool, model bird or fish; drawstring bag)

Spelling: Read and match

Revise
● Revise blending using sets of everyday objects, for example, items used for washing, model farm animals. Ensure that children are familiar with the GPCs involved. Arrange the objects attractively to engage children, for example, in a wash bag or on a farm mat.
● Take turns to choose an object and 'sound-talk' the name, (break it down into separate phonemes) for example, /s/ /oa/ /p/, /t/ /oo/ /th/ /br/ /u/ /sh/.
● Write these words on the board with children choosing which letters to use. Discuss and agree the final spelling of each word.
● Draw attention to any alternative graphemes, for example, *bear, chair*.

Assess
● Ask the children to sit in a circle and arrange the word cards upside down in the centre, along with a bag full of the matching objects.
● Invite all children to pick up a card and read it to themselves.
● Pull an object out of the bag and show it to the children.
● Ask the child with the corresponding card to read it aloud, first in 'sound-talk' and then as a complete word.
● Continue until all children have matched their cards to an object.
● Observe individual responses and note any difficulties with blending and particular GPCs.

Further practice
● Encourage children who struggle by praising their effort and then simplifying the activity to match their reading level.
● Extend the activity by using pictures rather than objects, so that more complex words can be introduced.

Curriculum objectives

● To read accurately by blending sounds in unfamiliar words containing GPCs that have been taught.
● To apply phonic knowledge and skills as the route to decode words.
● To read other words of more than one syllable that contain taught GPCs.
● To respond speedily with the correct graphemes for all 40+ phonemes, including alternative sounds for phonemes.

Resources

Photocopiable page 47 'Sort the sentences'; photocopiable page 'Extract from *Tyrannosaurus Drip*' from the CD-ROM

Reading: Sort the sentences

Revise

● Display 'Extract from *Tyrannosaurus Drip*' from the CD-ROM and recall work on this (week 4, lesson 1).
● Read the extract together and invite children to highlight words with the /e/ phoneme written in different ways, 'ee', 'ea', 'e', 'y'. Talk about how the name of a letter, 'T', has been used by the writer to create an /e/ sound and find words that rhyme with this. Use the correct terminology when discussing phonemes and graphemes.
● Talk about how other words are built up, for example, creating the past tense of *hatch* and *grumble* by adding a 'd'.
● Invite children to search for alternative graphemes related to words in the story, for example, finding a word to rhyme with *dinosaur* (*war*). Talk about the letters used ('aur', 'ar') and the sound created. Think of other words with the same phoneme and discuss their spelling (*corn, claw*).
● Draw attention to and revise other aspects of reading discussed previously. Ask children to identify the phrase that is repeated, *And she grumbled,* and recall previous discussion about the effect that repetition has in poetry and stories. Recall why the baby dinosaurs have capital letters in the description of them, to remind children of the need for capital letters for names.
● Display photocopiable page 47 'Sort the sentences'. Focus initially on continuing to look for alternative graphemes as in the extract work above, for example, *shouts, Down; on, swamp.*
● Invite the children to read through the words in the boxes. Divide the class in half and ask one half to read the box on the left and the other the corresponding box on the right. Begin with the first row of boxes and talk about whether reading the two boxes in order creates a sentence that makes sense and has an accurate meaning. Do the same with all of the boxes.
● Return to the left box of the first line and invite the children to read the other boxes with a partner and decide which one might be added to make a sentence that has the correct meaning.
● Share the decision and ask the partners to work together through the rest of the page.

Assess

● Read the instructions for completing the photocopiable sheet and make sure that children understand.
● Provide each child with the photocopiable sheet to complete independently.

Further practice

● Include all children who might be struggling with the reading level of this work in the discussion and reading of the extract and the photocopiable sheet, supporting and encouraging them in their attempts to read. However, create a different page for them to complete. Do not include cutting out, but ask children instead to read a simple sentence and then draw a picture about what they read, for example, *This dinosaur likes plants to eat.* Work alongside them to support blending.
● Extend the activity to challenge children's reading skills by writing more complex sentences on a blank page, for example, to include common exception words, contractions and '-ed' endings (*"I'm tired of looking for my friend," said the worried dinosaur*). Jumble the new sentences as they appear on the photocopiable sheet.

Curriculum objectives
● To write sentences by saying out loud what they are going to write about.
● To use the grammatical terminology in Appendix 2 in discussing their writing.
● To sequence sentences to form short narratives.
● To discuss what they have written with the teacher or other children.

Resources
Photocopiable page 46 'The sad little dinosaur'; the children's dinosaur stories (week 6, lesson 5)

Writing: When the dinosaur came to school

Revise
● Recall previous discussions about how a story follows a sequence of beginning, middle and end.
● Display photocopiable page 46 'The sad little dinosaur' and talk about how children followed this sequence to help them to sort out the jumbled sentences so that the story made sense.
● Refer to the displayed story and recall discussions about helping stories, and events within them, to flow along by using connecting words and phrases, such as *At last, Then, After that.*
● Ask the children to read their dinosaur stories (week 6, lesson 5) to a different partner from the last lesson and invite comments from the partners about how easy it is to identify a beginning, middle and end.
● Recall sentence writing and encourage children to use the correct grammatical terminology when talking about full stops, capital letters, question marks and exclamation marks.
● Talk about the need to leave spaces between words. Write a simple sentence on the board without spaces and ask how easy the children find this to read. Invite one child to write it again with spaces and discuss the effect.

Assess
● Write the title *When the dinosaur came to school* on the board and invite children to speculate about what they might do if this happened.
● Recall how humans did not live in dinosaur times, and talk about how a dinosaur might react when arriving in a noisy classroom.
● Consider how the story could be quite different, depending on whether the main character was a meat- or plant-eating dinosaur. Discuss how this could change events, for example, making the story frightening rather than amusing. Perhaps there could be a problem to solve, such as how to send the dinosaur back to his or her own time.
● Spend some time in groups following this discussion to extend ideas for the story plot. Encourage children to make notes of interesting suggestions before bringing them together as a class to share these.
● Ask children to consider story language and call out some suitable opening sentences, for example, *Once upon a time, Long, long ago, There was once a....*
● Talk about possible endings for the story. Will it be happy or sad?
● Write a list on the board, with the children's help, to remind them of things they need to include in their story, for example, title, at least three sentences – beginning, middle and end – capital letters, full stops, word spaces.
● Ask the children to write a story that has at least three sentences representing the beginning, middle and end.
● Invite children to read their finished stories to partners and discuss features such as sequence, sentence structure and punctuation.
● Choose stories at random to discuss with the class. Draw attention and give praise for correct sentence-punctuation features, and encourage children to include any missing aspects next time.

Further practice
● Support those who have difficulty by playing with model dinosaurs and people. Encourage them to re-enact a simple story of a dinosaur arriving amongst a group of people. Model appropriate voices and dialogue as you move the characters around. Help the children to write down three simple sentences about the story that emerges. Use correct terminology relating to sentence structure as you draw attention to the completed writing.
● Extend the activity by asking groups of children to produce a book of dinosaur stories. Encourage them to create an exciting title and book cover.

Describe the dinosaur

■ Cut out names of the dinosaurs and stick them at the top of a separate sheet of paper.

■ Draw the dinosaur under each name.

■ Cut out the words and stick them next to the right dinosaur.

■ Add more words of your own if you have space.

✂

Tyrannosaurus Rex	Tyrannosaurus Drip
scaly tail	beak nose
meat eater	plant eater
green	sharp teeth
can swim	strong

PHOTOCOPIABLE

Sensing the dinosaur

- Read the poem to your partner.
- Draw a circle around the rhyming words.

Sensing the Dinosaur

See the dinosaur's feet as they stomp,

Smell the dinosaur's teeth as they chomp,

Hear the dinosaur's jaws as they munch,

Taste the dinosaur's huge meaty lunch

See the dinosaur's tiny black eye,

Hear the dinosaur's frightening sigh,

Feel the dinosaur's pointed sharp claw,

Hear the dinosaur bellow and roar,

BUT...

If you dare touch the dinosaur's knee,

Then I'm sure it will eat you for tea!

by Jean Evans

I can read a poem aloud and find words that rhyme.

How did you do?

Name: _____ Date: _____

Dinosaur facts

- Colour the pictures.
- Fill in the missing words.

tail	back	neck	horns

Apatosaurus

This dinosaur has
a very long _____ .

Diplodocus

This dinosaur has
a very long _____ .

Triceratops

This dinosaur has
three _____ .

Stegosaurus

This dinosaur has
spiny plates on its _____ .

I can hold my pencil properly and form
letters correctly.

How did you do?

PHOTOCOPIABLE

Name: _____   Date: _____

Dinosaur information

- Draw a picture of each dinosaur.
- Finish the two sentences under each picture.
- Make up a sentence of your own about each dinosaur.

Tyrannosaurus Rex	**Stegosaurus**
I like to eat _____ _____ My teeth are _____ _____ _____ _____	I like to eat _____ _____ My back has _____ _____ _____ _____

I can finish a sentence and write a sentence
of my own.

How did you do?

Dinosaur display review

■ Read the questions. Write your answers in the spaces below.

1. What do you like about the display?

I like _____

_____

2. What does the display tell you?

The display tells me _____

_____

3. What would you change about the display?

I would change _____

_____

4. What did you learn when you helped with the display?

I learned _____

_____

Colour the face that shows what you think of the display.

I can review the dinosaur display.

How did you do?

PHOTOCOPIABLE

Dinosaur story map

- Answer the questions about your story map in the spaces below.
- Remember to write sentences.

I. What happens at the beginning of the path in your story map?

At the beginning of the path _____

_____

_____

2. What happens along the path in your story map?

Along the path _____

_____

3. How have you shown the setting on your story map?

I have shown the setting by _____

_____

4. What happens at the end of the path in your story map?

At the end of the path _____

_____

_____

I can arrange the sentences in the correct
order to tell the story.

How did you do?

Name: _____   Date: _____

The sad little dinosaur

- Cut out the sentences.
- Stick them on paper in the correct order to tell the story.
- Draw pictures around the sentences to illustrate your story.

At last she found a friend who looked just like her.
In the end the dinosaur was happy.
First she went to the swamp, but there was nobody there.
One day the dinosaur went out to look for a friend.
Then one day the dinosaur went to a different swamp.
Once upon a time there lived a sad little dinosaur.
Second she went into the woods, but there was nobody there.

Name: _____ Date: _____

Sort the sentences

- Cut out the boxes below.
- Arrange them in pairs to make sentences about the dinosaurs in the story of *Tyrannosaurus Drip*.

✂

The duckbill dinosaurs lived in a...	hill with no green plants.
Tyrannosaurus Rex shouts...	"Down with hunting! Down with war!"
The duckbill dinosaurs hoot...	bellyfuls of water weeds.
Tyrannosaurus Rex lived on a...	bellyfuls of duckbill dinosaur!
Duckbill dinosaurs eat...	swamp beside a river.
Tyrannosaurus Rex eat...	"Up with hunting! Up with war!"

Fairy stories and traditional tales

The theme of this half-term is fairy stories and traditional tales. Children spend the first two weeks exploring the traditional tales, 'The Enormous Turnip' and 'The Gingerbread Man', before spending a further three weeks enjoying activities relating to the fairy story, 'Cinderella'. The final week introduces exploration of traditional rhymes. Prior learning is revised and embedded, and exciting new learning opportunities are introduced throughout.

Expected prior learning
- Understand the terms plot, character and setting.
- Know in simple terms what is meant by a verb and a noun.
- Can read and understand simple sentences.
- Can use phonic knowledge to decode regular words and read them aloud.
- Can talk to others with understanding about what they have read.
- Can write words that reflect their spoken sounds.
- Can write simple sentences with some words spelled correctly and others phonetically plausible.

Overview of progression
- As the children explore traditional stories, they develop prediction skills, identify characters and events, explore word endings and enhance skills in writing dictated sentences and retelling stories. They extend awareness of formal writing conventions when reading and writing recipes.
- Fairy stories serve to revise character, plot and setting, and simple punctuation, including question marks and exclamation marks. Children read contraction words, learn the spelling rules for plural endings and learn how to read and write common exception words and the 'un-' prefix.
- Work with traditional rhymes encourages children to extend appreciation of rhymes and poems by reciting and performing favourites, and to break words down into syllables as a way of decoding them.

Creative context
- Children are encouraged to use drama, role play, puppets and small-world equipment to re-enact stories, and through accompanying rhyme performances with percussion instruments to highlight rhythm (links to music).
- PSHE links through discussing characters' feelings in hot-seating and role play.
- Discovering aspects of order and sequence when ordering story events and reciting number rhymes links to maths.

Preparation
You will need appropriate versions of 'The Enormous Turnip', 'The Gingerbread Man' and 'Cinderella' – any can be used.

You will also need:
A turnip; sticky notes; individual whiteboards and pens; large sheets of paper; yellow card; green pens; small-world characters; string; shallow trays filled with compost; dressing-up clothes; puppets; turnip soup and gingerbread men recipes; cooking ingredients and untensils; coloured pens and pencils; camera; role-play cleaning equiment; examples of diaries; voice recorder; newspaper headlines and children's pages; large sheets of paper; glue; wedding magazines; nursery rhyme books; percussion instruments;

On the CD-ROM you will find:
Interactive activities 'Sort the rhymes', 'Rhymes and patterns', 'Five Old Fishermen (1)', 'Five Old Fishermen (2)', 'The Princess and the Pea'; photocopiable pages 'The Enormous Turnip', 'Ugly sisters' letter', 'Cinderella endings', 'Tongue twisters', 'Fairy-tale review', 'The Little Red Hen word endings', 'The Princess and the Pea'

Chapter at a glance

An overview of the chapter. For curriculum objective codes, please see pages 8–10.

Week	Lesson	Curriculum objectives	Summary of activities	Outcomes
1	1	RC: 3, 11, 13	Read the traditional tale 'The Enormous Turnip'. Predict what might happen. Identify characters and setting.	• Can make predictions based on pictorial and contextual clues. • Can demonstrate understanding of what is read.
	2	RWR: 2, 9 RC: 4	Read another version of the story and compare to previous version. Identify repetitive phrases and join in.	• Can use correct sound for graphemes taught. • Can recognise and enjoy joining in with predictable phrases.
	3	RWR: 5 WT: 8, 10 WC: 11	Change the endings of words so that a sentence makes sense in the context. Write a dictated sentence from memory.	• Can read and write words with '-s','-es', '-ing', '-ed', '-er' and '-est' endings. • Can write from memory a dictated sentence.
	4	RC: 3, 13	Listen to retelling of 'The Enormous Turnip'. Discuss characters and event sequence. Retell story to a partner and the class.	• Can explain understanding of a story through retelling. • Can demonstrate familiarity with traditional stories and their characters and event sequences.
	5	RWR: 9 RC: 3, 13	Watch re-enactment of the story using small-world characters and props. Group re-enactments. Discussion about performances.	• Can re-enact a story using props, commenting on interpretations, and accuracy and order of events. • Can talk about what made performances enjoyable.
2	1	RC: 2, 7 WT: 14	Recall 'The Enormous Turnip'. Explore turnips. Find turnip soup recipe. Read the recipe, then discuss features and annotate copies. Form digits 0 to 9.	• Can use knowledge and information to discuss turnips. • Can read recipe and recognise features. • Can form digits 0 to 9.
	2	RC: 7, 8	Read 'The Gingerbread Man'. Find common features with 'The Enormous Turnip'. Search for gingerbread man recipe. Read and discuss ingredients.	• Can link what they read to own experiences. • Can check that text makes sense while reading.
	3	RC: 2, 8	Read the gingerbread recipe, checking it makes sense. Make gingerbread men, drawing on previous experience of baking.	• Can read a simple recipe and check it makes sense. • Can correct own inaccuracies when reading.
	4	WT: 9, 14 WC: 1	Write sentences recalling the making of the gingerbread men using template. Use sequence, numbering and accurate recall.	• Can explain the writing plan. • Can apply spelling rules to sentences. • Can number sentences to show correct sequence of actions.
	5	WT: 9, 14 WC: 4	Write recipe for gingerbread men. Emphasis on following rules and guidelines and re-reading work.	• Can produce instruction text applying spelling rules and guidelines and forming digits correctly. • Can check it makes sense.
3	1	RWR: 2 RC: 3, 6 WC: 3	Listen to 'Cinderella'. Identify fairy-story genre. Learn new vocabulary. Write sentences showing story sequence.	• Can identify fairy-story characteristics. • Can punctuate simple sentences and sequence them to outline a story.
	2	RWR: 5 WT: 6 WC: 11	Identify nouns in sentences. Learn rule for creating plural. Complete written exercise, inserting plural endings.	• Can identify and read plurals with '-s' or '-es'. • Can apply rule for adding these endings in written work.
	3	RWR: 4 WT: 2, 10	Discover common exception words in 'Cinderella'. Read paragraph, underlining exception words. Write a dictated sentence containing exception words.	• Can read common exception words in focused story. • Can write common exception words correctly in a dictated sentence.
	4	RC: 3, 10	Set up role-play castle kitchen. Act out scenes from story. Focus on how characters look, talk, move and feel.	• Can make inferences through actions and reactions during role play. • Can recognise features of fairy stories.
	5	WT: 2 WC: 3, 5, 9	Discuss diaries. Choose an event an ugly sister might write about. Write a diary page. Focus on sentence structure.	• Can write a character's account of an event. • Can use correct punctuation and sequence sentences to reflect narrative.
4	1	RWR: 5, 7 RC: 10 WC: 11	Read letter and infer feelings. Explore contractions, plurals, prefix 'un-', question marks.	• Can read taught GPCs and word endings. • Can make inferences based on what is said/done.
	2	WC: 2, 9	Identify question marks in sentences. Discuss meaning. Write questions.	• Can write sentences with correct punctuation, including appropriate use of question marks.
	3	WT: 1, 7 WC: 2, 11	Identify prefix 'un-' and discuss change to meaning. Use it in sentences.	• Can understand how 'un-' changes meaning. • Can compose a sentence the prefix 'un-'.
	4	WT: 6, 13 WC: 10	Write letters from Cinderella. Focus on capital letters and plural endings.	• Can use capital letters and apply spelling rules for plurals correctly when writing a letter.
	5	WC: 5, 12	Discuss written letters using grammatical terminology. Read with partner.	• Can discuss their written letters with class, using correct grammatical terminology.

Chapter at a glance

Week	Lesson	Curriculum objectives	Summary of activities	Outcomes
5	1	WT: 11, 12 WC: 7	Explore newspaper reports and discuss key features. Create report using template.	• Can form letters correctly, space words, and sit and hold pencil correctly when writing a report.
	2	WT: 8 WC: 9	Explore newspaper headlines/sentences with question and exclamation marks, '-ed' and '-est' endings.	• Can use '-ed' and '-est' endings, question marks and exclamation marks in writing.
	3	WC: 3, 12	Observe in role as 'Palace News' reporters, while groups act out scene. Discuss writing report in sequence.	• Can use grammatical terminology when discussing writing. • Can sequence events to form narrative report.
	4	WT: 1 WC: 2	Develop reports using notes from previous lesson. Focus on oral sentence composition and correct punctuation.	• Can compose sentences orally before writing. • Can use correct punctuation when writing sentences for reports.
	5	WC: 3, 12	Share reports and discuss correct sequence to tell 'Cinderella' story. Put reports together to form 'Palace News'.	• Can use grammatical terminology when discussing sentences in reports. • Can decide correct sequence to put narrative reports into a newspaper.
6	1	RWR: 4, 8 WT: 5	Explore nursery rhymes and choose favourites. Read nursery rhymes aloud from board. Matching rhyming words.	• Can read aloud rhymes at appropriate level. • Can match rhyming words and use letter names to distinguish those with alternative spellings.
	2	RWR: 6 RC: 5	Recite favourite rhymes by heart. Clap or beat time to the syllables of words read in rhymes and tongue twisters.	• Can appreciate and recite rhymes and poems by heart. • Can read words of more than one syllable. • Can identify syllables by beat and rhythm.
	3	RWR: 6 RC: 1	Listen to and discuss number rhymes beyond their reading levels. Highlight rhyming words in rhymes, including those with alternative spellings.	• Can read polysyllabic words with taught GPCs when exploring number rhymes. • Can listen to and discuss number rhymes.
	4	RWR: 8 WT: 9	Explore sequence and pattern in a displayed number rhyme. Read the poem aloud, highlighting rhyming words. Write own version of the poem.	• Can read poem aloud using existing phonic knowledge. • Can apply spelling rules when writing own poem.
	5	RC: 1, 5	Recall range of poems explored over week. Choose one to perform to class. Discuss choice, rhyme and content.	• Can recite poem to audience. • Can listen to and discuss poems beyond their reading level.

Background knowledge

Apostrophe: Punctuation used to indicate either the place of missing letters (*I'll*), or possession (*Peter's hat*).

Noun: Sometimes called naming words because they name people, places and things. However, this does not always apply.

Past tense: Verbs in the past tense are typically used to talk about the past.

Plural: A plural noun means more than one (*house/houses*).

Prefix: Letters added to the front of a word to change its meaning, such as the prefix 'un-' (*fasten/unfasten*).

Suffix: An ending which turns one word into another (*strong/stronger, call/called*).

Verb: Words that usually name actions.

Week 1 lesson plans

The lessons for this week focus on the traditional story, 'The Enormous Turnip'. Initially children are encouraged to listen to the story and identify the characters, plot and setting. They predict what might happen next at various points in the story and have fun joining in with predictable phrases. Subsequent lessons involve a more in-depth exploration of the story language and new vocabulary, as well as of the effect of adding the suffix '-ed'. Children work with partners and practise retelling the story to one another using the language they have explored. Finally, the week's work is consolidated as groups of children organise performances of the story for the rest of the class.

1: 'The Enormous Turnip'

Introduction
● Pass the turnip around and invite each child to say something about it, for example, how it smells, what colour it is or whether they like the taste.
● Explain that the turnip is a clue about the story you are going to read to them. Invite the children to guess the title.

Whole-class work
● Explore the book cover, asking the children to read the title. Encourage discussion about whether they have heard the story before. Look for the names of the author and illustrator and read them together. Some versions of the story might be by authors children have come across before, if so ask them to recall other titles by this author.
● Look closely at the illustration and ask if it gives us any clues about the story, for example, *It might be about a man and a woman and a big turnip.*
● Depending on your version of the story, focus on the back cover and read the blurb and quotes to the children, encouraging them to join in when they can. Discuss how these might help to predict the plot.
● Read the story, pausing to explain any new words, and to ask what might happen next. Encourage children to recognise the sequence of adding another character one by one until the turnip is finally pulled from the ground. Talk about how this sequence makes predicting easier.
● Once you have read the whole story, talk about where it is set and think of words to describe the turnip field. Explain that words that describe things are called *adjectives*.
● Invite children to identify the main character(s). Do they think the old man and woman are the most important characters? Consider the significant part that the tiny mouse plays to see whether this changes their opinions.

Paired work
● Divide the board into two sections headed *Characters* and *Setting*.
● Ask pairs to continue the class discussion about the main character(s). Suggest that they consider who does the most, or whether some have an equal part to play. Provide them with a sticky note to write down the name(s) they have chosen and attach it under the heading *Character(s)*.
● Now invite them to write words to describe the setting before choosing which ones are the most effective. Remind them that these words are known as *adjectives*. Ask them to write these on the board under *Setting*.

Review
● Bring the children together and ask pairs to remove and read out their character names. Discuss these choices, emphasising that there is no right or wrong answer.
● Read the setting words, adding more to the list as children think of them. Decide whether the lesson has helped the class to become more familiar with the story, and in what way.

Curriculum objectives
● To re-read books to build up their fluency and confidence in word reading.
● To respond speedily with the correct sound to graphemes for all 40+ phonemes, including those with alternative sounds for graphemes.
● To recognise and join in with predictable phrases.

Resources
The chosen version of 'The Enormous Turnip' used in the previous lesson; photocopiable page 'The Enormous Turnip' from the CD-ROM

2: And they pulled, and they pulled...

Introduction
● Read 'The Enormous Turnip' to the class, showing the illustrations.
● Display the photocopiable page 'The Enormous Turnip' from the CD-ROM and invite children to read it together. Compare this story with the book version. Discuss whether the story events and characters are the same and compare the language used. Decide which version is more interesting.
● Consider the importance of illustration. Is it as easy to imagine setting and events in the photocopiable story?

Whole-class work
● Invite children to highlight the repeated phrase, *They pulled and pulled*. Find further examples, such as: *They grew and they grew*; *bigger and bigger and bigger*, and underline these.
● Introduce the notion of sequencing events by asking children to number the characters (1 = the old man, 7 = the tiny mouse) every time they appear.
● Discuss how repeated events and phrases help us predict what happens next.

Group work
● Invite mixed-ability groups of four to read a paragraph each from the photocopiable sheet, so that every child reads twice. Encourage them to support one another with blends and words.

> **Differentiation**
> ● Simplify the story to reflect the reading level of those who struggle.

Review
● Ask groups to read the story to the class to build up their fluency and confidence, while those who struggled join in with predictable phrases.

Curriculum objectives
● To read words containing taught GPCs and '-s', '-es', '-ing', '-ed', '-er' and '-est' endings.
● To add prefixes and suffixes using '-ing', '-ed', '-er' and '-est' where no change is needed in the spelling of root words.
● To learn the grammar for Year 1 in Appendix 2.
● To write from memory simple sentences dictated by the teacher that include words using the GPCs and common exception words taught so far.

Resources
Photocopiable page 72 'Change the endings'; individual whiteboards

3: Changing endings

Introduction
● Write *help, helps, helped, helper* and *helping* on the board and ask the children to read them. Discuss what is different about the sound and the spelling. Which four letters remain the same?

Independent work
● Read out familiar verbs, such as *help* or *jump* and ask children to write them in the past tense. Dictate a simple sentence including one of these verbs.

Whole-class work
● Display photocopiable page 72 'Change the endings', and read the instructions together. Ensure that children understand what to do by working through the first box. Suggest that they try each ending if in doubt to see if the sentence makes sense. Remind them that the story is written in the past tense, so the word is *planted*.

Paired work
● Provide pairs of children with the photocopiable sheet and ask them to help one another in completing the page.

Review
● Write the dictated sentence on the board with help from the class. Encourage children to comment on their individual difficulties with writing this.
● Review the completed photocopiable sheet together.

Curriculum objectives

● To explain clearly their understanding of what is read to them.
● To become very familiar with key stories, fairy stories and traditional tales, retelling them and considering their particular characteristics.

Resources

Photocopiable page 'The Enormous Turnip' from the CD-ROM; interactive whiteboard; large sheets of paper

4: Tell the story

Introduction

● Retell 'The Enormous Turnip' story to the children, holding their attention, for example, with dialogue between the characters and variation in the tone of your voice. Deliberately omit a middle character in the story, such as the cat.
● Ask whether the children liked your retelling and if you missed any events.
● Suggest that they try to retell the story, emphasising the importance of introducing characters and events in order. Remind them of how they followed story events in the displayed version of 'The Enormous Turnip' by looking for repeated phrases and recognising the event sequence. Briefly display the photocopiable page 'The Enormous Turnip' from the CD-ROM to recap this.

Paired work

● Divide into pairs and suggest making notes before telling the story, for example, writing a list of characters in the order they appear.
● Once children are confident that they can remember the story, suggest that they tell it to one another and discuss omissions.

Differentiation

● Retell the story with those needing support, pausing for them to finish predictable words and phrases.
● Challenge those who manage the retelling easily to retell another traditional story to the class, such as 'The Little Red Hen'.

Review

● Bring the class together to listen to the retellings. Invite comments on how well individuals have understood and represented the key events in the story. Discuss whether all the characters have been included in the correct order.

Curriculum objectives

● To re-read books to build up their fluency and confidence in word reading.
● To explain clearly their understanding of what is read to them.
● To become very familiar with key stories, fairy stories and traditional tales, retelling them and considering their particular characteristics.

Resources

Different versions of 'The Enormous Turnip' including photocopiable page 'The Enormous Turnip' from the CD-ROM; small turnips; yellow card; green pens; small-world people and animals to represent the characters from the story; string; shallow trays filled with compost; dressing-up clothes; puppets

5: Playing with performance

Introduction

● Put the compost tray in the centre of the room with a turnip pushed into it to look as if it is growing. Arrange small yellow card circles on the compost to represent smaller turnips.
● Re-enact the story, inviting individual children to place small-world characters in place on the compost to help you with this. Pull up the turnip and make the characters fall over at the end of the story.
● Explain that this is one way of re-enacting the story and invite children to suggest others, such as putting on a play, making a story bag or using puppets.

Group work

● Divide the children into mixed-ability groups and supply a bank of resources they might use. Be ready to add more if children have new ideas.
● Suggest that they begin by deciding on their method of re-enactment and then choose a book or photocopied story to refer to when they are planning it.
● Encourage confident members of the group to support those who struggle with remembering aspects of the story.

Review

● Invite groups of children to re-enact the story to the class using their chosen method.
● Encourage comments on the different interpretations, and the accuracy and order of events. Talk about what made performances enjoyable, for example, lively repetition, amusing characterisation and clever use of props.

Curriculum objectives
● To draw on what they already know or on background information and vocabulary provided by the teacher.
● To be encouraged to link what they read or hear read to their own experiences.
● To form digits 0 to 9.

Resources
A turnip; book of 'The Enormous Turnip' story used in week 1; cookery books containing turnip soup recipes (as simple as possible); children's cookery books; photocopiable page 73 'Turnip soup recipe'; coloured pencils and pens

Week 2 lesson plans

This week's lessons begin with a recall of 'The Enormous Turnip' story explored in week 1. A link is made between fiction and non-fiction with the introduction of informative text in the form of a recipe for turnip soup. Children spend time reading the recipe, understanding the content and exploring the features of a recipe. They return to fiction to find similarities between 'The Enormous Turnip' and 'The Gingerbread Man' stories, such as sequencing and repetition. A recipe for gingerbread is located using cookery books before children make gingerbread people. They write sentences recalling how they did this as a follow up. Finally, they write their own recipes for gingerbread people.

1: Tasty turnips

Introduction
● Recall the story of 'The Enormous Turnip', re-reading the book if necessary.
● Pass around the turnip and ask children to recall things they have learned. Ask questions about how and where it grows and ways of eating it.
● Recall ways that the characters in the story ate the enormous turnip.
● Ask where someone would look to find out how to cook turnips.

Whole-class work
● Show the children the cookery books. Ask whether they are fiction or non-fiction and how they can tell. Discuss where recipes for turnip soup might be found in each book, for example, in the soup or vegetable section.
● Find the words *turnip soup* in the index, asking children to decide where the letter 't' will fall in alphabetical order.
● Read some of the recipes aloud and talk about common ingredients.
● Display photocopiable page 73 'Turnip soup recipe' and ask children to read the headings together.
● Suggest that a substitute heading for *You will need* could be *Utensils* and ask children to name items that fall into this category.
● Discuss the meaning of *Ingredients* and read the list together.
● Read the *What to do* section together, supporting with tricky words where necessary, for example, *minutes* and *vegetables*. Ask: *Does this follow a sequence from the start of preparation to the finished soup?* Talk about how the inclusion of numbers for each point might help readers when they are making the soup.
● Look at a turnip soup recipe in a cookery book and draw attention to illustrations and photographs. Ask children how these might help them when they are cooking. Now look at the displayed photocopiable sheet and point to the empty boxes. Suggest children illustrate these as they choose.

Group work
● Provide mixed-ability groups with the photocopiable sheet. Suggest that they make notes about how they could improve it, for example, by numbering things to do and providing cartoon-like drawings in the box alongside the instructors.

Independent work
● Provide each child with the photocopiable sheet to annotate.

Review
● Bring the class together to share their recipe pages (save these for lesson 5). Discuss how the addition of numbers and drawings has helped. Talk about any new words learned, such as *ingredients* and *utensils* and tricky words encountered.
● Ask the children what they have learned about the features of a recipe and whether they think they could now write their own recipes incorporating these features.

Curriculum objectives
- To check that the text makes sense to them as they read and correcting inaccurate reading.
- To draw on what they already know or on background information and vocabulary provided by the teacher.

Resources
A book telling the traditional story of 'The Gingerbread Man', for example, *Usborne First Reading: Level 3* by Mairi Mackinnon, book of 'The Enormous Turnip' story used in week 1 lessons; recipe books containing simple recipes for gingerbread men

2: 'The Gingerbread Man'

Introduction
- Explain that 'The Enormous Turnip' is a traditional tale and has probably been handed down from one generation to another. Suggest that the children's family members may have read this story as children.
- Talk about how building up a sequence is a common feature of traditional stories.
- Explain that they are going to explore another traditional story together.

Whole-class work
- Read 'The Gingerbread Man' and ask children to compare it with 'The Enormous Turnip', identifying any common features, such as the gradual build-up of a sequence as characters in both stories help, either to pull up the turnip or to chase the gingerbread man.
- Invite them to suggest other traditional tales they may recall with the same sort of sequence, for example, 'The Big Pancake'.
- Recall how the turnip soup recipe linked to 'The Enormous Turnip' story and ask what sort of recipe might link to 'The Gingerbread Man' story.

Group work
- Provide a selection of cookery books for children to browse to find a recipe for gingerbread men.
- Ask them to read the recipe together and check that the text makes sense.

Review
- Bring the class together to read their recipes to one another. Encourage discussion about the recipe features and links to the children's experiences of cooking and baking. Decide on the most popular recipe.

Curriculum objectives
- To check that the text makes sense to them as they read and correcting inaccurate reading.
- To be encouraged to link what they read or hear read to their own experiences.

Resources
Gingerbread man recipe chosen in lesson 2 (either project an image of this from a cookery book or create a simple typed version); ingredients and utensils as defined by the recipe; access to oven; aprons; camera

3: Follow the recipe

Introduction
- Recall the previous lesson and explain that the children are going to make gingerbread men using their chosen recipe.

Whole-class work
- Display the chosen recipe and ask the children to read it with you, joining in where they can, applying spelling rules as applicable.
- Go through it again, making sure that children understand vocabulary and what to do. Emphasise safety issues, such as the hot oven.
- Show them the resources and name each item together.
- Explain that the camera is for you to record their actions for lesson 4.

Group work
- Arrange groups to cook together, assisted by appropriate adult support.
- Work with groups while they are busy, checking that they know which stage of the recipe they are on and what comes next by referring to the recipe.
- Put the finished trays of gingerbread men into the oven for the children.
- Take photographs throughout the session to show the stages of the recipe.

Review
- Bring the class together to enjoy the gingerbread men. Discuss how the baking went, for example, how easy it was to read and follow the recipe.
- Talk about how past baking experiences helped children to read and understand more difficult words, such as *knead, dough, method, weighing, quantity*.

Curriculum objectives
● To write sentences by saying out loud what they are going to write about.
● To apply simple spelling rules and guidelines, as listed in Appendix I.
● To form digits 0 to 9.

Resources
Photocopiable page 74 'Making gingerbread men'; children's photographs of their baking session

4: How did you do it?

Introduction
● Invite children to recall when they helped with baking, or followed recipes.
● Explain they are going to write about how they made the gingerbread men.

Whole-class work
● Display some photographs from the baking session and discuss what is happening in each one. Arrange them in sequence, from the first to the last.
● Display photocopiable page 74 'Making gingerbread men'. Explain that filling it in will help children remember the order in which they did things, and will remind them of ingredients and utensils used.
● Read the title and the headings, *My ingredients* and *My utensils*. Ask for things that might be written under these headings.
● Read the words starting each sentence and discuss ways of completing them.

Paired work
● Divide children into pairs and supply the photocopiable sheet.
● Encourage them to talk to one another about what they plan to write in the boxes and the order of their sentences.

Independent work
● Ask children to complete their photocopiable sheets, paying attention to spelling and formation of numbers.

> **Differentiation**
> ● Invite those who are struggling to draw pictures and write simple sentences.

Review
● Gather the class to share their written work (save this for lesson 5). Invite constructive comments about overall accuracy and ordering of sentences.

Curriculum objectives
● To apply simple spelling rules and guidelines, as listed in Appendix I.
● To form digits 0 to 9.
● To write sentences by re-reading what they have written to check that it makes sense.

Resources
Children's completed photocopiable sheets 'Turnip soup recipe' and 'Making gingerbread men' from lessons I and 4; paper or card; recipe books used in lesson 2; coloured pencils and pens; a template with the headings from photocopiable page 73 'Turnip soup recipe'

5: Follow my recipe

Introduction
● Ask the children to recall the turnip soup recipe they annotated in lesson I, the written work describing how they made gingerbread men completed in lesson 4, and the cookery books they browsed.
● Explore what they have in common and identify the features of a recipe.

Whole-class work
● Explain that the children will have their past written work available as they write their own gingerbread recipes.
● Display the template you have created and explain that these empty boxes are the same as those on the photocopiable page 73 'Turnip soup recipe'. Tell the children that they can use these to write their recipes on if they wish to.

Paired work
● Provide each child with their written work and your template. Leave the photographs and books on display for everyone to refer to.
● Ask them to share their ideas with one another and consider features that need to be remembered before working on their own to complete their recipe.
● Once they have done this, suggest they read their recipes to one another.

Review
● Invite the class to share recipes, praising them for good number formation and spelling. Encourage discussion about resources that helped with the final recipe, such as their written sentences and annotated recipe page.

Week 3 lesson plans

This week, the fairy story 'Cinderella' is introduced. Children listen to the story and identify what makes it a fairy story. They recall how a story is structured and learn new vocabulary. Lessons 2 and 3 focus on exploring the plural endings, '-s' and '-es', and reading exception words taken from the story. Role play follows to encourage children to explore characters in more detail and consider how they would react at different points in the story. Finally, this is extended with deeper focus on the ugly sisters, and children write a diary page depicting the point of view of one of them. There is strong focus on punctuation and spelling of exception words and plurals.

Expected outcomes
● All children can begin to punctuate simple sentences.
● Most children can form plurals ending with '-s' and '-es'.
● Some children can offer an opinion about a character's behaviour.

Curriculum objectives
● To become very familiar with fairy stories, retelling them and considering their particular characteristics.
● To respond speedily with the correct graphemes for all 40+ phonemes, including alternative sounds for graphemes.
● To sequence sentences to form short narratives.
● To discuss word meanings, linking new meanings to those already known.

Resources
Books telling the traditional 'Cinderella' story

1: The story of Cinderella

Introduction
● Recall work on the traditional tale, 'The Enormous Turnip', and explain that children are now going to explore a popular fairy story.
● Ask them to name some titles in this genre, for example, 'Sleeping Beauty'.

Whole-class work
● Read a traditional version of 'Cinderella'. Ask children to suggest why this is classified as a fairy story.
● Consider some key elements of a fairy story together, for example, mythical characters such as fairies, goblins, trolls and giants; a conflict between good and evil; magical happenings; often a king and queen, prince or princess, or a poor person struggling with adversity.
● Write any new vocabulary on the board. Explain and discuss the meaning in the context it is used, for example, *The ugly sisters lacked beauty.* Invite children to think of different ways of saying the same thing, such as *The ugly sisters were not beautiful.*

Group work
● Recall the words *sequence, beginning, middle* and *end.*
● Suggest that groups compose three sentences to describe what happens at these points in 'Cinderella'.
● Emphasise the need for correct sentence punctuation, such as inclusion of a capital letter and full stop. Suggest using an exclamation mark for a more punchy ending, for example, *...and she never wore rags again!*
● Remind children that 'Cinderella' is a fairy story and ask them to recall the phrases that such stories usually begin and end with (*Once upon a time, And they lived happily ever after*).
● Suggest that they spend time deciding what they think is the most important event in the middle of the story, for example, the arrival of the Fairy Godmother or when the clock strikes midnight.
● Provide copies of 'Cinderella' for reference. While they complete their sentences, praise correct punctuation and respond to any spelling queries.

> #### Differentiation
> ● If children are struggling, write the first part of the opening sentence, *Once upon a time there was...* and support them as they complete this. Do the same with a simple middle and end sentence.
> ● Invite those ready for a challenge to write the whole story in a logical sequence.

Review
● Bring the class together and ask a child from one group to write their first sentence the top of the board. Follow this with a child from another group writing their middle sentence, and finally ask a child from a different group to write the closing sentence. Read the sequence together to check it makes sense.

Curriculum objectives
● To read words containing taught GPCs and '-s', '-es', '-ing', '-ed', '-er' and '-est' endings.
● To use the spelling rule for adding '-s' or '-es' as the plural marker for nouns and the third-person singular marker for verbs.
● To learn the grammar for Year 1 in Appendix 2.

Resources
Photocopiable page 75 'Make it plural'

2: Exploring plurals

Introduction
● Recall the story 'Cinderella'.
● Define the words *noun* and *plural*, explaining with written examples.
● Explain that this lesson is about writing nouns with correct plural endings. (You could use starter activity 7 'More than one' to begin the task.)

Whole-class work
● Write a noun on the board, such as *cat*, and ask a volunteer to change the ending so that it means more than one cat. Say the /s/ sound at the end.
● Now write the word *dress* and add '-es' to read *dresses*. Ask children to say the /iz/ sound at the end.
● Explain the rule that if the plural ending sounds like /s/ or /z/ it is written '-s', but if the plural ending sounds like /iz/, then it is written '-es'.
● Work a few examples until the children understand the rule.

Paired work
● Provide each pair with photocopiable page 75 'Make it plural', encouraging them to apply the rule they have been practising and agree the ending together before completing their sheets.

> **Differentiation**
> ● Create a simple version of the photocopiable sheet for those requiring more support, concentrating on words with just '-s' endings, for example, *1 cat, 2 cat_*.

Review
● Display the photocopiable sheet to the class. Invite individuals to insert the correct endings so that pairs can check one another's work.
● Discuss how the lesson helped children to remember the rule.

Curriculum objectives
● To read common exception words, noting unusual correspondences between spelling and sound and where these occur in the word.
● To spell common exception words.
● To write from memory simple sentences dictated by the teacher that include words using the GPCs and common exception words taught so far.

3: Exception words

Introduction
● Write a common exception word from 'Cinderella' on the board, for example, *love*.
● Invite children to read the word. Talk about the split digraph 'o-e' and the sound it usually represents. Give examples, such as *bone, alone, choke*.
● Look at *love* again and question why it does not sound like the other words with 'o-e' in them. Explain that *love* is known as an *exception word* as it does not follow the rules that children have been taught.
● Write a paragraph on the board containing several common exception words taken from 'Cinderella', such as *said, once, she, were, there, where, one, have*. Include *love* as well. Read the paragraph together. Explain that many exception words in this paragraph are easy to read as they are recognisable from reading books.
● Invite children to underline the exception words. Discuss the spelling of these words and note unusual correspondences.

Paired work
● Dictate to mixed-ability pairs a sentence containing several exception words, for example, *Once there were two ugly sisters who were cruel to their lovely sister.*
● Invite children to write the sentence and discuss the spelling of the exception words in their pairs, and provide support if necessary.

Review
● Write the dictated sentence on the board and ask children to check and discuss the work of their partners. Review their successes.

Curriculum objectives
● To make inferences on the basis of what is being said and done.
● To become very familiar with fairy stories, retelling them and considering their particular characteristics.

Resources
Role-play cleaning equipment, such as brushes and mops; old dress cut into rags; apron; party dresses; smart clothes for Prince; other resources suggested by children, such as a safety mirror; pumpkin; different versions of 'Cinderella'

4: Exploring characters

Introduction
● Recall the story 'Cinderella'. Make a list of the characters on the board and write words alongside them defining what is known about them, for example, whether they are jealous, kind or cruel.
● Suggest that role play might help children discover more about how characters might look, talk, move and feel in different situations.

Whole-class work
● Show children the resource bank. Invite them to suggest ways to create a role-play castle in which they can re-enact scenes from 'Cinderella'.

Group work
● Work together to develop the castle, allocating different tasks to groups of children, for example, making signs and captions to indicate rooms, arranging furniture and setting out props appropriately.
● Invite children to act out their favourite story scenes that involve interaction between two characters, such as Cinderella's encounter with the Fairy Godmother. Allocate roles to two people while others support and observe.
● Encourage children to make inferences through their own actions, and observation of actions and reactions of others.
● Ask children to take turns to use the role-play area.

Review
● Bring the groups together to re-enact their scenes in the role-play area while others act as the audience. Discuss how children's opinions of characters may have been changed by the role play.

Curriculum objectives
● To discuss what they have written with the teacher or other children.
● To begin to punctuate sentences using a capital letter and a full stop, question mark or exclamation mark.
● To sequence sentences to form short narratives.
● To spell common exception words.

Resources
Examples of different kinds of diary, for example, desk diary, daily and weekly diaries

5: My secret diary

Introduction
● Show the children some diaries. Hold up a large desk diary and explain that this is used to keep dates for meetings. Compare this with a page-a-day diary for writing personal recollections.
● Encourage children to share their experiences of diaries.

Whole-class work
● Write yesterday's date on the board and explain to children that this is going to be a diary page about a fictional event that happened at school.
● Recall work on sequencing sentences and stories and ask how this might help when writing a diary.
● Write on the board some common exception words that might occur on a diary page, for example, *do, today, school, friend, was, house,* and ask children to read them.
● Invite children to suggest possible diary entries involving these words.

Paired work
● Invite mixed-ability pairs to support one another in writing a diary page for an ugly sister. Ask them to imagine she is writing in her diary about how she feels, for example, when the glass slipper would not fit her foot.
● Ask the children to think about the ugly sister's character and point of view.
● Remind them to focus on using the correct punctuation and also to think about the way in which they order their sentences.

Review
● Invite pairs to share their diary pages. Ask the class whether these pages help them to consider an event from another point of view.

Week 4 lesson plans

This week's lessons continue to focus on the 'Cinderella' story, beginning with a letter of apology from the ugly sisters to Cinderella. Children consider key features of a letter as they examine this in detail. They revise use of capital letters, learn what is meant by a contraction, and explore the prefix 'un-'. The meaning of the question mark is discussed when children compose answers to questions posed in the letter. They write their own letters from Cinderella to include these answers. Finally, they act out short scenarios involving the exchange of the two letters. They discuss what they have written, and speculate on whether their opinions of the characters have changed.

1: A letter of apology

Introduction
● Recall the 'Cinderella' story. Focus on the way that the ugly sisters treated Cinderella. Ask children to think of words to describe this behaviour.
● Display photocopiable page 'Ugly sisters' letter' from the CD-ROM and read it to the class. Ask them to comment on what the sisters say, and talk about whether they find this unexpected in any way.

Whole-class work
● Read the opening sentence of the letter and focus on the word *We're*. Introduce the word *contraction* and explain that, in a contraction, the apostrophe represents a missing letter(s). Explain that we often speak in this way, for example, *can't, won't, shouldn't*, but that we usually write words without missing letters. Suggest that the ugly sisters are writing in this way to sound relaxed and friendly. Find the other contractions (*can't, you'll, we'll*) and decide which letters have been missed out.
● Ask individuals to circle the plurals in the letter. Recall previous work on the plural endings '-s', '-es' and remind children of the rule. Identify words ending in '-s' and check whether they end with the sound /s/ or /z/. Read plurals ending in '-es' and check whether these endings sound like /iz/.
● Revise the '-es', '-ed' and '-ing' endings of words (*dresses, jumped, helping*).
● Introduce the prefix 'un-', and give examples of words without and then with this prefix, for example, *happy/unhappy*. Ask what this does to the meaning of the word. Invite children to highlight words with this prefix (*unkind, unhappy*). Decide which words have the opposite meaning. Underline them.
● Discuss the way the letter is written, for example, the friendly approach and the decisions to improve their behaviour towards Cinderella. Question if they think the sisters will really change the way they treat Cinderella. Perhaps they are just being kind to receive an invitation to her wedding?

Paired work
● Ask pairs of children to take on the role of the sisters arguing with each other about what they will write to Cinderella and why.
● Suggest that they try to take opposite viewpoints, with one sister wanting to try and be kind and the other still reluctant to do this.

> **Differentiation**
> ● Simplify the letter so that it has mainly previously taught GPCs and just one focus objective, for example, using the prefix 'un-'.

Review
● Bring the class together to share their discussions. Encourage some of the children to re-enact them. Come to a class decision about whether the sisters have changed permanently and ask children to give reasons for this decision.
● Discuss how exploring this letter has helped them to revise grammar and spelling rules.

2: What a question!

Introduction

Curriculum objectives
● To begin to punctuate sentences using a capital letter and full stop, question mark or exclamation mark.
● To compose a sentence orally before writing it.

Resources
Photocopiable page 'Ugly sisters' letter' from the CD-ROM; voice recorder

● Display photocopiable page 'Ugly sisters' letter' from the CD-ROM. Recall previous explorations of the content, grammar and spelling in the letter.
● Talk about conclusions reached during discussions about the apparent change in the character of the sisters.

Whole-class work

● Ask children to spot the question marks in the letter. Circle these and underline the whole sentences to which they belong. Read them together.
● Define a question mark as a form of punctuation at the end of a sentence to indicate that it is a question.
● Read out the questions again, one at a time, and ask children to think of interesting answers that Cinderella might give to each, for example: *No, thank you, I wouldn't like any of your dresses because they would be far too big for me!*

Group work

● Invite mixed-ability groups to think of suitable questions for Cinderella to ask the ugly sisters so that she can find out if they really mean what they say in the letter. Suggest that they compose them orally first and then write them down. Remind them to concentrate on correct punctuation.

Review

● Invite two children to sit in the hot-seat pretending to be the ugly sisters while the groups take turns to read their questions to them. Use a voice recorder to record the questions and answers. Play back the recording and discuss the sisters' responses.

3: Using prefixes

Introduction

Curriculum objectives
● To use the prefix 'un-'.
● To spell words containing each of the 40+ phonemes already taught.
● To compose a sentence orally before writing it.
● To learn the grammar for Year 1 in Appendix 2.

Resources
Photocopiable page 'Ugly sisters' letter' from the CD-ROM

● Use starter activity 9 'Add my prefix' to start the lesson.
● Display photocopiable page 'Ugly sisters' letter' from the CD-ROM and recall lesson 1 discussions about the prefix 'un-'. Underline the words in the letter starting with this prefix and read the sentences. Talk about how the meaning would change if the prefix was removed.

Group work

● Write some suitable words that can be prefixed by 'un-' on the board (try not to repeat those in the letter), such as *tie, popular, done, well, comfortable*.
● Ask groups to read them together, and then say the word that would be created by adding the prefix, for example, *untie, unpopular, undone, unwell, uncomfortable*.
● Invite them to compose sentences together orally and then write them down, checking spelling and punctuation and confirming that they make sense.

Differentiation
● Modify the words used to reflect the reading levels of individuals, for example, *happy, lock, pack, do*.
● Challenge children to use a word and its 'un-' prefix in one sentence, for example: *The girl turned the key in the lock but it got stuck and so she could not unlock it again.*

Review

● Invite groups to write one of their sentences on the board and read it to the class. Talk about correct use of the prefix, spelling and punctuation.
● Ask children to consider how working in a group can help with reading and sentence composition.

Curriculum objectives
● To use a capital letter for names of people, places, the days of the week, and the personal pronoun *I*.
● To form capital letters.
● To use the spelling rule for adding '-s', or '-es' as the plural marker for nouns and the third-person singular marker for verbs.

Resources
Photocopiable page 'Ugly sisters' letter' from the CD-ROM; photocopiable page 76 'Cinderella's letter'

4: Letters from Cinderella

Introduction
● Display photocopiable page 'Ugly sisters' letter' from the CD-ROM and recall discussions about Cinderella's possible responses to it.
● Explain that the children are going to write letters from Cinderella replying to the ugly sisters' letter.

Whole-class work
● Ask children to name some key letter features, such as name and address of recipient, name of sender, opening and closing words.
● Discuss letter language, for example, recalling the contractions used by the ugly sisters to reflect their relaxed style. Discuss what might be different about a formal letter, such as paying a bill.
● Emphasise the need to use capital letters for names and the personal pronoun *I*, and revisit the spelling rule relating to '-s' or '-es' endings for plurals.
● Display photocopiable page 76 'Cinderella's letter'. Go through each section, reading the questions and asking children what they might write for each one.
● Discuss suitable ways to begin and end the letter.

Independent work
● Provide individual children with photocopiable page 76 'Cinderella's letter' to assist their plans. Once they are satisfied, ask them to write their letters.
● Praise them for correct punctuation and support those who need help.

Review
● Bring children together to read their letters to the class. Encourage positive comments about their use of suitable language.

Curriculum objectives
● To discuss what they have written with the teacher or other children.
● To use the grammatical terminology in Appendix 2 in discussing their writing.

Resources
Photocopiable page 'Ugly sisters' letter' from the CD-ROM, children's completed letters from Cinderella

5: Letter sharing

Introduction
● Recall the ugly sisters' letter and the letters that the children wrote.

Whole-class work
● Display photocopiable page 'Ugly sisters' letter' from the CD-ROM and revise grammatical terminology introduced so far, for example, *sentence, capital letter, punctuation, question mark,* using examples from the letter.

Group work
● Provide the children with the individual letters they wrote from Cinderella and the ugly sisters' letter.
● Invite them to discuss which of the individual letters they think is the most interesting reply to the ugly sisters.
● Suggest that children work in groups of three, using role-play, to act out a short scene involving the two letters.
● Explain that the scene should involve Cinderella receiving and reading the ugly sisters' letter and speaking aloud her thoughts about it. Follow this with the ugly sisters reading and commenting on Cinderella's letter.

> **Differentiation**
> ● Help less confident learners to write a short sentence inviting the ugly sisters to Cinderella's wedding. Encourage them to discuss what they have written.

Review
● Encourage the groups to act out their scenes for the class and share responses. Ask children to discuss and review their Cinderella letters using the correct grammatical terminology.

Week 5 lesson plans

Lessons this week focus on conventional newspaper reports in order to revise previous work. Children explore newspapers and then plan and write their own reports. This involves revisiting punctuation rules, including the use of word spaces, question marks and exclamation marks, and '-s', '-es', '-ing', '-ed', '-er' and '-est' endings. Groups of children share their reports and make sure that sentences follow a narrative sequence. They are encouraged to use appropriate grammatical terminology as they engage in these discussions. Finally, reports are put together for the 'Palace News', telling newsworthy events from 'Cinderella'.

1: News reporters

Introduction
● Invite children to explore newspaper reports from children's newspapers, and distribute some of these around the classroom.
● Choose a newspaper report to display on the board.
● Explore the report with the children and point out specific features, such as the headline, picture, caption and opening sentence. Label these.

Whole-class work
● Read the report, pointing to words as you do so. Discuss what it is about.
● Ask the children to read the headline, supporting them with any new vocabulary or exception words. Talk about what they notice about it, for example, large bold lettering in an unusual font. Discuss punctuation, asking children to circle any capital letters, full stops, question or exclamation marks.
● Explain that a headline is usually there to catch the reader's eye and ask whether this headline does this, for example, with exciting or amusing word choices, interesting lettering and an exclamation mark.
● Display photocopiable page 77 'Read all about it' on the board and explain that it is a template to create a report. Read the instructions together and highlight the words describing what the report should be about.
● Ask the children for suggestions about what Jack in 'Jack and the Beanstalk' might write in a report to a local newspaper about arriving in the land of giants, and how they might make the headline eye-catching.
● Consider different suggestions for the main picture and caption.
● Talk about things to remember when writing their report sentences, for example, correct punctuation, a definite sequence and good letter formation.

Group work
● Divide into groups and provide paper for notes and the photocopiable sheet.
● Ask children to discuss each template section in turn and make notes on a piece of paper.

Paired work
● Invite pairs of children to complete the photocopiable sheet individually, supporting one another with recall of group discussions.
● Once they have finished, ask them to read each other's work and make constructive comments on ideas and omissions.
● Praise children for correct posture as they are writing.

> **Differentiation**
> ● For those who are struggling, discuss what Jack might see at the top of the beanstalk and draw a picture of this. Support the children as they write a sentence about it.

Review
● Invite the class to share some of their completed report pages. Discuss whether the headline, picture and caption would attract the interest of readers. Praise evidence of correct letter formation and appropriate punctuation.

Expected outcomes
● All children can sit correctly at a table, hold a pencil correctly and form letters in the right direction.
● Most children can write a sequence of sentences and begin to use appropriate conventions.
● Some children punctuate sentences with a question mark or exclamation mark.

Curriculum objectives
● To begin to form lower-case letters in the correct direction, starting and finishing in the right place.
● To sit correctly at a table, holding a pencil comfortably and correctly.
● To leave spaces between words.

Resources
Short reports with punchy headlines cut from newspapers, for example, 'First News' (a newspaper written for children); children's pages in daily newspapers; photocopiable page 77 'Read all about it'

Curriculum objectives
● To use '-ing', '-ed', '-er', and '-est' endings where no change is needed in the spelling of root words.
● To begin to punctuate sentences using a capital letter and a full stop, question mark or exclamation mark.

Resources
Photocopiable page 78 'Headline punctuation'; photocopiable page 'Cinderella endings' from the CD-ROM

2: Punctuation and word endings

Introduction
● Recall the previous lesson and discuss what makes an attractive headline. Remind children of the importance of appropriate punctuation and word choice in capturing the reader's attention.

Whole-class work
● Write some punchy headlines on the board for children to read, deliberately leaving out the question mark or exclamation mark, for example: *Who will the glass slipper fit* or *Will the fairy godmother save the day*.
● Read the first sentence together and ask what is missing. Invite a child to add the appropriate punctuation mark. Do the same with the rest of the headlines, establishing whether they are questions, needing question marks, or punchy lines, requiring exclamation marks.

Paired work
● Provide each child with photocopiable page 78 'Headline punctuation'.
● Ask pairs to read the headlines together and support one another with adding punctuation.

Group work
● Display photocopiable page 'Cinderella endings' from the CD-ROM. Explain that this work will help them to revise endings they have used previously.
● Ask mixed-ability groups of seven children to copy a sentence each from the board and then discuss each sentence in turn, deciding which ending is correct.

Review
● Gather the class to review paired and group work. Encourage them to talk about new things they have learned in the lesson.

Curriculum objectives
● To use the grammatical terminology in Appendix 2 in discussing their writing.
● To sequence sentences to form short narratives.

Resources
Dressing-up clothes and props to re-enact the Cinderella story; box; clipboards

3: Breaking palace news

Introduction
● Recall the newspaper reports explored and written in the previous lessons. Discuss the role of a newspaper reporter covering national or local events.
● Explain that children are going to work in groups, with some children acting out important events from 'Cinderella', while others act as reporters writing notes for their newspaper reports.

Whole-class work
● Write significant story events, such as the arrival of the invitation to the ball or losing the slipper, as sentences on the board, making sure that there is a different one for each group. Ask children to ensure correct sequencing, rearranging sentences if necessary. Praise children's use of correct terminology when discussing sentence structure.
● Write each sentence on a slip of paper and put them into a box.

Group work
● Show the groups the bank of resources they can use.
● Ask them to pull a slip of paper from the box to act out.
● Invite them to allocate the roles of reporter and characters.
● Allow time for groups to plan the sequence of their actions.
● Invite reporters to watch their group act out the scene and to make notes.

Review
● Ask groups to act out their scenes, and have reporters explain their notes. Consider how this activity will support sequencing of events in future writing.

Curriculum objectives
- To compose a sentence orally before writing it.
- To spell words containing each of the 40+ phonemes already taught.

Resources
Reporters' notes from last lesson; photocopiable page 77 'Read all about it'; large sheets of paper; coloured pens

4: Reports from the palace

Introduction
- Display the sentences relating to story events created in the previous lesson.
- Invite groups to talk briefly about their experiences of acting out the events and note taking.
- Explain that these recollections and notes will support the newspaper report they are going to write.

Whole-class work
- Revise key aspects of a newspaper report, such as an eye-catching headline, pictures, captions and sequenced sentences.

Group work
- Invite children to form the same groups as in the previous lesson.
- Provide them with their reporter's notes from yesterday and photocopiable page 77 'Read all about it' (explain that this is to remind them of what to include in their report).
- Ask children to create an attractive newspaper report, encouraging them to be adventurous with their use of writing tools and materials, for example, including several small pictures with captions, or enclosing the headline within a colourful design. Encourage oral composition of sentences before writing.
- Once children finish, ask pairs of groups to swap reports. Encourage them to read each other's reports, looking for the key features discussed at the start of the lesson. Ask them to make notes on this for review.

Review
- Invite the pairs of groups to feed back to the class, taking turns to read and show their own report and to explain the comments and notes they made on the other group's report.

Curriculum objectives
- To use the grammatical terminology in Appendix 2 in discussing their writing.
- To sequence sentences to form short narratives.

Resources
Children's reports from previous lesson; examples of newspaper supplements about royal events, such as weddings; large sheets of white and coloured paper; coloured pencils; glue; scissors; wedding magazines

5: Tell the story

Introduction
- Display the events list from lesson 3 and talk about the chosen sequence.

Whole-class work
- Explain that the palace has a newspaper for those who live and work there.
- Talk about how the story of the Prince meeting and marrying Cinderella is something that the palace residents want to know more about.
- Show examples of newspaper supplements created for memorable royal events in this country, such as the birth of a prince or princess.
- Suggest that children create a supplement for the 'Palace News', answering the questions about the love story of the Prince and Cinderella.
- Consider a suitable title for this, such as *A happy ending*.
- Decide together on tasks that need to be done when compiling the supplement. Write these on the board, for example, arranging reports attractively and in the correct sequence, creating the cover, adding artwork, character information (a sort of *Who's who* at the palace).

Group work
- Allocate individual tasks to groups and provide resources to use creatively.
- Assemble each section of the supplement ready for review.

Review
- Bring the class together to explore the finished supplement. Read it through, commenting on sequencing, and inviting suggestions for improvement, for example, numbered pages, a contents page.

Expected outcomes
● All children learn to appreciate rhymes and poems, and to recite some by heart.
● Most children can listen to and discuss a wide range of poems at a level beyond that at which they can read independently.
● Some children can use letter names to distinguish between alternative spellings of the same sound.

Curriculum objectives
● To read aloud accurately books that are consistent with their developing phonic knowledge and that do not require them to use other strategies to work out words.
● To use letter names to distinguish between alternative spellings of the same sound.
● To read common exception words, noting unusual correspondences between spelling and sound and where these occur in the word.

Resources
Selection of nursery rhyme books, including 'Twinkle, Twinkle, Little Star'; interactive activity 'Sort the rhymes' on the CD-ROM

Week 6 lesson plans

This week, children explore a wide range of traditional rhymes. They begin by choosing their favourite nursery rhymes and reading them aloud. Matching rhyming words are identified and children use letter names to distinguish those with alternative spellings. They enjoy reciting rhymes by heart that are beyond their reading levels, and clapping or beating time to the syllables of words in rhymes and tongue twisters. There are opportunities to listen to number rhymes, and to explore sequence and pattern in these. They write their own version of a focused poem, applying spelling rules, before finally choosing a favourite poem to perform to an audience.

1: Rhymes we remember

Introduction
● Show the children the nursery rhyme books and explain that they are going to recite some of their favourites together.
● Invite them to name some nursery rhymes they are familiar with.
● Explain that most nursery rhymes are traditional. Recall the meaning of the word *traditional* from previous work on traditional tales.

Whole-class work
● Choose a few children to volunteer to recite a favourite nursery rhyme. Ask them to repeat the rhyme while others join in.
● Display the rhyme 'Twinkle, Twinkle, Little Star', and ask the children to read it together. If possible, include the second verse.
● Invite someone to highlight the rhyming words at the end of each line in the first verse. Continue with the remaining verses if you have them.
● Discuss the spellings of these rhyming words and highlight or underline alternative graphemes, such as *star* and *are*, *high* and *sky*, *gone* and *upon*.
● Introduce the term *common exception words* and consider why *are* and *gone* fit into this category.
● Read the remaining consistent pairs of rhyming words and identify their graphemes.
● Try another rhyme, such as 'Mary Had a Little Lamb', and explore the rhyming words *snow* and *go*, *rule* and *school* in the same way.
● Ask pairs to try interactive activity 'Sort the rhymes' on the CD-ROM together in order to develop confidence and awareness.
● Display the interactive activity on the board and read the instructions as a class to ensure that children feel comfortable with what is expected of them. Recall the meaning of the term *drag and drop*, working through examples on the first screen together.

Paired work
● Ask pairs to write down the rhyming words next to each other on a sheet of paper while they are completing the interactive activity.
● Once they have done this, suggest that they underline the words with alternative graphemes, such as *prune* and *soon*, *clear* and *peer*, *alert* and *squirt*.
● Ask them to add pairs of their own rhyming words to the list.
● Encourage them to use letter names when discussing alternative spellings.

> **Differentiation**
> ● For pairs of children who need practice, provide a set of rhyming word cards with consistent GPCs to match, for example, *moon* and *soon*, *toy* and *boy*, *ship* and *chip*.

Review
● With the class read out and compare their lists of rhyming words.
● Decide how much the activities helped them to identify and spell rhyming words with alternative graphemes.

SCHOLASTIC

2: Exciting rhythms

Introduction
● Suggest that children clap in time to emphasise rhythm as they recite a favourite nursery rhyme.
● Introduce the word *syllable* and discuss the meaning. Break the word *Twinkle* into syllables and clap at the same time, *twin-kle*.
● Display 'Twinkle, Twinkle, Little Star' and encourage children to clap the syllables as they say the rhyme. Draw dashes in words to indicate separate syllables. Try clapping syllables in more rhymes.

Whole-class work
● Have fun playing with strings of words.
● Begin by asking children to chant someone's name while clapping the syllables, for example, *Mai-sy, Mai-sy, Mai-sy*.
● Extend this to chanting nonsense strings such as *boom-er-ang-bing, floom-er-ang-fling, boom-er-ang-bing, floom-er-ang-fling*.

Group work
● Ask groups to play with repeating syllable strings in unison based on their names, objects and nonsense words.
● Provide percussion instruments for children to tap or beat out the syllables.

> **Differentiation**
> ● Challenge children to try chanting and clapping syllables from the tongue twisters on photocopiable page 'Tongue twisters' from the CD-ROM. Consider why this is so tricky when reading the words is easy. Discuss the meaning of *tongue twisters*.

Review
● Ask them to perform their word strings and tongue twisters to the class. Talk about how playing with words, syllables and rhythms can help us to appreciate rhymes and poems.

3: Number rhymes

Introduction
● Invite children to recall number rhymes from the Early Years Stage.
● Recite a few together, introducing actions if applicable.

Whole-class work
● Display the traditional 'One, Two, Buckle my Shoe' number rhyme. Read it to the children, explaining any words not yet encountered.
● Invite individuals to highlight the pairs of rhyming words in the middle and at the end of each line. Go through them and identify any with alternative grapheme spellings. Circle these, for example, *six* and *sticks*. Search for exception words and underline these, such as *shoe* and *four*. Draw attention to the pairs of words that do not really rhyme, for example, *fourteen* and *courting* and talk about why that might be.
● Display interactive activity 'Rhymes and patterns' on the CD-ROM and read the instructions together. Demonstrate how to use the controls.

Independent work
● Invite children to complete the interactive activity, highlighting the rhyming words on each of the two screens.

Review
● Gather together to discuss the success of the activities in revising GPCs and learning new words.

Curriculum objectives
● To apply simple spelling rules and guidelines, as listed in Appendix 1.
● To read aloud accurately books that are consistent with their developing phonic knowledge and that do not require them to use other strategies to work out words.

Resources
Interactive activities 'Five Old Fishermen (1)' and 'Five Old Fishermen (2)' on the CD-ROM

4: 'Five Old Fishermen'

Introduction
● Discuss the pattern and sequence within number rhymes, for example, starting with five or ten objects and counting down or counting up, for example, 'One, Two, Three, Four, Five, Once I Caught a Fish Alive'.

Whole-class work
● Display the interactive activity 'Five Old Fishermen (1)' on the CD-ROM, click on the poem link and read it together. Encourage children to build up words using existing phonic knowledge, for example, *fish-er-men*, *per-am-bu-lat-or*.
● Discuss the positioning of rhyming words at the end of alternate lines.
● Close the poem to display the template and read the instructions together.
● Explain that children will have to think of their own rhyming words to replace those that are missing.

Paired work
● Organise the children into pairs of similar ability.
● Leave the rhyme 'Five Old Fishermen (1)' on display and provide each child with access to the interactive template to write their poem.
● Support those who need help with choosing appropriate rhyming words and checking spelling.
● Once the poems are written, invite children to read them to each other.

> **Differentiation**
> ● Challenge more confident learners to rewrite more of the poem using the interactive activity 'Five Old Fishermen (2)' from the CD-ROM.

Review
● Bring the class together to share their poems. Ask for positive comments on the choice of words and application of spelling rules.

Curriculum objectives
● To learn to appreciate rhymes and poems, and to recite some by heart.
● To listen to and discuss a wide range of poems at a level beyond that at which they can read independently.

Resources
A range of nursery- and number-rhyme books; typed nursery rhymes explored during the week; percussion instruments; children's poems written in the previous lesson

5: Poetry performance

Introduction
● Recall the range of poems explored over the week. Identify which ones the children enjoyed most and why.
● Suggest that they put on a performance of favourite rhymes and poems.

Whole-class work
● Discuss the form the performance will take, for example, split into sections of different kinds of poem.
● Write a list of section headings on the board, for example, *nursery rhymes*, *number rhymes*, *nonsense chants* and *class compositions*.
● Agree the order of these sections so that the performance has variety. Write these on the board with spaces between.
● Ask the children to decide which section their favourite poem fits into and write their name in the appropriate space.

Paired work
● Invite children to find partners and provide them with a bank of resources, including their past written work, to find possible poems to recite.
● Encourage them to spend time performing to/with one another and making constructive comments before settling on final choices.

Review
● Practise the performance as a class before performing for an audience. Review how well the performance went afterwards.

Curriculum objectives
● To learn to appreciate rhymes and poems, and to recite some by heart.
● To draw on what they know or on background information provided by the teacher.
● To begin to punctuate sentences using a capital letter and a full stop, question mark or exclamation mark.
● To leave spaces between words.

Resources
Selection of books containing fairy tales; photocopiable page 'Fairy-tale review' from the CD-ROM

Grammar and punctuation: Fairy-tale review

Revise
● Recall lessons focusing on fairy tales and identify the children's favourites.
● Explain that the children are going to write a review of their favourite fairy tale to encourage others to read it. Discuss the meaning of *review* and list key features of a good fairy tale.
● Display and read photocopiable page 'Fairy-tale review' from the CD-ROM.
● Focus on the first box asking for the title. Remind children that the response must be written as a sentence, for example: *The title of my favourite fairy tale is Sleeping Beauty.*
● Continue through the boxes, recalling previous lessons involving sentence writing and noting things to remember, such as capital letters and full stops.
● Suggest that children discuss their initial thoughts with a partner. Leave the page on display to support the structure of their interaction.

Assess
● Provide each child with photocopiable page 'Fairy-tale review' from the CD-ROM to complete. Repeat the need to answer in sentences, paying attention to aspects of punctuation and grammar already discussed.

Further practice
● Support struggling children by adapting the photocopiable sheet so that there are fewer questions. Alternatively, you could ask them to write a simple sentence, for example: *I like the story of Cinderella best.* (The aim is to check sentence grammar and punctuation rather than content.)
● Challenge more confident learners to write contrasting reviews comparing their favourite story with one that they did not enjoy as much.

Curriculum objectives
● To use '-ing', '-ed', '-er', and '-est' where no change is needed in the spelling of root words.
● To apply simple spelling rules and guidelines, as listed in Appendix 1.
● To spell words containing each of the 40+ phonemes already taught.

Resources
Photocopiable page 'The Little Red Hen word endings' from the CD-ROM

Spelling: Adding endings

Revise
● Explain that children are going to demonstrate what they know about the spelling of word endings by using them in their own sentences.
● Use the starter activity 8 'Make me different'.
● Display photocopiable page 'The Little Red Hen word endings' from the CD-ROM. Ask the children to read the instructions with you.
● Read the first sentence together and decide if it makes sense in this context. Look at the choice of word endings and try each one before deciding which completes the sentence.
● Continue in the same way through the sentences reminding children to test each sentence by reading it aloud after they have made their choice of ending.
● Highlight the words that have been changed and explain that children are going to write three new sentences using one of these words in each.

Assess
● Provide paper and pencils for children to write their three new sentences.
● Leave the completed photocopiable page on display for reference.

Further practice
● Concentrate on completing '-ed' endings in simple sentences with those who struggle, for example: *The hen plant__ the seeds.*; *The hen fill__ the sack.*
● Challenge more confident learners to write sentences of their own using '-er' and '-ing' word endings.

Curriculum objectives
● To apply phonic knowledge and skills as the route to decode words.
● To read words containing taught GPCs and '-s', '-es', '-ing', '-ed', '-er' and '-est' endings.
● To respond speedily with the correct sound to graphemes for all 40+ phonemes, including alternative sounds for phonemes.

Resources
Interactive activity 'The Princess and the Pea' on the CD-ROM; photocopiable page 'The Princess and the Pea' from the CD-ROM

Reading: 'The Princess and the Pea'

Revise
● Recall fairy stories the children are familiar with, and discuss some of the key features.
● Invite those who have heard the story of 'The Princess and the Pea' to talk about what they remember of the events.
● Display interactive activity 'The Princess and the Pea' on the CD-ROM and click on the text button.
● Read the story to the children so that they become familiar with it before inviting them to read sections with you.
● Focus on punctuation and ask one child to highlight the speech marks. Explain that these indicate when someone is speaking. Read the story again, stopping to ask children to join in with the spoken words.
● Remove the highlighting and invite children to find the questions spoken by characters. Ask how they know that they are questions. Circle the question marks. Do the same with the exclamation marks and discuss their purpose.
● Draw attention to and revise other aspects of reading discussed previously. Look for alternative graphemes representing the same sound, for example, highlight words with the /e/ phoneme written in different ways, 'ee', 'ea', 'e', 'y', 'e-e'. Discover *exception* words that do not fit the usual rules, such as *heard, there, said*.
● Recall the meaning of the term *contractions* and ask if the children can find one in the text (*don't*).
● Talk about the effect of changing the ending of a word, for example, changing *open* or *ask* by adding '-ed', or changing *low* or *tall* with '-est', and *mattress* with '-es'.
● Display the first activity screen of 'The Princess and the Pea', read any instructions together and discuss what children are expected to do.
● Read the first box together and decide which picture it describes. Once all children understand what is required of them they are ready to start the activity.
● Suggest that they go through the story with a partner initially to discuss the allocation of the pictures and support one another with reading.

Assess
● Explain that the aim of the activity is to see how well they can read and understand a story, using their previous reading skills to help with this. Remind them of the way that they explored the text in detail as a class and in pairs to revise these skills.
● Provide each child with access to the interactive activity to complete.
● Ask them to save their work on completion.

Further practice
● Involve all children in the class analysis of the text, but provide those who struggle with the reading level with photocopiable page 'The Princess and the Pea' from the CD-ROM for their assessment. Explain what is expected of them and support and encourage them in their attempts to read the sentences.
● Extend the activity by challenging children to read a book version of the story to the class for their assessment.

Curriculum objectives

● To say out loud what they are going to write about.
● To use the grammatical terminology in Appendix 2 in discussing their writing.
● To sequence sentences to form short narratives.
● To punctuate sentences using a capital letter and a full stop, question mark or exclamation mark.
● To discuss what they have written with the teacher or other children.

Resources

Books of the traditional story 'The Little Red Hen'; photocopiable page 79 'The Little Red Hen'; coloured pens and pencils

Writing: 'The Little Red Hen'

Revise

● Show the children the front covers of the books and ask if they know the story. Encourage those who know the story to recall events.
● Explain that the children will be writing their own versions of this story and that this discussion will help them to remember important things they have already learned about story writing.
● Choose one of the versions of 'The Little Red Hen' to read to the children, asking them to join in with the repeated phrases, *"Who will help me to..."*, *"Not I!" said the...*, *"Then I'll do it myself"*.
● Ask children to consider story language and suggest some suitable opening sentences, for example: *Once upon a time, One day, There was once a...*.
● Consider suitable words to end the story, for example, *So the Little Red Hen shared the bread with her chicks.*
● Write *who will help me to plant these seeds* and ask the children to add the punctuation. Introduce or revise the term *speech marks* and add a capital letter and question mark.
● Draw attention to any contractions in the story by writing the sentence on the board, for example: *"Then I'll do it myself", said the Little Red Hen.*
● Discuss the effect of exclamation marks, for example, *"Not I!" said the cat.*
● Display the story told in pictures on photocopiable page 79 'The Little Red Hen'. Encourage children to discuss the sequence of events from planting the seeds to eating the bread. Use the words *beginning* and *end* to define the first and last events.
● Recall the repeated phrase that often marks the end of each event in this story, for example, *And so she did.* Recall discussions about helping stories, and events within them, to flow along by using connecting words and phrases, such as *Then, After that, In the end.*
● Ask groups to list the action words (verbs) used on the displayed story to describe what the hen does as she grows and harvests the wheat and bakes her bread. Encourage them to think of what each of these actions involves, for example, *Plant: dig a hole, drop in the seed, cover it, rake it over.*
● Recall sentence writing and encourage children to use the correct grammatical terminology when talking about full stops, capital letters, question marks, exclamation marks and so on.
● Emphasise the need to leave spaces between words. Write a sentence from the story on the board without spaces and ask how easy the children find this to read. Invite someone to write it again with spaces and discuss the effect.
● Encourage children to talk about what they plan to write with a partner before working on their own.

Assess

● Provide each child with the photocopiable sheet to serve as an event reminder, along with paper and writing materials.
● Ask the children to write a story with at least one sentence for each event.
● Invite children to read their finished stories to partners and discuss features such as sequence, sentence structure and punctuation.
● Choose stories at random to discuss with the class. Draw attention to and give praise for correct sentence punctuation features. Encourage children to include any missing aspects next time.

Further practice

● Support those who struggle to write a simple sentence about each picture in turn, for example, *The Little Red Hen plants seeds.* Use correct terminology relating to sentence structure as you draw attention to the completed writing.
● Extend the activity by asking groups of six children to produce a book about 'The Little Red Hen' based on the pictures, with each child producing several sentences about a picture. Encourage them to put the events into a sequence to create the pages and then make an attractive book cover.

Change the endings

- Read the sentence in each box.
- Add the correct ending. Choose from these four endings:

's'   **'ed'**   **'ing'**   **'er'**

The old man plant_____ some turnip seed_____.
The old woman help_____ the old man.
The turnip kept on grow_____.
It grew fast_____ and fast_____ every day.
The boy call_____ to the girl.
They kept on pull_____ and pull_____ the turnip.
They cook_____ the turnip for tea.

I can choose the correct endings for the words.

How did you do?

■SCHOLASTIC
www.scholastic.co.uk

Turnip soup recipe

■ Read the recipe and draw pictures in the blank boxes to help explain how to make turnip soup.

You will need: ● Vegetable peeler ● Wooden spoon ● Small knife ● Soup ladle ● Chopping board ● Blender ● Large pan ● Soup bowls	
Ingredients: 4 turnips 1 onion 1 potato 1 vegetable stock cube 4 cups of water	
What to do: Peel and chop the turnip into small cubes. Peel and chop the potato into small cubes. Peel and chop the onion. Put the chopped vegetables into the pan. Add the water. Bring to the boil. Crumble the stock cube into the soup. Simmer the soup for about 15 minutes until all the vegetables are soft. Leave the soup to cool. Blend the soup and pour into bowls.	

Name: _____ Date: _____

Making gingerbread men

■ How did you make your gingerbread men? Remember to number the sentences you write.

My ingredients:	My utensils:

☐ First I _____

_____

☐ After that I _____

_____

☐ Then I _____

_____

☐ Last of all I _____

_____

I can finish a sentence.
I can number my sentences in order.

How did you do?

PHOTOCOPIABLE

SCHOLASTIC
www.scholastic.co.uk

Make it plural

- Read each sentence.
- Make the words plural by adding '-s' or '-es'.

Cinderella lived in a castle with her two ugly sister_____.

Every day she washed the dish_____ and mopped the floor_____.

One day the sister_____ were invited to a ball in their new dress_____.

Cinderella could not go because her dress was in rag_____.

She sat by the fire among the cinder_____ and cried.

Her fairy godmother granted her wish_____.

Cinderella wore glass slipper_____ to the ball but she lost one.

The Prince found her slipper and took her in his arm_____.

They were married and lot_____ of their friend_____ came to a big party.

I can make words plural by writing the correct letters at the end.

How did you do?

Cinderella's letter

- Use this page to help you to plan your letter.
- Remember to use capital letters, full stops, question marks and exclamation marks.

Who is your letter to?
How will you start your letter?
What is your letter about?
Do you have any questions to answer?
How will you finish your letter?

I can plan a letter before writing it.

How did you do?

PHOTOCOPIABLE

SCHOLASTIC
www.scholastic.co.uk

Read all about it

■ Jack is arriving in the land of giants. Plan his newspaper report.

Write your headline.
Draw a picture about the main event in the report.
Write a caption for your picture.
Write sentences about what happens.

I can write a newspaper report.

How did you do?

Headline punctuation

- Read the newspaper headlines.
- Add a question mark or an exclamation mark to complete each one.

Who is the girl who slept among the cinders___

Will the stepsisters ever change___

She waved her wand and... *FLASH*___

Why did the pumpkin change___

Boom__ The clock struck midnight___

Will the servant in rags marry the handsome Prince___

Did they live happily ever after___

I can punctuate a sentence correctly.

How did you do?

PHOTOCOPIABLE

SCHOLASTIC
www.scholastic.co.uk

The Little Red Hen

■ Use these pictures to help you to tell the story.

1. Plant	2. Grow

3. Harvest	**4.** Mill

5. Bake	**6.** Eat

I can tell the story of 'The Little Red Hen'.

How did you do?

Plants

The theme of this half-term is plants. Children spend the first two weeks exploring the fairy tale, 'Jack and the Beanstalk', before investigations into plants are introduced during the next two weeks. They return to 'Jack and the Beanstalk' in the fifth week to consider alternative versions. The final week introduces exploration of plant-related poems.

Expected prior learning
- Know that stories contain characters, a plot and a setting.
- Can recognise the exception words said.
- Know how to write simple short sentences.
- Understand the meaning of non-fiction.

Overview of progression
- As children explore 'Jack and the Beanstalk' in depth, they gain confidence in expressing opinions about a character's behaviour and begin to visualise events from another character's viewpoint.
- To support plant investigations, they learn to point out relevant features in an information text and use effective words to describe objects. They write simple recounts of the growth of bean seeds, revise the use of '-ed' to denote past tense, and use plural nouns with '-s' and '-es' endings. They begin to combine sentences with *and*. Exploring plant poems encourages children to use their senses to describe plants in their own poems.

Creative context
- The children are encouraged to express their ideas creatively by writing alternative versions of stories, creating non-rhyming and sensory poems, making 'magic beans' and designing posters. They use drama, role play, hot-seating, puppets and small-world characters to visualise events from the viewpoints of different characters.
- Exploring plants through non-fiction books, growing seeds and going for observation walks links to science.
- Discussing how characters might be feeling supports PSHE.
- Discovering aspects of order and sequence when ordering story events, and measuring plant growth and using comparative adjectives to describe plants links to maths.

Preparation
For this chapter you will need different versions of 'Jack and the Beanstalk'.

You will also need:
Broad bean seed; large sheets of paper; creative materials; dressing-up clothes; small-world figures; large, medium and small cubes; fiction and non-fiction books about plants; clipboards; camera; printer; objects for comparison; different types of plant; fast-growing seeds and materials to grow them; small rulers; selection of poetry books; collection of leaves and/or books and images of leaves; labelled herb pots.

On the CD-ROM you will find:
Media resource 'Plants'; interactive activities 'Plant growth', 'How would you feel?', 'Spot the stops!'; photocopiable pages: 'Wanted!', 'Jack and the Beanstalk prompts', 'Plant labels', 'Little Brown Seeds', 'A tree', 'Exploring 'A tree'', 'The parts of a plant', 'Real or nonsense?', 'Jack and the Beanstalk in pictures'

Chapter at a glance

An overview of the chapter. For curriculum objective codes, please see pages 8–10.

Week	Lesson	Curriculum objectives	Summary of activities	Outcomes
1	1	RC: 3, 4, 6, 11	Read 'Jack and the Beanstalk'. Compare with other key stories. Predict what might happen next. Join in the giant's chant.	• Can make predictions based on pictorial and contextual clues. • Can join in repeated phrases.
	2	RWR: 5 WT: 8 WC: 11	Explore story page for examples of given endings. Write words with correct endings to make sense in given sentences.	• Can recognise effect of given endings on words and use correct endings in context or written work.
	3	RWR: 4 WT: 2	Play 'Beanstalk Bingo' to develop their ability to read common exception words.	• Can read common exception words and use them in sentences.
	4	RC: 8 WC: 1, 6, 12	Write class character profile about Jack. Create 'wanted' poster for giant to catch Jack using profile ideas.	• Can say what they are going to write in character profile. • Can read this aloud to class.
	5	RC: 3, 10, 13	Explore other story characters by going in the hot-seat. Ask characters how they felt about events of the story.	• Can make inferences during group interaction. • Can explain understanding of what is read through oral responses. • Can begin to explore characters' points of view.
2	1	RC: 3, 10, 12	Break down story into scenes. Discuss characters' differing viewpoints and possible reactions during them to develop character profiles further.	• Can compare traits in characters in story. • Can make inferences about characters based on discussions.
	2	RC: 10, 12	Dramatise events using yesterday's lists to gain deeper understanding of characters and their reactions. Sharing opinions following this.	• Can take turns and listen in discussions involving reading aloud. • Can make inferences based on what they hear and see.
	3	WT: 6, 8 WC: 11	Explore word endings for comparisons. Revise plural endings '-s' and '-es'.	• Can use '-er' and '-est' endings for adjectives to denote comparisons. • Can use '-s' or '-es' to form noun plurals.
	4	WC: 2, 9	Consider a character's point of view and use this to write about a key story event.	• Can work with partner to compose and write sentences, focusing on correct punctuation.
	5	WC: 3, 12	Write a scene from the story taking into account views of characters involved.	• Can sequence sentences to form narrative scene.
3	1	RC: 1, 12	Recall 'Jack and the Beanstalk'. Introduce plants using bean as link. Revise fiction/non-fiction and search books for information about plants.	• Can listen to and join in with discussions about books explored. • Can explain and identify differences between fiction and non-fiction.
	2	RC: 12 WT: 12	Go for a walk to identify plants, such as trees, wild and garden plants. Make drawings and notes. Discuss on return.	• Can discuss walk and respond to others. • Can make notes, forming lower-case letters correctly.
	3	WT: 8, 12	Put plants in order according to height, size and so on. Draw plant comparison images and write adjective with correct ending underneath.	• Can use correct ending for adjectives that make comparisons. • Can form lower-case letters in correct direction.
	4	RWR: 1 WT: 12 WC: 6	Label a plant drawing with root, bud, leaf, stem, flower. Create captions for plants and read them to group members.	• Can write labels and captions, forming lower-case letters correctly.
	5	WC: 3, 9	Label the growing sequence. Write sentences in same sequence.	• Can recognise a sequence. • Can write sentences in a sequence.
4	1	RC: 10, 11, 12	Recall 'Jack and the Beanstalk'. Make beans 'magic' with glitter and sand. Invent 'bean' stories based on fairy tales.	• Can make up own 'magic bean' stories based on what has been read.
	2	RC: 11 WT: 13 WC: 10	Plant mustard and cress in pots and predict what will happen. Create name labels to identify own plants.	• Can predict what will happen to seeds based on previous information read. • Can use capital letters for name labels.
	3	WT: 3, 13 WC: 10	Record daily growth changes on chart by writing down measurements and notes about appearance. Use of capital letters.	• Can use capital letters for the days of the week and own name. • Can form capital letters correctly.
	4	RC: 12 WT: 6 WC: 6	Recall previous plant labelling. Explore parts in detail. Write sentences to explain plant parts. Make into zigzag book.	• Can join in discussion appropriately, taking turns and listening to others. • Can read their written work to class.
	5	WT: 8 WC: 3, 11	Write instructions to tell Jack how to grow a plant, writing sentences in the correct sequence and using appropriate endings.	• Can write sequence of sentences to form narrative. • Can use correct word endings.

Chapter at a glance

Week	Lesson	Curriculum objectives	Summary of activities	Outcomes
5	1	RC: 3, 12 WC: 9	Compare the way Jack's beans grew with their own beans. Recall sentence writing and define features of a sentence.	• Can discuss fairy stories. • Can show understanding of the term *sentence*. • Can use correct punctuation in sentences.
	2	WC: 8, 9	Learn to write sentences with correct punctuation and join sentences with *and*.	• Can punctuate sentences correctly. • Can join words and sentences together using *and*.
	3	RC: 3, 10	Recall beginning, middle and end sequence in stories. Consider alternative events that change middle and end using previous knowledge.	• Can show increasing familiarity with fairy-tale genre. • Can sequence sentences to define beginning, middle and end.
	4	WC: 3, 9	Write stories, focusing on sentence sequence and correct punctuation.	• Can use correct sequence and punctuation when writing sentences in a story.
	5	RC: 12 WC: 6	Groups read their stories to class who comment on content and discuss the most effective versions of 'Jack and the Beanstalk'.	• Can take part in discussion about what is read to them. • Can read aloud their stories so that others can hear clearly.
6	1	RWR: 1, 5 RC: 1	Read and discuss plant-themed poems. Close eyes and listen to poem to form 'mind's eye' picture. Draw and discuss.	• Can read poems using skills to decode words. • Can listen to and discuss poems beyond reading levels.
	2	RC: 2 WC: 8	Collect leaves. Make up non-rhyming poem using descriptive words about leaves.	• Can link experience of leaf exploration with non-fiction books read about trees. • Can join words using *and*.
	3	RC: 2 WC: 1	Explore unusual close-up pictures of plants and describe them in poems.	• Can look at images and discuss what they are going to write about them. • Can link what is read to these experiences.
	4	WC: 1, 2, 6	Use senses of smell and touch to identify plants. Write poems about this. Read them aloud to class.	• Can discuss what they are going to write about with peers. • Can compose poem lines orally before writing and can read them clearly.
	5	WT: 8 WC: 8	Write word strings about plant parts using *and* to join them.	• Can write strings of words with same endings, using *and*.

Background knowledge

Adjective: Sometimes called a describing word because it picks out single characteristics such as size or colour. However, verbs, nouns and adverbs can do the same thing. They can be used before a noun to make the noun's meaning more specific (*The children did some really **good** work*), or after the verb *be* as its complement (*Their work was **good***).

Conjunction: A word that inks two words or phrases together.

Consonant: A sound produced when the speaker closes off or obstructs the flow of air through the vocal tract, usually using lips, tongue or teeth.

Ellipsis: The omission of a word or phrase which is expected and predictable.

Phrase: A group of words that are grammatically connected.

Vowel: A speech sound produced without any closure or obstruction of the vocal tract.

Week 1 lesson plans

The lessons this week focus on the fairy tale, 'Jack and the Beanstalk'. Initially, children listen to the story and predict what might happen next at various points. They have fun with repetition as they join in the giant's chant. Subsequent lessons involve exploration of the effect of adding the suffixes '-ed' and '-ing' and writing sentences using them. Common exception words are identified in the story and children play 'Beanstalk bingo' to revise their recognition of these. The character of Jack is discussed in detail as they create a 'Wanted!' poster for Jack to assist the Giant's search. Finally, they take the hot-seat to explore the reactions of different characters to story events.

1: 'Jack and the Beanstalk'

Introduction
- Pass the bean around and invite the children to decide the type of seed it is and what it will grow into.
- Tell them that it is a clue to help them to guess which fairy tale you are going to read.
- Invite those familiar with the story to talk about what they remember of it.

Whole-class work
- Explore the book cover, asking the children to read the title. Look for the name of the author (and illustrator, if applicable) and read this together.
- Look closely at the artwork and ask if it helps us to predict what they story might be about, for example, *It looks as if it is about a boy climbing a huge plant.* Develop children's prediction skills by asking questions about this, for example, *Who is the boy? Where is he going? Do you think he is being sensible when he tries to climb this tall plant? What might happen? What sort of plant is it? Can you spot any beans?*
- Depending on your version of the story, focus on the back cover and ask the children to read any blurb or quotes, supporting them with words not previously taught and exception words. Discuss how these might help to predict the plot.
- Read the story, pausing at suitable points and discussing the illustration to extend descriptions of what is happening. Invite children to predict what might happen next, for example, when Jack starts to climb up the beanstalk. Encourage children to predict the meaning of new vocabulary, such as *fearsome*, substituting known words, if necessary, to aid their understanding.
- Identify the repeated chant of the giant, *Fee-fi-fo-fum!...To make my bread*, and ask children to join in with these words. Encourage them to modify their voices to reflect the anger of the giant.
- Extend children's familiarity with key stories by asking them to compare elements of repetition in this story with others they have recently explored, such as *They pulled and they pulled and they pulled but...* ('The Enormous Turnip'), *"Not I," said the cat, "Not I," said the dog...* ('The Little Red Hen').

Group work
- Move into a large space and invite the children to recreate the giant's chant. Encourage them to consider how the giant would speak and move, and the sound his huge boots would make as he stamped towards Jack. Have fun stamping and chanting in time.

Review
- Recall the initial class discussions about the story. Ask those who have heard it before if they have discovered anything new. Ask those who are less familiar with it about what they have enjoyed most. Invite the groups to perform their chants and decide which one has created the most effective representation of the giant.

Expected outcomes
- All children have an opinion about a character's behaviour.
- Most children can read and spell common exception words.
- Some children understand the suffixes '-ed' and '-ing' and begin to use them.

Curriculum objectives
- To become very familiar with fairy stories and traditional tales, retelling them and considering their particular characteristics.
- To predict what might happen on the basis of what has been read so far.
- To recognise and join in with predictable phrases.
- To discuss word meanings, linking new meanings to those already known.

Resources
A broad bean seed; a traditional version of 'Jack and the Beanstalk', for example, the *First Fairy Tales* version or *The Ladybird Tales* version by Vera Southgate

Curriculum objectives
● To read words containing taught GPCs and '-s', '-es', '-ing', '-ed', '-er' and '-est' endings.
● To use '-ing', '-ed', '-er' and '-est' where no change is needed in the spelling of root words.
● To learn the grammar for Year 1 in Appendix 2.

Resources
A version of 'Jack and the Beanstalk'; photocopiable page 104 'Add the endings'

2: Different endings

Introduction
● Read 'Jack and the Beanstalk' and encourage children to participate.
● Recall work on '-ed' and '-ing' endings and find examples in 'Jack and the Beanstalk'. Write these on the board in the context of the sentence.

Whole-class work
● Display photocopiable page 104 'Add the endings' and read the instructions.
● Read the words in the bottom boxes and identify the graphemes used, 'ou', 'ow', 'ea' and 'ar'. Write these on the board and invite children to think of different words that use them to represent the same phonemes, for example, *house, snow, heat, chart*. Challenge them to lengthen words by adding new endings, such as *houses, snowing, heated, charts*.

Paired work
● Provide each child with the photocopiable sheet and ask them to work with a partner to decide which words and endings they will use.
● Once they have completed the sheet individually, ask them to read their sentences to each other to check whether they make sense.

> **Differentiation**
> ● Simplify the words and sentences to reflect the reading level of those struggling.
> ● Challenge learners to think of different words with '-ed' and '-ing' endings.

Review
● Go through children's completed photocopiable sheets together as a form of self-assessment. Discuss their understanding of changed word endings.

Curriculum objectives
● To read common exception words, noting unusual correspondences between spellings and sound where these occur in the word.
● To spell common exception words.

Resources
Photocopiable page 105 'Beanstalk bingo' to make sets of playing boards; card for groups of five children (four players and one caller)

3: Beanstalk bingo

Introduction
● Recall discussions about *exception words* and recap the meaning of this term.
● Write familiar exception words on the board and read them together. Explain that the more children come across these words in their reading, and use them in their writing, the easier it will be to remember them.

Whole-class work
● Demonstrate the Beanstalk bingo game to the class (from photocopiable page 105 'Beanstalk bingo'). Explain that the words on the cards are all exception words that they should already be able to read. Display the list of words discussing unusual correspondences between spellings and sound.

Group work
● Divide half the class into groups of five, each with a set of game boards and cards. Explain to each group how to play the game, following the instructions on the photocopiable sheet.
● If any child cannot read a word ask others in the group to help.

Paired work
● Invite remaining children to work in pairs to compose and write down sentences using these common exception words.
● Swap the activity so that all children experience paired and group work.

Review
● Bring the class together to talk about their successes in reading and writing the words and any difficulties they encountered. Ask whether they think this will help them to read and write common exception words.

Curriculum objectives
- To say out loud what they are going to write about.
- To read aloud their writing clearly enough to be heard by their peers and the teacher.
- To check that the text makes sense to them as they read and correct inaccurate reading.
- To use the grammatical terminology in Appendix 2 in discussing their writing.

Resources
Different versions of 'Jack and the Beanstalk'; large sheets of paper; creative materials such as paint, collage, coloured card, coloured and black pens; photocopiable page 'Wanted!' from the CD-ROM

4: Wanted criminal

Introduction
- Read a traditional version of 'Jack and the Beanstalk' and ask children what evidence there is about Jack's character in the text and illustrations.

Whole-class work
- Recall recent explorations into story characters and explain that children are going to look more closely at the character of Jack.
- Tell the children that the Giant wants their help in designing a *Wanted!* poster so that he can catch Jack and get his gold coins, hen and harp back.
- Display the photocopiable page 'Wanted!' from the CD-ROM to stimulate ideas for what they should include. Discuss how each poster has a picture and a short description of the wanted person.

Group work
- Ask the children to look for ideas about Jack's appearance in the story.
- Suggest that they discuss his character, for example, was he sensible or did he make some wrong decisions? Was he right to take the Giant's possessions?
- Encourage them to consider whether the Giant is right to try and catch Jack.

Paired work
- Ask them in pairs to design a wanted poster about Jack.
- Invite them to include at least a sentence about Jack. Encourage them to use grammatical terminology when discussing this, such as *sentence* or *capital letter*.

Review
- Ask pairs to display their posters and clearly read out what they have written. Discuss which posters best describe Jack's character. Praise correct punctuation and ask children to point out where exclamation marks or question marks have been used.

Curriculum objectives
- To make inferences on the basis of what is being said and done.
- To explain clearly their understanding of what is read to them.
- To become very familiar with key stories, fairy stories and traditional tales, retelling them and considering their particular characteristics.

Resources
A version of 'Jack and the Beanstalk'; photocopiable page 106 'In the hot-seat'; simple dressing-up clothes

5: In the hot-seat

Introduction
- Compile a list of the six characters on the board (*Jack, Jack's mother, the man with the beans, Giant, Giant's wife, harp*).
- Encourage children to consider the part played by each character.

Whole-class work
- Recall previous sessions involving hot-seating, or explain what this involves.
- Show children the prepared character cards (create them from photocopiable page 106 'In the hot-seat').
- Explain that they will turn the cards upside down, take turns to pick one, and then dress up as that character to sit in the hot-seat.

Group work
- Suggest that, while the character is choosing a costume, the rest of the group need to be preparing questions to find out as much a possible about how this character feels.
- Encourage children to ask the same question to different characters and compare the answers.
- Suggest they write each character's name on a sheet of paper and write notes during each hot-seat interview.

Review
- Bring the class together to discuss their notes and experiences. Have they changed their opinions or learned anything new about the characters?

Expected outcomes
● All children can participate in discussion about what is read to them, taking turns and listening to what others say.
● Most children can write sentences.
● Some children can visualise some events from another character's viewpoint.

Curriculum objectives
● To become very familiar with key stories, fairy stories and traditional tales, retelling them and considering their particular characteristics.
● To participate in discussion about what is read to them, taking turns and listening to what others say.
● To make inferences on the basis of what is being said and done.

Resources
A selection of books telling the story, 'Jack and the beanstalk'

Week 2 lesson plans

This week's lessons continue to discuss events from the viewpoints of 'Jack and the Beanstalk' characters. Children begin by dividing the story into separate scenes. They then dramatise these events in order to consider how characters will react. Much emphasis is on discussion and sharing of ideas. They revise '-s' and '-es' endings to create noun plurals, and written work involves '-er' and '-est' endings in comparison adjectives. Children choose an item linked to an event and then write a sequence of sentences about this event from a character's viewpoint. Finally, groups of children write a favourite scene from a character's viewpoint. Emphasis during sentence writing is on revising punctuation and using correct grammatical terminology.

1: Character reactions

Introduction
● Recall last week's work when children built up ideas about the characters in 'Jack and the Beanstalk', for example, with hot-seat questioning and creating 'Wanted!' posters. Talk about how this helped them to 'get inside' each character and think more about how they might be feeling. Explain that this week's lessons will help to extend this understanding of the characters.
● Talk about how exploring the viewpoints of characters also involved them in considering the significance of story events in more detail.
● Explain that they are going to continue thinking about characters' points of view in other ways. For example, using props such as small-world people or puppets to represent characters and making up dialogue between them, or by dramatising events involving interaction between characters.

Whole-class work
● Suggest to the class that they consider points in the story when characters talk to one another about something important, for example, the discussion between Jack and his mother about selling the cow. Also ask them to consider when they do something to affect another character, for example, when Jack steals the Giant's coins.
● Explain that you would like the children to go through the story in groups and write down key events involving the characters that could be dramatised, or re-enacted with props, during the next lesson.

Group work
● Divide into mixed-ability groups so that children can support one another in their reading, writing and discussion.
● Provide each group with access to a bank of 'Jack and the Beanstalk' books, and large sheets of paper and pencils to create their lists.
● Ask each group to choose a book to refer to as they recall the sequence of events.
● Suggest that they discuss the events and take turns to write each one down.
● Once they are happy with their event list, they should discuss the characters involved in each one and write the relevant names next to it.
● Suggest that they number the events in the order they occur in the story to ensure that they are following the correct sequence and not leaving out anything significant.
● Once the lists are created ask children to go through them together and select the ones that they think show characters reacting in different ways.

Review
● Bring the class together to share their lists and the reasons for their choice of events. Decide together which is the first significant event in the story and write this on the board. Continue adding events until children are satisfied with the sequence.

Curriculum objectives

- To participate in discussion about what is read to them, taking turns and listening to what others say.
- To make inferences on the basis of what is being said and done.

Resources

Various versions of 'Jack and the Beanstalk'; the list of events created in the previous lesson; dressing-up clothes and props; small-world people or puppets suitable to dramatise events from the story

2: Revealing reactions

Introduction

- Display the event list created in the previous lesson and recall the way it was compiled.
- Explain that children are going to take on the roles of the characters, or create voices for small-world people and puppets, to dramatise the events.

Whole-class work

- Look at the list together and ask children which events they think are the most dramatic in the story.
- Suggest that, as the lesson is about characters, it may be best to choose two events and share them equally amongst the groups. If one event featured Jack, Jack's mother and the man with beans, and the other Jack, the Giant and the Giant's wife, then all characters would be covered.

Group work

- Circle the chosen events and allocate groups equally between them.
- Ask children to decide who will play the characters and to choose suitable resources to help them dramatise their scenes.
- Remind them to include lots of dialogue and dramatic reaction, for example, gasping in horror.
- Provide writing materials so that children can note down their ideas.

Review

- Bring the class together to watch each other's events. Discuss things they have discovered about the characters. Did they find anything unexpected in the characters' reactions? How did this help them with character explorations?

Curriculum objectives

- To use '-ing', '-ed', '-er' and '-est' where no change is needed in the spelling of root words.
- To use the spelling rule for adding '-s' or '-es' as the plural marker for nouns and the third-person singular marker for verbs.
- To learn the grammar for Year 1 in Appendix 2.

Resources

Photocopiable page 107 'Choosing adjectives'; large, medium and small cubes

3: Plurals and adjectives

Introduction

- Recall previous work on word endings and ask children for some examples of those they have encountered previously.
- Remind children how plurals can be created by adding '-s' or '-es', for example, *beans, wishes*.
- Write singular nouns on the board and ask children to add the correct letter(s) to make them plural.

Whole-class work

- Introduce the word *adjective* and explain its function when in front of a noun, as in *Jack saw a tall beanstalk,* or after a verb, as in *Jack's mother was kind.*
- Arrange three cubes in size order. Say, *This brick is small, but this brick is smaller, and this brick is the smallest,* pointing to the correct one.
- Discuss how the adjective endings tell us how small the brick is compared with the others in the group.
- Display photocopiable page 107 'Choosing adjectives' and read through the instructions. Work through the first sentence, trying the adjectives to find the correct one. Explain how the adjectives give us information about comparisons.

Independent work

- Provide each child with the photocopiable sheet to complete.
- If necessary, ask a more confident learner to work with one who is less confident, to provide peer support.

Review

- Bring the class together to share their work. Go through the answers on the board to reinforce understanding and support self-correction.

Curriculum objectives
● To compose a sentence orally before writing it.
● To begin to punctuate sentences using a capital letter and a full stop, question mark or exclamation mark.

Resources
Photocopiable page 106 'In the hot-seat' and the cards prepared from this (as for week 1, lesson 5); a box to draw them from; photocopiable page 'Jack and the Beanstalk prompts' from the CD-ROM

4: What happened?

Introduction
● Invite children to recall the story and their experiences of exploring the characters through role play, hot-seating and discussion. Explain that their work will help them to write from the viewpoint of one of the characters.

Whole-class work
● Display photocopiable page 'Jack and the Beanstalk prompts' from the CD-ROM. Discuss an event that happened involving each image. Then display photocopiable page 106 'In the hot-seat' to remind children of the characters.

Paired work
● Explain that they will be writing sentences about an event involving one of the characters and one of the images, such as Jack receiving the beans.
● Invite pairs to choose a character card from the box (see Resources). Explain that they will write their sentences from the point of view of this character.
● Provide photocopiable page 'Jack and the Beanstalk prompts' so that children can choose one event to write about.
● Suggest that they compose their sentences orally before writing them.
● Emphasise that they should be in order and correctly punctuated.

> **Differentiation**
> ● Provide less confident learners with a printed image from the CD-ROM selection and ask them to complete a sentence about it.

Review
● Gather the class to read their written work. Invite constructive comments about whether children successfully wrote from the point of view of a character, and also consider accuracy of punctuation.

Curriculum objectives
● To sequence sentences to form short narratives.
● To use the grammatical terminology in Appendix 2 in discussing their writing.

Resources
Completed sentences from lesson 4; different versions of 'Jack and the Beanstalk'

5: Picture the scene

Introduction
● Ask the children to recall their investigations into the story characters, culminating with writing sentences from the viewpoint of a given character.
● Talk about how exploring viewpoints will help them to understand the roles and reactions of characters during important events.

Whole-class work
● Explain that you would like children to rewrite their favourite scene from the viewpoint of a character rather than from their own point of view.
● Invite children to tell the class their favourite scenes and why they like them. Talk about the characters involved in each scene.

Group work
● Divide into groups of three to discuss and choose the scene and the characters involved (groups of three ensures one child for each character).
● Provide them with their sentences from lesson 4 and the story.
● Ask them to decide which character's viewpoint they will be writing from.
● Suggest that they role-play the scene to help with sequence and dialogue.
● Encourage them to take turns to act as scribe, writing at least a sentence each, and emphasise the importance of sequence.

Review
● Invite groups to share their scenes, with each child reading the sentences they wrote. Analyse some sentences together on the board. Encourage the use of grammatical terminology, for example, to describe punctuation.

Week 3 lesson plans

This week's lessons focus on plants, linking with 'Jack and the Beanstalk' explorations the previous week. Children revise differences between fiction and non-fiction, and search books for information about plants. They discover the variety of plants in their local area as they go for a walk to identify and record trees, wild plants and garden plants. Grammar and sentence structure are revised throughout the week with strong focus on punctuation and letter formation. Adjectives with '-er' and '-est' endings are revisited in order to make comparisons between plants. Children label plant drawings with *root*, *bud*, *leaf*, *stem* and *flower*, and create captions for different types of plant. They explore the growing sequence and write sentences to describe this.

Expected outcomes
● All children can begin to describe objects.
● Most children can point out features in an information text.
● Some children can write a sequence of sentences to describe a process.

Curriculum objectives
● To listen to and discuss a wide range of poems, stories and non-fiction at a level beyond that at which they can read independently.
● To participate in discussion about what is read to them, taking turns and listening to what others say.

Resources
Fiction books linked to plants, including 'Jack and the Beanstalk', such as, *The Tiny Seed* by Eric Carle (1997, Puffin), *Jasper's Beanstalk* by Nick Butterworth and Mick Inkpen (2008, Hodder Children's Books); non-fiction books about common plants, for example, *Plant* by Penelope Arlon (2006, Dorling Kindersley), *What is a Plant?* by Louise and Richard Spilsbury (2006, Heinemann Library), *Trees* by Lisa Jane Gillespie (2009, Usborne)

1: Fiction and non-fiction

Introduction
● Recall 'Jack and the Beanstalk' and discuss how Jack's bean seed grows into a bean plant with roots, a stem, flowers, leaves and tiny beans.
● Revise the terms *fiction* and *non-fiction* and remind children about when they sorted dinosaur books into fiction and non-fiction titles. Discuss how they decided on the correct categories. Talk about occasions when they would choose a fiction book, and times when a non-fiction book would be more suitable.

Whole-class work
● Explain that this week's lessons will be all about plants.
● Discuss ways of locating plant facts, such as searching books and the internet, visiting garden centres, and talking to local experts. It is important that children are made aware of the wide range of information resources available to them.
● Show children a range of plant-related books and ask what they notice about them. Encourage use of the words *fiction* and *non-fiction* in their responses. Invite two children to hold up a fiction and a non-fiction book. Talk about differences in title and cover.
● Discuss whether plant facts in fiction books can be relied upon, for example, could a beanstalk really grow into the sky, could one turnip fill a field?
● Read a page from a non-fiction book and ask children to listen for interesting facts. Take turns to share a fact and write it on the board. Read the page again to check that all facts have been written down.
● Write down the different types of common plant (garden or cultivated plants, wild plants and trees) and invite children to give examples.

Group work
● Suggest that children work in groups to research plants. Invite them to choose two suitable books each from the selection and to swap books with each other once they have searched them thoroughly.
● Divide the types of common plant among the groups, for example, ask two groups to research cultivated plants, two trees and two wild plants.
● Ask the children to write down the facts they find. Support children with tricky new vocabulary they may encounter and encourage them to note these words, for example, describing trees as *deciduous* or *evergreen*.

Differentiation
● Challenge confident children to write a simple book or sequence of instructions about a plant, for example, how to plant, grow, harvest and cook beans.

Review
● Bring the groups together to read out their information about their plant categories. Encourage others to listen and comment on what has been read.

Curriculum objectives
• To participate in discussion about what is read to them, taking turns and listening to what others say.
• To begin to form lower-case letters in the correct direction, starting and finishing in the right place.

Resources
Clipboards; cameras; printer

2: Plant detectives

Introduction
• Plan an outing and go through safety rules with children.
• Explain that the purpose of the outing is to find different plants.
• Describe the resources available and invite some children to be responsible for taking photographs.

Group work
• Encourage groups to look for the three categories of plant discussed in lesson 1: trees, wild plants and cultivated plants.
• Emphasise the importance of recording their finds by taking photographs, drawing accurate pictures, writing labels and notes.
• Stress that plants should not be disturbed from their habitat.

Whole-class work
• Bring the class together to discuss their findings. Encourage children to take turns and to listen when others are speaking.
• Draw three columns headed *Wild plants*, *Garden plants* and *Trees*. Print off the photographs and stick these into the correct columns during the discussion.
• Invite children to write the plants they found under the appropriate heading, paying particular attention to letter formation so that others can read them.

Review
• Review the success of the walks and ask individuals to describe their favourite plant and what they liked about it.

Curriculum objectives
• To use '-ing', '-ed', '-er' and '-est' where no change is needed in the spelling of root words.
• To begin to form lower-case letters in the correct direction, starting and finishing in the right place.

Resources
Suitable objects to make comparisons, for example, different-sized apples, lengths of ribbon, plants; photocopiable page 108 'Comparing plants'

3: Plant comparisons

Introduction
• Recall previous work on adjectives of comparison, for example, between the size of cubes, and 'Jack and the Beanstalk' characters (week 2, lesson 3).
• Discuss how comparison adjectives could be used to help to describe objects, for example: *This towel is rough, this one is rougher, but this one is the roughest; This bell sounds loud, but this gong is louder, and this cymbal is the loudest.* Explore how these examples link to the senses of touch.

Whole-class work
• Use sets of three real objects for comparison, for example, different sized apples, various lengths of rope, plants of different heights.
• Invite individuals to choose three objects to arrange in order and then ask the class to use suitable adjectives and nouns to describe each one.
• Display photocopiable page 108 'Comparing plants' and read the instructions together. Work through the first example to make sure that children understand what to do.

Independent work
• Provide each child with the photocopiable sheet to complete.
• Observe children as they work and praise them for correct letter formation.

> **Differentiation**
> • Support less confident learners by adapting the photocopiable sheet so that the adjectives are all shown for them to read. They then draw the corresponding picture.

Review
• Go through the photocopiable sheet together and write the correct words on the board. Discuss how the lesson has helped them to revise endings and letter formation.

4: Labels and captions

Introduction

Curriculum objectives
● To apply phonic knowledge and skills as the route to decode words.
● To begin to form lower-case letters in the correct direction, starting and finishing in the right place.
● To read aloud their writing clearly enough to be heard by peers and the teacher.

Resources
Photocopiable page 'Plant labels' from the CD-ROM; card; different kinds of plant, for example, flowering plant, spider plant, bean plant, tiny tree, herbs such as rosemary, mint and thyme, lemon plant

● Recall children's plant search, look at the photographs and discuss the main types of plant that they found.

Whole-class work

● Show children the plants and ask individuals to choose one, name it if possible and describe how it looks, smells and feels.
● Recall work on writing captions and discuss what should be included.
● Establish that the children should write two sentences about each plant. Ask for suggestions and write the resulting caption on the board, for example: *This is a spider plant. It has long green striped leaves that look like a spider's legs.*

Group work

● Invite mixed-ability groups to choose two plants to create a caption about.
● Encourage them to think of what makes the plant different from others.
● Stress that letters should be correctly formed to make reading easier.
● Arrange completed captions on a table alongside the appropriate plant.

Individual work

● Provide individuals with photocopiable page 'Plant labels' from the CD-ROM. Go through the instructions, and use a real plant to identify the parts.

Review

● Invite groups of children to read their captions to the class. Ask the listeners to make decisions about whether the captions contain interesting information. Discuss how successful the photocopiable sheet was in helping them to remember the parts of a plant.

5: Growing order

Curriculum objectives
● To sequence sentences to form short narratives.
● To begin to punctuate sentences using a capital letter, full stop, question mark or exclamation mark.

Resources
Interactive activity 'Plant growth' on the CD-ROM

Introduction

● Recall stories that follow a sequence. Ask children to name some, for example, 'The Enormous Turnip', 'The Gingerbread Man'.
● Remind children that this week's focus is on plants and explain that they are going to look at how the growth of a plant follows a sequence.

Whole-class work

● Display interactive activity 'Plant growth' on the CD-ROM and identify the plant (sunflower). Talk about what is happening in each picture.
● Use correct vocabulary, such as *roots, shoots, stem, leaves, flower*, and connective words, such as *first, next, then, last*.
● Invite the children to decide which picture would come first in the sequence and why. Drag the pictures into the correct order on screen and then move to the next screen for self-correction. If the children are wrong, try again.
● Leave the correct image sequence on display.

Group work

● Invite groups of children to write a sequence of four sentences describing the growth of a sunflower. Encourage them to number their sentences.
● As they work, praise correct punctuation and provide support with spelling.

Review

● Invite groups to share their sentences and ask listeners to comment on the vocabulary used and sequence created. Ask the class how much this work has helped with sequencing sentences.

Expected outcomes

● All children can participate in discussion about what is read to them, taking turns and listening to others.
● Most children can write a simple recount.
● Some children can add '-ing', '-ed', '-er' and '-est' endings where no change is needed in the spelling of root words.

Curriculum objectives

● To participate in discussion about what is read to them, taking turns and listening to what others say.
● To make inferences on the basis of what is being said and done.
● To predict what might happen on the basis of what has been read so far.

Resources

Broad bean seeds; PVA glue; squeezy paint; powder paint; small collage materials such as glitter, coloured sand, rice, sesame seeds, sequins, tiny beads

Week 4 lesson plans

This week children focus on plant growth. They recall the way that Jack's 'magic' beans grew, make magic beans of their own using shiny collage materials and bean seeds, and invent magic bean stories. This is followed by planting fast-growing seeds and predicting what will happen, writing labels, and focusing on use of capital letters as they fill in a growth chart for their seedlings. They further extend their awareness of the parts of a plant by creating zigzag books about them. Here, the focus is on the correct use of word endings and sentence grammar. Finally, children help Jack to plant and look after his seeds correctly by writing instruction sheets for him.

1: Magic beans

Introduction

● Recall the story of 'Jack and the Beanstalk'. Focus on the beanstalk and how it grew from the magic beans given to Jack, even though he carelessly threw the beans out of the window instead of planting them carefully in the soil.
● Pass around some broad bean seeds and ask the children to describe how they look, smell and feel.
● Revise facts about how a beanstalk is a type of plant that grows from a bean seed just like these.

Whole-class work

● Emphasise again that the beans given to Jack were magic and that is why such a huge beanstalk grew from one of them.
● Discuss whether Jack's beans would have looked like the children's beans, and consider whether any of these beans could grow into huge beanstalks.
● Invite children to share their recollections of magic in fairy tales and traditional stories already read, for example, a broomstick that can fly or a pumpkin that turns into a golden coach.
● Speculate what a magic bean might look like. Perhaps it will twinkle and shine, or have spiky lumps and gooey bumps all over it?
● Show the children the resources available and suggest that they use them to transform the broad bean seeds into magic ones.

Independent work

● Encourage children to be as zany and imaginative as they like. Demonstrate techniques, such as covering one side of the bean in PVA glue and decorating it with collage materials. Once beans have dried on one side children can turn them over and do the same, or something completely different, on the other.
● Some children might like to paint their beans before applying glue, or mix squeezy paint with glue to form a coloured mixture. They can then apply the paint and sprinkle sand on before it dries to create interesting textures.

Paired work

● While the magic beans dry, invite children to discuss with partners what sort of magic their beans might have, for example, they could grow into fearsome creatures or alien plants. Some may have magic powers to enable the owner to transform themselves into anything they wish.
● Encourage children to make use of their stored 'magic memory' bank and explain how reading and listening to lots of stories helps this to develop.

Review

● Invite pairs of children to show the class some of the magic beans they made. Ask them to explain the powers that the beans have and the sorts of thing that might happen. Make positive comments about the most inventive magic ideas and talk about how the activity will help with their future story writing.

2: Growing seeds

Curriculum objectives
● To predict what might happen on the basis of what has been read so far.
● To use a capital letter for names of people.
● To form capital letters.

Resources
Fast-growing seeds such as mustard and cress; small recycled plastic food containers such as yoghurt pots, take-away containers or margarine tubs; compost; small watering cans; small trowels; buckets; sticky tape

Introduction
● Recall previous work on the growth sequence of a plant. Identify the different stages, such as roots growing down into the soil and shoots appearing above the soil.
● Talk about the key conditions necessary for growth (water and sunlight).

Whole-class work
● Make comparisons between the size and appearance of the chosen seeds and the beans explored in the previous lesson.
● Suggest planting these seeds and recording growth in a week.
● Ask children to predict what is likely to happen.
● Talk about what children need to do to start their seeds growing.
● Decide where to leave seed-growing containers to catch maximum sunlight and make watering easy, for example, along windowsills.

Group work
● Invite groups to water a bucketful of compost and use this to fill plastic containers, leaving a centimetre at the top to observe the seedling growth.
● Demonstrate how to sprinkle seeds thinly on the top of the compost and lightly press them down before sprinkling more compost on top.
● Remind children to water their seeds daily.

Independent work
● Invite each child to make a name label for their container and stick it on. Praise appropriate use and correct formation of capital letters.

Review
● Review the success of the planting process and predict what might happen.

3: Weekly growth chart

Curriculum objectives
● To spell the days of the week.
● To form capital letters.
● To use capital letters for the days of the week.

Resources
Photocopiable page 109 'My plant growth chart'; small rulers

Introduction
● Recall lesson 2 and discuss ways of recording how the plants grow, for example, drawing pictures, taking photographs, measuring, making notes.
● Introduce the word *chart* and suggest using one to record the growth process.

Whole-class work
● Display photocopiable page 109 'My plant growth chart'. Explain that the first row is to record the days of the week, and emphasise the need for capitals.
● Suggest that children use the middle row for drawings and notes about changes they observe, for example, the appearance of a leaf.
● Explain that the last row is to record measurements in centimetres.

Group work
● Provide small rulers to measure seedlings, and give children the photocopiable sheet to fill in. Encourage them to discuss their observations of any growth so far and decide how to record them.

Differentiation
● Challenge confident children to record in millimetres as well as centimetres.

Review
● Allow time for children to record growth and fill in their charts every day. Discuss the seedlings' growth regularly and review the charts after a week. Compare results and decide which growth stages have been observed.

Curriculum objectives
● To participate in discussion about what is read to them, taking turns and listening to what others say.
● To use the spelling rule for adding '-s' or '-es' as the plural marker for nouns and the third-person singular marker for verbs.
● To read aloud their writing clearly enough to be heard by their peers and teacher.

Resources
Non-fiction books in different formats about plants, for example, lift-the-flap books, 'feely' books, books with buttons to press; card to make zigzag books; coloured pens and pencils

4: Parts of a plant

Introduction
● Recall previous lessons involving plant parts. Ask children to write those that they remember on the board, for example, *root, stem, bud, flower, leaf*.
● Demonstrate some of the more unusual non-fiction books, for example, 'lift-the-flap' and 'feely' books.

Whole-class work
● Suggest that children might like to make their own unusual books to explain the function of the parts of a plant.
● Introduce the idea of a zigzag book. Fold a piece of card into a zigzag and explain how each page could be about a different plant part, in the order they appear: seed, root, shoot, stem, leaf, bud, flower, fruit.
● Suggest children complete their sentences, illustrations and labels on paper, and then stick them onto the card zigzag in the correct order.

Group work
● Provide a selection of non-fiction plant books for them to refer to.
● Suggest that they begin by writing a list of parts they plan to cover and allocate parts for group members to work on.
● Emphasise use of correct word endings so that sentences make sense in this context, for example, *seeds, grows, taller, plants, leaves, patterned*.
● Remind children to work together to ensure their pages are in the correct order before they stick them into the zigzag book.

> **Differentiation**
> ● Help children to fold their card into pages and support simple sentence composition.

Review
● Ask groups to read their books aloud. Encourage positive comments about sentence structure, correct word endings, order and content.

Curriculum objectives
● To sequence sentences to form short narratives.
● To use '-ing', '-ed', '-er' and '-est' where no change is needed in the spelling of root words.
● To learn the grammar for Year 1 in Appendix 2.

Resources
Photocopiable page 110 'How to grow a beanstalk'; children's partially completed photocopiable sheets 'My plant growth chart' (lesson 3); coloured pencils and pens; large sheets of paper

5: How to grow a beanstalk

Introduction
● Recall 'Jack and the Beanstalk' and ask the children how Jack grew his beans. Consider why he carelessly threw them out of the window rather than planting them in a pot so that he could look after them carefully.

Whole-class work
● Suggest that Jack did not know how to look after plants properly and invite the children to create a sheet of instructions to help him, based on how they planted their own beanstalks (lesson 2).
● Write a list of useful action words, such as *plant, cover, water*, and plant parts.
● Display photocopiable page 110 'How to grow a beanstalk'. Remind children that they are telling Jack what they did, and so they need to add the correct endings to action words to write in the past tense, such as *planted*.
● Remind them to write in sentences and to create a sequence.

Individual work
● Provide each child with the photocopiable sheet to complete. Allow them to refer to their plant growth charts. Explain that, when they have finished, they can cut out their sentences and stick them in order on a large sheet of paper. They can then extend them with drawings, labels and numbers.

Review
● Gather the children together to comment on the way the instructions are presented. Decide which ones will help Jack most and why.

Week 5 lesson plans

Children begin lessons this week by comparing the careless way that Jack treated his beans with how they nurtured their own seeds. The focus here is on sentence writing and defining the features of a sentence. Children begin to join sentences with *and* and complete written work to embed this learning. The 'beginning, middle and end' sequence in stories is revised and children enhance their awareness of the fairy-tale genre by reading and writing alternative versions of 'Jack and the Beanstalk'. As they write, emphasis is placed on sentence sequence and correct punctuation. They share their stories with others for constructive comment, and are encouraged to read aloud so that others hear them clearly.

1: Careless Jack

Introduction

● Recall past explorations of 'Jack and the Beanstalk'. Focus on the incident when Jack throws the beans out of the window. Speculate what might have happened if the beans had fallen on a stony path or a wooden seat. Discuss others things that might have happened, for example, it might not have rained and so the seeds would not have grown.
● Link this discussion to recall of conditions needed for seeds to grow. Decide where Jack's beans probably landed for this to happen, for example, in soil.
● Invite children to describe how they made sure that conditions were ideal for their own seeds to grow.

Whole-class work

● Remind children of their past work involving sentence writing, for example, making zigzag books and writing instruction sheets for Jack.
● Invite them to say some key features of a sentence, for example, it begins with a capital letter and ends with a full stop, question mark or exclamation mark; it makes complete sense without having to add anything else.
● Write some complete and incomplete sentences on the board and read through them together, for example: *Jack went up the beanstalk/the man asked jack for/"You are a silly boy, Jack!"/the giant reached the top of/The Giant yelled.*
● Ask children to decide which ones are in complete sentences. Invite individuals to add what is necessary to make all sentences complete.
● Display the first screen of interactive activity 'How would you feel?' on the CD-ROM, and read through the instructions together. Discuss the content of the two pictures and explain that children must write a complete sentence to explain how they would feel if they were in each picture.

Paired work

● Divide into pairs of similar ability and suggest that children support one another as they write and read through their sentences.
● Once the children have written their two sentences ask them to read their partner's work. Encourage them to discuss whether the sentences are complete, contain the information asked for and make sense.
● Display the second screen for the children to complete.

> **Differentiation**
> ● Help those struggling to write a simple sentence, for example, *I am happy on my birthday*.
> ● Challenge more confident learners to ask their partners questions about how they feel in different situations, and invite partners to answer in written sentences.

Review

● Invite the children to read each other's sentences and discuss. Praise evidence of effective sentences with correct punctuation and appropriate use of capitals.

Curriculum objectives
● To begin to punctuate sentences using a capital letter and a full stop, question mark or exclamation mark.
● To join words and join sentences using *and*.

Resources
A version of 'Jack and the Beanstalk'; photocopiable page 111 'Joining words and sentences'

2: Punctuation and word endings

Introduction
● Hold up 'Jack and the Beanstalk' and read the title. Recall discussions about what this might tell us about the story.
● Ask children to consider why the word *and* is included. Talk about how the story is about Jack and what happens to him with the beanstalk.
● Recall other fairy tales with the word *and* in the title, for example, 'The Princess and the Pea', 'Hansel and Gretel'.

Whole-class work
● Explain that the word *and* helps to group words together and create longer sentences.
● Write two sentences on the board that can be linked by *and*, for example: *I came to school this morning/I forgot to bring any lunch*. Invite children to add *and* in the correct place and read it aloud. Try linking different sentences.
● Display photocopiable page 111 'Joining words and sentences' and read the first set of instructions to make sure children understand what is required.
● Read the next set of instructions, once again commenting on punctuation.

Paired work
● Provide mixed-ability pairs with the photocopiable sheet to complete.
● Ask them to support one another by checking punctuation and whether the sentences make sense.

Review
● Review written work together. Encourage children to consider how they will use *and* in future work. Praise correct punctuation.

Curriculum objectives
● To become very familiar with key stories, fairy stories and traditional tales, retelling them and considering their particular characteristics.
● To make inferences on the basis of what is being said and done.

Resources
A version of 'Jack and the Beanstalk'

3: What if?

Introduction
● Recall lessons involving story language and sequencing of events to identify the beginning, middle and end of stories.
● Read 'Jack and the Beanstalk'. Ask children to name things that happen during each section of the story.

Whole-class work
● Read the beginning of the story, stopping when Jack's bean starts to grow.
● Ask children to consider an alternative event to change the whole story, for example, the seeds grow into an entirely different plant or alien creature. Write ideas on the board in a section headed *Beginning*.
● Consider events in the middle of the story, such as when Jack climbs up the new plant or meets the alien creature. Encourage children to come up with interesting adjectives to describe the appearance of the plant or creature. Perhaps it is a man-eating plant or a shy alien? Make notes on the board under the heading *Middle*.
● Finally, invite children to consider a different ending to the story, for example, with Jack travelling through space to meet the alien's family. Note ideas under the heading *End*.

Group work
● Divide into groups to write their own story using the board notes. Emphasise that each story should follow a sequence and use correct punctuation.

Review
● Ask groups to read their stories aloud. Consider how the finished stories differ despite starting from the same board notes.

Curriculum objectives
● To sequence sentences to form short narratives.
● To begin to punctuate sentences using a capital letter and a full stop, question mark or exclamation mark.

Resources
A version of 'Jack and the Beanstalk' and an alternative version of the story, such as *Jim and the Beanstalk* by Raymond Briggs or *Jack and the Baked Beanstalk* by Colin Stimpson; large sheets of paper; coloured pens

4: Alternative tales

Introduction
● Recall how children planned an alternative version of 'Jack and the Beanstalk' as a class in the last lesson. Write down each stage of this planning process on the board.

Whole-class work
● Read another alternative version of the story.
● Compare this with 'Jack and the Beanstalk', identifying any similarities and differences in characters, setting and events.

Paired work
● Ask pairs of children to write an alternative version of the story, following the same stages as in lesson 3.
● Provide access to 'Jack and the Beanstalk' and your chosen alternative story.
● Suggest that they decide on the name(s) of their main character(s) and make notes about the sequence of events. Encourage them to consider what changes to make at the beginning, middle or end of the story.
● Ask children to take turns to write a sentence while their partner checks that it has the correct punctuation.
● Encourage them to join some of their sentences with *and*. Remind them to think about the sequence of events and to organise their sentences in the correct order.

Review
● Bring the class together and ask what they enjoyed most about the lesson. Discuss whether the activities have increased their confidence in sequencing sentences to form a narrative.

Curriculum objectives
● To participate in discussion about what is read to them, taking turns and listening to what others say.
● To read aloud their writing clearly enough to be heard by their peers and the teacher.

Resources
Children's stories from lesson 4

5: Let's listen to a new story

Introduction
● Recall the previous lesson's versions of 'Jack and the Beanstalk'.
● Ask questions to engage interest, for example: *Did anyone change the main characters? What names were used? Can you describe any magic in your story?*

Whole-class work
● Invite three pairs of children to share their stories with the class, reading alternate sentences clearly.
● Ask the remaining children to listen initially for the names of the characters so that they can join in a discussion about them. When the stories have been heard, ask specific questions, for example, *Did any of the stories introduce new characters? Can you name them? Which characters did you like/dislike?*
● Continue in this way with another three pairs, this time asking about the opening sentence, for example: *One of the stories had a really unusual beginning. Can you say anything about it?*
● Consider setting, events and endings as the remaining pairs read.

Paired work
● Ask pairs of children to write a short review about their favourite story and the way it was read. Suggest that they comment on clear reading, good sentence sequencing and exciting new ideas.
● Explain that they should write at least three sentences in their reviews.

Review
● Bring the pairs together to read their reviews aloud. Comment positively on clear reading and imaginative ideas.

Expected outcomes
● All children can listen to and discuss a wide range of poems at a level beyond that at which they can read independently.
● Most children can join words and join sentences with *and*.
● Some children can use their senses to write a poem.

Curriculum objectives
● To apply phonic knowledge and skills as the route to decode words.
● To listen to and discuss a wide range of poems, stories and non-fiction at a level beyond that at which they can read independently.
● To read words containing taught GPCs and '-s', '-es', '-ing', '-ed', '-er' and '-est' endings.

Resources
Selection of poetry books including plant poems; photocopiable pages 'Little Brown Seeds', 'A tree' and 'Exploring 'A tree'' from the CD-ROM

Week 6 lesson plans

This week the focus is on plant-themed poems. Children read poems using their existing phonic skills to decode words, and listen to and discuss poems at a level beyond that of their independent reading levels. They enjoy collecting interesting leaves outdoors and making up non-rhyming poems about them, using pairs of descriptive words joined by *and*. Unusual close-up plant photographs are introduced and children are encouraged to create imaginative poems about them. They close their eyes in order to focus on the senses of smell and touch as they identify herbs before transforming their ideas into poems to read aloud to the class. Finally, children use words with familiar endings to create catchy and interesting plant poems.

1: Plant poems

Introduction
● Show the children the poetry books and explain that they are there to explore in spare moments.
● Ask children to recall rhymes that they already know about plants and recite some of these together, for example: *Once I found a cherry stone, Oats and beans and barley grow.*

Whole-class work
● Display photocopiable page 'Little Brown Seeds' from the CD-ROM and read the poem together.
● Talk about the poem and ask questions to encourage closer observation of detail, for example, *Can you find any rhyming words? Are any of the words repeated?*
● Invite someone to highlight the rhyming words and discuss their spelling. Identify the sound made by the 'ou' and 'ow' graphemes. Consider the different phonemes created by the same graphemes in *brown* and *grow*.
● Display photocopiable page 'A tree' from the CD-ROM.
● Ask children what they notice before you start to read the poem. Discuss the way the words are arranged to create a tree shape. Invite children to make comments about their initial impressions.
● Read the poem aloud while children listen with their eyes closed. When you have finished, ask children to describe the picture they have in their *mind's eye*.
● Focus on new vocabulary, such as *modesty, generosity, shimmy,* and explain the meaning in this context. Draw attention to the metaphor *clothed* and discuss what this means when applied to a tree.
● Suggest that pairs of children work together to answer questions about the poem on photocopiable page 'Exploring 'A tree'' from the CD-ROM, in order to develop their reading skills and awareness of different styles of poetry.

Paired work
● Ask the pairs to read one question at a time and write an answer on a separate sheet of paper. Tell them to write in sentences and to number their answers to correspond with the questions.

> **Differentiation**
> ● Ask less confident learners to draw a picture of the tree depicted in the poem. Give them word cards at their reading level to remind them of items to include and label.

Review
● Bring the class together to read out and discuss their answers to the questions. Decide how much the lesson's activities have helped them to develop their reading skills and extend their vocabulary. Invite them to explain what they have learned about different ways of presenting a poem.

Curriculum objectives
● To be encouraged to link what they read or hear read to their own experiences.
● To join words and join sentences using *and*.

Resources
Collections of leaves (if available); books containing information about leaves, images of leaves from the internet; bucket; clipboards

2: Out and about

Introduction
● If possible, take the children outdoors to find interesting leaves to examine. Otherwise, have books and images of leaves available.
● Explore non-fiction books to find out about the function of leaves.
● Recall the poem about a tree that you explored in lesson 1.
● Establish that poems do not have to rhyme and suggest creating a 'leaf poem' to demonstrate this.

Whole-class work
● Ask each child to look at a leaf in detail and to think of words to describe how it looks, smells, sounds or feels. Encourage them to describe a time when they walked in leaves or played with them.
● Draw a long thin leaf on the board and write the children's words inside it in a column, for example: *green, lumpy, veiny, colourful, crumply, smelly, scrunchy.*
● Tell the children that this is a class poem. Invite them to read the poem they have made up and discuss the effect, changing the order of the words, or arranging them in groups, until they are satisfied with the sequence.
● Write a suitable title at the top of the leaf and repeat this as the last line, for example, *Our leaves*.

Group work
● Ask groups to write their own non-rhyming poem about leaves, but this time joining words with *and*, for example, *long and narrow, bumpy and prickly*.

Review
● Ask groups to read their poems to the class for constructive comments. Observe how children have used *and* in their descriptions.

Curriculum objectives
● To say out loud what they are going to write about.
● To be encouraged to link what they read or hear read to their own experiences.

Resources
Media resource 'Plants' on the CD-ROM

3: Plant pictures

Introduction
● Recall the leaf poems created in the previous lesson and discuss any plant pictures you have looked at in class.

Whole-class work
● Display the first photograph from 'Plants' on the CD-ROM and invite children to comment on it. Ask if they can identify the plant and explain that this is a photograph that has been taken from an unusual angle, or very close to the plant, so that we see it in a different way.
● Look through the images one by one, talking about what children can see.
● Suggest that children use these unusual images to help them to write unusual group poems.

Group work
● Print off a set of images and ask each group to take one and write a poem to describe it.
● Encourage children to discuss how they will write their poem, starting by writing down descriptive words and then arranging them in a pattern.
● Stress the unusual nature of the photographs and encourage children to consider what they might remind them of, for example, a row of peas in a pod might look *like shiny green teeth in a smiling mouth!*
● Suggest that they add a title and some illustrations.

Review
● Display the poems beside their images. Ask the class to explore the photographs and read the poems, commenting on creative use of words.

Curriculum objectives
● To say out loud what they are going to write about.
● To compose a sentence orally before writing it.
● To read aloud their writing clearly enough to be heard by their peers and the teacher.

Resources
A selection of labelled herbs in pots with different shapes, textures and smells, for example, chives, parsley, fennel, mint, lemon balm, marjoram, thyme, rosemary; coloured pencils

4: Feel and smell

Introduction
● Recall observing plant photographs on the CD-ROM and in non-fiction books. Consider the notion that photographs cannot show how a plant smells and feels.
● Show the children the labelled herbs and explain that they are used to flavour foods. Ask if they recognise any.

Whole-class work
● Ask a child to close his/her eyes and try to identify the smell of a herb, such as mint or lemon balm. Pass it to the next child to do the same. Explain that closing the eyes concentrates the sense of smell.
● Read the label and write this on the board along with words suggested by the children to describe how the herb smells.
● Repeat with several herbs.
● Pass the same herbs around again, this time asking children to feel them with closed eyes. Write their words on the board.

Group work
● Organise children into mixed-ability groups. Ask them to choose three herbs and write a poem about how they smell and feel (one verse for each herb).
● Encourage children to compose short sentences, saying each one aloud before writing it down.
● Once poems are written, invite children to read them to each other, making modifications until they are satisfied.

Review
● Invite the groups to share their poems. Ask for comments on word choices that reflect the senses of smell and touch.

Curriculum objectives
● To use '-ing', '-ed', '-er' and '-est' where no change is needed in the spelling of root words.
● To join words and join sentences with and.

Resources
Coloured pencils

5: Pleasing endings

Introduction
● Recall the plant-related poetry that you have read and created together.
● Discuss familiar word endings and write examples on the board, such as tall, taller, tallest, planted, planting, seeds, bushes.
● Talk about how the children connected words with and, and suggest that they do this with words with the same endings to use in their plant poems.

Whole-class work
● Write the parts of a plant on the board in the order they appear: seeds, roots, stems, buds, leaves and flowers. Invite children to think of words ending in '-ing' to describe each part, such as seeds: swelling, bursting; stems: stretching, curling; buds: uncurling, unfurling and so on.
● Suggest joining these pairs with and, for example, swelling and bursting, fat brown seeds; stretching and curling, bright green stems; uncurling and unfurling, tight round buds.
● Finally, try writing or colouring letters to describe the word, for example, twisting, using a wavy line, green using the colour. Discuss the effects.

Paired work
● Divide children into pairs to try and compose some plant poems.
● Ask them to spend time reading them to one another and making modifications before settling on their final poems.

Review
● Invite pairs to read their poems to the class for comment. Discuss how the experience has helped children to remember how to use word endings.

■ SCHOLASTIC

Curriculum objectives
● To begin to punctuate sentences using a capital letter and a full stop, question mark or exclamation mark.
● To leave spaces between words.
● To use a capital letter for the names of people, places, the days of the week, and the personal pronoun *I*.

Resources
Access to computers and interactive activity 'Spot the stops!' on the CD-ROM

Grammar and punctuation: Spot the stops!

Revise
● Recall lessons focusing on defining a sentence, emphasising the need to start with a capital letter and end with a full stop, question mark or exclamation mark.
● Write a sentence on the board without punctuation, for example: *the children looked out of the window* (no capital letter and no full stop). Invite children to take turns to add punctuation until they have a complete sentence.
● Recall other times when a capital letter is used, for example, for names of people, places, the days of the week and the personal pronoun *I*. Invite children to write examples on the board.
● Display interactive activity 'Spot the stops!' on the CD-ROM.
● Display the first screen, and ask what the children notice (no punctuation).
● Explain that there are two stories and show the second screen.

Assess
● Provide each child with the interactive activity to complete. Repeat the need to punctuate sentences correctly and to look out for any other words that should have a capital letter.

Further practice
● Support less confident learners by asking them to punctuate simple sentences, for example, *my name is tom.* (The aim is to check sentence punctuation and use of capital letters rather than reading skills.)
● Challenge children to compare the stories in the interactive activity and to write, and correctly punctuate, a short review saying which one they prefer.

Curriculum objectives
● To apply simple spelling rules and guidelines, as listed in Appendix 1.
● To use words containing each of the 40+ phonemes already taught.
● To use the spelling rule for adding '-s' or '-es' as the plural marker for nouns and the third-person singular marker for verbs.

Resources
Scissors; glue sticks; photocopiable page 'The parts of a plant' from the CD-ROM

Spelling: The parts of a plant

Revise
● Use starter activity 7 'More than one?' to revise plural endings.
● Explain that children are going to revise their spelling skills by writing sentences about a sequence of pictures.
● Display photocopiable page 'The parts of a plant' from the CD-ROM.
● Locate the first picture of the sequence and decide what it shows. Ask children how they would write this in a sentence, for example: *Here* (or *This*) *is a seed with some roots growing from it.* Talk about the spelling of the key words *seed* and *roots*, recalling how to spell the phonemes /ee/ and /oo/. Discuss how to spell the word *growing*, first identifying the grapheme for the phoneme /ow/ and then deciding how to spell the '-ing' ending.
● Continue through the pictures, reminding children of the rule for plural noun endings, '-s' or '-es', for example, *branches, buds, apples* and *flowers*. Discuss how the word *leaf* changes to *leaves*.
● Recall how the same grapheme can sometimes represent different phonemes, for example, *growing, flowers*.

Assess
● Provide scissors, glue, paper, pencils and the photocopiable sheet for children to complete.

Further practice
● Simplify the page for less confident learners by supporting spelling of simple captions for plant parts, for example: *This is a seed; Here is a root.*
● Challenge more confident learners to write sentences in the past tense, for example: *First the seed was planted...*

Curriculum objectives

● To apply phonic knowledge and skills as the route to decode words.
● To read words containing taught GPCs and '-s', '-es', '-ing', '-ed', '-er' and '-est' endings.
● To respond speedily with the correct sound to graphemes for all 40+ phonemes, including alternative sounds for phonemes.
● To check that the text makes sense to them as they read and correct inaccurate reading.

Resources

Photocopiable page 'Real or nonsense?' from the CD-ROM

Reading: Real or nonsense

Revise

● Use starter activity 8 'Make me different' to revise word endings.
● Recall fairy stories the children are familiar with to link with the content of the assessment page.
● Display photocopiable page 'Real or nonsense?' from the CD-ROM and read through the instructions together so that children are aware of what they need to do.
● Cover the sentences in the left-hand column and together read the words in the first box in the right-hand column, using phonic knowledge of taught GPCs. Talk about how all three words sound the same and ask children to spot the nonsense word among them. Invite them to explain the meaning of the two remaining words.
● Reveal the left-hand column and read the sentence together. Choose which word to write in the space so that it makes sense, given the meaning of the additional word.
● Draw attention to and revise other aspects of reading discussed previously that are evident in this sentence, for example, how the '-ed' ending changes the word *pick* into *picked* to indicate that this event happened in the past. Ask children to spot the grapheme that creates the phoneme /er/ in *flower* in other words (*her, godmother*) and highlight both word endings.
● Do the same with the next box, discussing how the graphemes 'ow' and 'ou' in the words create the same phoneme.
● Point out capital letters in the sentences to indicate the names of characters and circle them.
● Underline the endings '-ed', '-er', '-est', and draw attention to plural ending '-s'. Ask children to think of words with the plural ending '-es', such as *dresses* and *buses*.
● Split the word *coach* into phonemes and discuss the letters that form the vowel digraph 'oa' and the more familiar consonant digraph 'ch'.
● Find examples of split digraphs, such as *made, broke* and *like* and read these words aloud, discussing how the vowel sounds change in these words.
● Remove all annotations from the displayed screen and suggest that children go through each sentence with a partner initially before completing it. Explain that this is so that they can discuss the reason for their choice of words, and support one another with reading.

Assess

● Explain that the aim of the activity is to see how well the children can read the sentences and the words in the boxes alongside. Talk about how their previous reading will help them to identify nonsense words, and support them as they make their choices. Remind them of the way that they explored the sentences and words in detail as a class to revise these skills, and in pairs to support one another.
● Provide each child with the photocopiable sheet to complete.

Further practice

● Involve all children in the class analysis of the text on the photocopiable sheet but provide those who struggle with the reading level with an alternative page for their assessment based on their current ability. Give them a choice of two words but omit any nonsense words. Explain to them what is expected of them and support and encourage them in their attempts to read sentences and choose words.
● Create a more challenging assessment page for children who are reading at a higher level, making up sentences to reflect their reading abilities.

Curriculum objectives

● To compose a sentence orally before writing it.
● To sequence sentences to form short narratives.
● To punctuate sentences using a capital letter and a full stop, question mark or exclamation mark.
● To use '-ing', '-ed', '-er' and '-est' where no change is needed in the spelling of root words.
● To discuss what they have written with the teacher or other children.

Resources

Different versions of 'Jack and the Beanstalk'; photocopiable page 'Jack and the Beanstalk in pictures' from the CD-ROM; coloured pens and pencils; scissors; glue

Writing: 'Jack and the Beanstalk'

Revise

● Show children the books they have explored to remind them of the story.
● Recall how they planned their own stories using storyboards. Display photocopiable page 'Jack and the Beanstalk in pictures' from the CD-ROM and discuss how it is in storyboard style. Go through the pictures one by one and discuss events they represent.
● Explore the first image, identifying Jack and the man with the beans. Are they as the children imagined them, an old man with a beard and a boy dressed as a fairy-tale character? Perhaps they imagined a clever young man tricking Jack? Explain that this is the artist's impression of these characters and is there to remind children about what happened. It is up to them how they imagine characters, settings and events.
● Discuss each picture in the same way, commenting on the artist's impression of the Giant's wife, the Giant and the magic harp.
● Decide whether any key events are missing, for example, the hen that lays golden eggs and the Giant chanting.
● Explain that the children are going to write their own versions of this story and that this page, along with the discussion, will help them to remember important things they have already learned about story writing. For example, sequencing events, using story language and including repeated phrases.
● Recall how many fairy tales and traditional tales include memorable phrases, and 'Jack and the Beanstalk' is no exception. Repeat the Giant's chant together to help children to remember it. Write *fee fi fo fum i smell the blood of an Englishman* on the board and ask children to add punctuation. Remind them about speech marks, and suggest use of exclamation marks to emphasise the shocking nature of the Giant's words.
● Ask children to consider story language and suggest suitable opening sentences, such as *Once upon a time, There was once a....*
● Consider suitable endings to the story, for example, *And that was the end of the Giant!/Jack and his mother never had to go hungry again!*
● Recall discussions about helping stories, and events within them, to flow along using connecting words, such as *Then, After that, In the end.*
● Ask the children to go into pairs to list action words (verbs) represented by the images. Remind them to add suitable endings to indicate that the story is in the past, for example, *dropped, was climbing, opened, was chopping.*
● Encourage children to use correct grammatical terminology when discussing full stops, capital letters, question marks and exclamation marks.
● Invite children to compose sentences orally to a partner before writing them.

Assess

● Provide each child with the photocopiable sheet to serve as an event reminder, and paper, scissors, glue and writing tools.
● Ask the children to write a story that has at least one sentence for each event. Suggest that they cut out the pictures and stick them at suitable points in their story.
● Invite children to read their finished stories to partners and discuss features such as sequence, choice of word endings and punctuation.
● Choose stories to discuss with the class. Draw attention to and give praise for correct sentence punctuation features.

Further practice

● Support sentence writing by helping less confident learners to write a simple sentence about each picture, for example: *The man gave Jack some beans.* Use the words *capital letter, full stop* and *sentence* to reinforce these terms.
● Challenge groups of children to write a different story in the same way. Invite each member of the group to choose an event to draw and write about. Put this writing into a sequence and ask the children to read the story to others, with each child reading their own work.

Add the endings

■ Each sentence has a missing word. The words you need are in the box below. You will need to add '-ed' or '-ing' to the words.

shout	show	start
grow	sleep	steal

The giant _____ at Jack.

The beanstalk is _____ outside Jack's window.

Jack _____ the coins to his mother.

The giant came in while Jack was _____.

Jack _____ to climb up the beanstalk.

"Jack is _____ me!" tinkled the harp.

I can use add the correct ending to a word
so that it makes sense in the sentence.

How did you do?

Name: _____   Date: _____

Beanstalk bingo

Instructions:

■ To make up the game, print two copies of the page and stick them onto thick card.

■ Cut one page into individual words for the playing cards.

■ Cut the second page into four larger lotto boards.

■ Laminate the four playing boards and the smaller cards, which children will place on the matching squares as the game progresses.

To play the game:

■ Divide children into groups of five. Invite one child to hold the small cards while the others have a game board each.

■ The child who has the word on the card on his/her game board should read it aloud and put it over the matching word on the game board.

■ The first child to fill the game board is the winner.

■ Suggest that children in the same group take turns to hold up small cards and swap their boards after each game so that they have the opportunity to read all of the words.

the	today	says	there	come	do
once	she	little	friend	when	are
they	one	said	were	into	what
like	have	some	out	was	climb

In the hot-seat

Jack	Jack's mother

Giant	Giant's wife

Man with the beans	Harp

PHOTOCOPIABLE

SCHOLASTIC
www.scholastic.co.uk

Choosing adjectives

■ Choose the correct adjective to describe the noun in each sentence. The adjectives are in the boxes on the right.

Jack's mother was a _____ widow.	poor poorer poorest
Jack climbed to the _____ branch of the beanstalk.	high higher highest
The Giant had the _____ voice in the land.	loud louder loudest
The Giant had a very _____ wife.	kind kinder kindest
The harp played the _____ music Jack had ever heard.	sweet sweeter sweetest
Jack ran much _____ than the Giant.	fast faster fastest
Jack and his mother were much _____ by the end of the story.	rich richer richest

I can choose the adjective with the correct ending to fit in the sentence.

How did you do?

Comparing plants

■ Draw pictures in the boxes and write the correct adjective above each one. The first row has been done for you.

tall	taller	tallest
short		
small		
long		

I can choose the adjective with the correct ending to compare objects.

How did you do?

PHOTOCOPIABLE   ■SCHOLASTIC
www.scholastic.co.uk

Name: _____   Date: _____

My plant growth chart

- Write the days of the week in column 1.
- Draw pictures and write notes about your seeds in column 2.
- Write how tall your plants are every day in column 3.

1. Day	2. Pictures and notes	3. Height

I can keep a record of the growth of a plant.

How did you do?

How to grow a beanstalk

- Write a sentence in each box about how you planted and grew your beanstalk.
- Remember to write your sentences in the correct sequence.
- Here are some words to help you:

fastened	filled	taller	lifted
watered	pushed	planted	covered

I can write instructions in the correct order.

How did you do?

PHOTOCOPIABLE

Joining words and sentences

- Join the words in the boxes with *and* to make a fairy-tale title.
- Write the titles next to each pair of words.
- Remember capital letters for names!

the princess	_____
the pea	_____
goldilocks	_____
the three bears	_____

- Join the two sentences in the boxes below with *and* to make a longer sentence.
- Write the new sentence underneath each pair.
- Remember to change punctuation!

Jack took the beans to the market. He sold them to a man on the way.

_____

_____

The princess slept in a very tall bed. She still felt the pea.

_____

_____

I can join words and sentences with *and* to make longer phrases and sentences.

How did you do?

Julia Donaldson

This half-term's Julia Donaldson theme is designed to engage children with the rich patterned language and strong exciting characters that abound in her books, and provides opportunities to experience the joy of the rhyming word. After absorbing some of her most popular stories, children move on to enjoying her songs and rhymes. Prior learning is embedded and new learning opportunities are introduced.

Expected prior learning
- Can listen and concentrate when stories are read to them.
- Has begun to use adjectives.
- Understand what a setting is.
- Can discuss an opinion.
- Can write simple sentences.
- Understand what is meant by a rhyme.

Overview of progression
- Children write about their experiences in greater detail, using *and* confidently to join sentences. They learn the importance of re-reading their work to ensure it makes sense.
- Story characters are analysed in greater depth, and children represent them with puppets during story retelling.
- They write stories using both text and images, and confidently express their opinions on books in book reviews.
- Awareness of story features is enhanced by discussing the significance of the role of author and illustrator. Children learn to search for appropriate information to write simple biographies.
- Poetry appreciation is greatly supported by Julia Donaldson's songs, rhymes and phrases. Children recite some of these with drama, adding percussion to demonstrate syllabic rhythm of words.

Creative context
- The children are encouraged to express their ideas creatively using paint and collage to create pictures, and book images, drama, small-world and role play to re-enact stories and character conversations.
- Aspects of order and sequence are included in activities involving alphabetical order and ordering of story events, which links to maths.

Preparation
We recommend certain texts by Julia Donaldson, including: *Tyrannosaurus Drip*, *Superworm*, *Monkey Puzzle*, *Sharing a Shell*, *The Gruffalo's Child*, *The Snail and the Whale*, *Room on the Broom*, *Tabby McTat*, but any Julia Donaldson texts could be used.

You will also need:
Sticky notes; percussion instruments; books featuring superheroes; coloured pens; collage materials and materials to enhance retellings; outdoor access; images of dinosaur display from Autumn 1; materials to make puppets; upper- and lower-case alphabet lists

On the CD-ROM you will find:
Media resources '*Tyrannosaurus Drip* book cover', '*Superworm* book cover', 'Monkey puzzle tree', 'The Gruffalo's Child song'; interactive activities 'Finding rhymes', 'Jumbled words'; photocopiable pages: 'Extract from *Superworm*', '*Superworm* events', 'Puppets from gloves', 'Julia Donaldson', 'Axel Scheffler facts', 'Extract from *Sharing a Shell*', 'Tabby McTat's favourite song', 'Start and finish the sentence'

Chapter at a glance

An overview of the chapter. For curriculum objective codes, please see pages 8–10.

Week	Lesson	Curriculum objectives	Summary of activities	Outcomes
1	1	RC: 3, 10, 11	Introduce *Superworm*. Explore cover for clues and prediction of content. Make inferences after group discussion.	• Can predict based on clues and prior reading. • Can infer based on what is said and done.
	2	RWR: 8 RC: 4, 9	Read and explore extract. Listen to full story. Discuss title and events. Enjoy group and class repetition of chant.	• Can join in with predictable phrases. • Can discuss significance of title and events. • Can read extract accurately.
	3	RWR: 1, 3 RC: 10	Explore term *superhero*. Outline a superhero's skills. Invent superhero characters and make inferences.	• Can read words in text to identify skills. • Can make inferences about superheroes.
	4	RWR: 6, 7	Explore contractions in a story and how these help lines to scan. Read and clap syllables. Look for contractions.	• Can identify contractions. • Can recognise the difference in syllables for sentences with and without contractions.
	5	RC: 3, 4	Retell *Superworm* using props, emphasising repeated phrases. Make worms from wool. Watch others and comment constructively.	• Can retell a story using props. • Can comment on interpretations, and accuracy and order of events.
2	1	WC: 1, 4	Explore different settings in a story. Create a setting and then write sentences to describe it.	• Can say aloud what they are going to draw and write about. • Can re-read their writing to check it makes sense.
	2	RC: 2 WC: 1	Make underground environment for treasure hunt. Write sentences about the treasure finding.	• Can link activity to story and own experience. • Can plan and explain a sentence before writing it.
	3	WT: 8 WC: 8	Identify adjectives used to describe characters. Choose correct endings to fit sentence. Use *and* to join words.	• Can use *and* to join adjectives. • Can choose appropriate endings for words to make sense in sentences.
	4	RWR: 9 RC: 2, 8	Read *Superworm* and discuss events, setting and characters. Create display about the story.	• Can read story and link to own experiences. • Can show confidence in reading and correct own inaccuracies.
	5	WT: 2 WC: 4, 8	Add captions and labels to display made in lesson 4. Use exception words and join labels and captions with *and*.	• Can spell common exception words, join words with *and* on labels and captions. • Can re-read to check it makes sense.
3	1	RC: 1, 9, 11	Introduce *Monkey Puzzle*. Predict and compare common features and events with other books by same author/illustrator. Discuss title and events.	• Can make predictions based on previous reading of books by same author. • Can discuss significance of title and events.
	2	RC: 7 WT: 9 WC: 5	Make comparisons of characters in stories explored so far. Use adjectives to describe them. Discuss written work with others.	• Can use adjectives to describe characters from stories explored. • Can discuss written ideas with others.
	3	RWR: 1 RC: 7	Follow instructions to make finger puppets to represent characters in stories. Plan how to re-enact story with puppets.	• Can use information provided to make puppet. • Can apply phonic knowledge and skills to decode words on instruction sheet.
	4	RC: 1, 10 WC: 2	Use puppets to re-enact an event from a story. Write sentences to identify action sequence. Modify in light of the discussion.	• Can discuss an event from a story beyond their reading level. • Can compose sentences orally before writing.
	5	WC: 2, 7, 8, 9	Write book reviews about favourite Julia Donaldson books in sentences with correct punctuation. Discuss orally before writing.	• Can compose sentences orally. • Can punctuate sentences correctly, leave spaces and use *and* to join words. .
4	1	RC: 7, 9	Identify book covers. Pairs design own cover, as author and illustrator. Choose appropriate title to reflect proposed events.	• Can use previous experiences and teacher input to support ideas. • Can discuss significance of title and events.
	2	RWR: 3 RC: 1, 4	Discuss and repeat memorable phrases from books explored. Identify which characters said phrases. Blend unfamiliar words containing taught GPCs.	• Can recognise and join in with phrases. • Can blend unfamiliar words containing taught GPCs.
	3	WT: 4 WC: 4	Create a Julia Donaldson corner, arranging books in alphabetical order.	• Can name letters in alphabetical order. • Can write book titles. • Can re-read to check writing makes sense.
	4	RC: 67 WT: 8 WC: 11	Read and discuss facts in a simple biography. Recognise '-er' endings and apply '-ing' and '-ed' endings.	• Can read and understand a simple biography. • Can recognise and use appropriate suffixes.
	5	WC: 4, 5	Use biographies from lesson 4 to create questions and answers for a hot-seat activity.	• Can write questions and re-read writing to check it makes sense. • Can discuss writing with teacher and peers.

Chapter at a glance

Week	Lesson	Curriculum objectives	Summary of activities	Outcomes
5	1	RC: 1, 3, 10	Read a story with no illustrations. Make inferences about effect of this. Introduce new Julia Donaldson story. Note key features.	• Can listen to and discuss new key story. • Can compare features with other books by same author. • Can make inferences following discussion.
	2	WT: 11, 12, 13	Discuss good story features. Create story plans in pairs identifying title, characters, setting and events. Focus on writing posture and letter formation.	• Can adopt good writing posture. • Can correctly form letters while writing story plans.
	3	WC: 2, 3	Begin to write own stories. Write events as sequence of sentences. Compose orally first after role play.	• Can compose sentences orally after role play. • Can write sentences in sequence to form short narrative.
	4	WC: 3, 9	Write own stories in full in roles as authors and illustrators. Focus on sequencing sentences, using correct punctuation.	• Can sequence sentences to form own story. • Can punctuate correctly with capital letter and full stop, question mark or exclamation mark.
	5	RC: 12 WC: 5	Complete books. Talk about content with class. Read aloud to class for discussion.	• Can discuss writing of story books with teacher and peers. • Can participate in discussion about stories read to them by other children.
6	1	RC: 4, 5	Learn a Julia Donaldson song and sing it. Explore other songs she has written. Discuss rhyme and structure of the song.	• Can join in with a song. • Can identify predictable phrases and repeat together. • Can appreciate rhymes, poems and songs by one author.
	2	WT: 5 WC: 8	Find rhyming words on photocopiable sheet. Join words with *and*. Match rhyming words. Discuss alternative GPCs.	• Can discuss alternative GPCs in words using correct letter names. • Can match rhyming words. • Can use *and* to join words.
	3	RWR: 6 WT: 5	Read sentences from Julia Donaldson's books. Choose missing rhyming words from selection.	• Can read words of more than one syllable in sentences. • Can use letter names to distinguish between alternative graphemes when choosing words.
	4	RC: 4, 5	Use instruments to beat rhythm. Recall chants and make new ones using rhyming words on photocopiable sheet.	• Can recognise and say by heart previously identified rhyming phrases. • Can appreciate rhymes in new chants and enjoy reciting them.
	5	RC: 5 WT: 5, 9	Explore *Tabby McTat's favourite song*. Learn and recite. Choose their own favourite rhymes, write short reviews and share them.	• Can appreciate rhymes and recite them. • Can use letter names to distinguish alternative GPCs. • Can apply spelling rules to write reviews.

Background knowledge

No new terms have been introduced in this chapter but terms from Autumn 1, 2, and Spring 1 are revisited and revised in this chapter.

■SCHOLASTIC

Week 1 lesson plans

This week's lessons begin an exploration into the stories of Julia Donaldson. Children's initial interest is engaged by revisiting *Tyrannosaurus Drip* before they are introduced to the popular *Superworm*. They predict the story content using clues apparent from the cover before listening to the story and discussing the significance of the title and events. Subsequent lessons extend enjoyment through exploration of the meaning of *superhero* and invention of children's own superheroes. Revision of contractions, and clapping of syllables, encourages children to become aware of the satisfaction that can be derived from rhythmic text. Finally, they re-enact story scenarios using props.

1: *Superworm*

Expected outcomes
● All children can recite a repeated phrase with drama.
● Most children are able to predict what might happen on the basis of what has been read so far.
● Some children can read words with contractions and understand that the apostrophe represents the omitted letter(s).

Curriculum objectives
● To become very familiar with key stories, fairy stories and traditional tales, retelling them and considering their particular characteristics.
● To predict what might happen on the basis of what has been read so far.
● To make inferences on the basis of what is being said and done.

Resources
Tyrannosaurus Drip and *Superworm* by Julia Donaldson; media resources 'Tyrannosaurus Drip book cover' and 'Superworm book cover' on the CD-ROM; sticky notes

Introduction
● Show children the book *Tyrannosaurus Drip* and ask them what they remember about the story, for example, the plot, contrasting characters and illustrations.
● Invite children to recall the author's name. Encourage them to predict what these stories will be like, for example, memorable rhymes and chants, quirky characters and amusing events.
● Recall discussions about *Tyrannosaurus Drip* illustrations and discuss what they like/dislike about David Roberts' work.

Whole-class work
● Display media resource 'Tyrannosaurus Drip book cover' on the CD-ROM, and look at the front and back covers to encourage children to recall discussions about characters and possible events. Remind them how they read the quotes on the back cover to help them to predict the plot.
● Introduce, *Superworm*, and display media resource 'Superworm book cover' on the CD-ROM. Invite children to point out differences in the two covers. Ask questions to encourage more detailed observation, for example: *Do you think the artist is the same in both books? Do you notice any differences in the style of the illustrations?* Introduce the name Axel Scheffler and ask if children can remember any other books by Julia Donaldson and Axel Scheffler.

Group work
● Display the front cover and encourage children to discuss the image of Superworm and the other creatures. Invite them to decide whether Superworm is the main character and ask: *Do you think the other characters like or dislike Superworm? Why do you say that?* Suggest that they write their thoughts on sticky notes and attach them down one side of the board.
● Display the back cover of *Superworm* and invite children to read the words of the chant and use this information to predict what they think might happen in the story. Ask them to stick their predictions down the other side of the board.
● Promote taking turns to listen and speak and encourage children to make their own inferences, taking into account the ideas of others in the group.

> **Differentiation**
> ● If any children are struggling to talk about the image of Superworm, join them and encourage discussion about how he looks and his facial expression. Ask: *Do you think Superworm looks happy or sad/kind or unkind?*

Review
● Bring the children together and ask groups to remove and read out their sticky-note thoughts and predictions.
● Use this evidence to assess children's ability to make predictions based on pictorial and contextual clues on the cover, and inferences based on what is said. Refer to children's notes during subsequent readings.

Curriculum objectives
● To recognise and join in with predictable phrases.
● To discuss the significance of title and events.
● To read aloud accurately books that are consistent with their developing phonic knowledge and that do not require them to use other strategies to work out words.

Resources
Superworm by Julia Donaldson; photocopiable page 'Extract from *Superworm*' from the CD-ROM; percussion instruments

2: A super-chant

Introduction

● Read *Superworm* to the class and discuss the significance of the title. Touch briefly on the term *superhero* (this will be explored in more depth in lesson 3).
● Discuss the main events, such as the capture of Superworm by Wizard Lizard, and how they impact on the story.

Whole-class work

● Display photocopiable page 'Extract from *Superworm*' from the CD-ROM and ask children to identify two points in the story when this same text appears. Read it together, building up words using existing phonic knowledge.
● Highlight familiar punctuation in the extract, such as capital letters, full stops and exclamation marks. Discuss why speech marks are used.
● Ask children to identify the chant and encourage them to join in as you say this. Clap the rhythm and emphasise phrases with exclamation marks at the end. Notice the capital letters for the final word, SUPERWORM. Ask why children think the word is written this way. Suggest that they should chant the word loudly.

Group work

● Divide into groups to practise the chant together, using percussion to emphasise syllables.
● Suggest that children take turns to be Superworm, wiggling and squirming in and out of a circle of chanting children, and flexing muscles.

Review

● Invite groups to perform their chants around Superworm to the class. Comment on the rhythm and accuracy of the chants.

Curriculum objectives
● To apply phonic knowledge and skills as the route to decode words.
● To read accurately by blending sounds in unfamiliar words containing GPCs that have been taught.
● To make inferences on the basis of what is being said and done.

Resources
Superworm by Julia Donaldson; books featuring superheroes, for example, *Super Daisy* by Kes Gray and Nick Sharratt, *Eliot Jones Midnight Superhero* by Anne Cottringer and Alex T Smith; coloured pens

3: Superheroes

Introduction

● Ask the class to help read *Superworm*, tackling words using their existing decoding skills, for example, *skipping-rope, servant, fearful*.
● Explain that Superworm is a *superhero* and ask children what this means. Encourage them to name other superheroes, such as Batman and Superman, and to explain the powers they have.
● Discuss the role of superheroes in coming to the aid of those in trouble. Talk about how Superworm provides endless help and entertainment for his friends, and what they do to help him in return.

Whole-class work

● Re-read the story, asking children to indicate when they hear a description of one of Superworm's skills, for example, turning into a skipping-rope or a slide. Write these on the board, asking children to help with spelling.

Paired work

● Invite pairs of children to invent a superhero, decide upon a name and list the superpowers they have.
● Ask the children to draw a picture of their superhero and annotate it.

Review

● Ask pairs to share their superhero ideas with the class. Invite them to take turns to sit in the hot-seat while others ask questions about how the superhero has helped someone in distress or provided fun for friends.
● Discuss the influence of the story in deciding attributes for their superheroes, and whether children changed their ideas in the light of discussion.

4: Clever contractions

Introduction
● Recall where you have come across apostrophes in lessons and books.

Whole-class work
● Find a good example of the use of an apostrophe in the story, not featured on the photocopiable page, for example, *BANG! CRASH! THUMP! The wizard's in the rubbish dump!* Write this on the board and circle the apostrophe. Talk about which letter(s) have been removed when adding the apostrophe. Write the words in full with no apostrophe.
● Invite children to clap the syllables and read the apostrophe version. Discuss the satisfying rhythm it makes. Do the same with the second sentence. Does this still have a satisfying rhythm? What is different? Count the syllables as you clap. Explain that poets sometimes shorten words to make lines flow in a predictable rhythm.
● Write some contractions on the board and give their full equivalents, for example, *I'll* is short for *I will* and *isn't* is short for *is not*.
● Display and read photocopiable page 136 'Clever contractions'.

Paired work
● Provide pairs with the photocopiable sheet.
● Suggest that they read each sentence aloud together before deciding where the contraction is.

Differentiation
● Provide a simplified version of the sheet, using only the example *It is*.

Review
● Review the completed photocopiable sheet together. Discuss how the sentences would sound if written in full, without the apostrophe.

Curriculum objectives
● To read words with contractions and understand that the apostrophe represents the omitted letter(s).
● To read words of more than one syllable that contain taught GPCs.

Resources
Superworm by Julia Donaldson; photocopiable page 136 'Clever contractions'

5: Miniature performances

Introduction
● Read *Superworm* and recall the role of a superhero and the powers possessed by Superworm. Encourage children to join in with familiar phrases.
● Explain that the children are going to retell short scenes from the story to others. Discuss interesting props that would enhance this retelling, for example, model creatures, woollen worms and leafy compost landscapes.
● Suggest dividing into groups so that each group can focus on one event.
● Display photocopiable page 'Superworm events' from the CD-ROM, read each event together and discuss what was happening. Cut out each event.

Group work
● Supply resources and ask each group to pull an event from the box.
● Suggest that they represent characters with models, or make them from collage materials, for example, a Superworm made from pink wool tied to thin string that can wriggle and change shape.
● Suggest using trays filled with natural materials as landscapes.
● Allow time for children to set up props and plan interpretations. Discuss dialogue and character voices.

Review
● Invite groups of children to re-enact their events to the class using their chosen props. Encourage comments on interpretations and accuracy of events. Talk about what made performances enjoyable, for example, chanting.

Curriculum objectives
● To become very familiar with key stories, fairy stories and traditional tales, retelling them and considering their particular characteristics.
● To recognise and join in with predictable phrases.

Resources
Superworm by Julia Donaldson; photocopiable page 'Superworm events' from the CD-ROM; small collage materials such as pink wool, buttons, string; glue; scissors; box to draw from; shallow trays; compost and natural materials such as leaves and twigs; fabric; small-world minibeast models

Curriculum objectives
● To re-read what they have written to check that it makes sense.
● To say out loud what they are going to write about.

Resources
Superworm by Julia Donaldson; other books written by Julia Donaldson and illustrated by Axel Scheffler; paint and collage materials; natural materials such as leaves, grass and moss; scissors; glue; large paper in a variety of colours

Week 2 lesson plans

This week, children continue *Superworm* explorations, starting by examining how the illustrations add detail to the author's description of a setting. They create pictures of story settings and write sentences to describe them. They explore the underground setting where Superworm hunted for treasure and link this to their own experiences by organising outdoor treasure hunts with their own written clue cards. Character descriptions are enhanced with adjectives, joined using *and*. They revise appropriate word endings and check by reading to make sure they make sense. Finally, children create a story display depicting the setting, characters and some events. They add informative captions and labels, and revise common exception words.

1: Picture the scene

Introduction
● Look at the cover of *Superworm* and establish the illustrator's name, Axel Scheffler. Talk about other Julia Donaldson books with the same illustrator, showing a few covers.
● Ask children to identify the key features of Axel's work, for example, quirky characters with big eyes, human-like facial expressions, tiny detail.
● Explain that children are going to use Axel's illustrations to discover more about the setting for *Superworm*.

Whole-class work
● Look at the book illustrations and establish that the main activity takes place in the open countryside. Ask what we can tell about this countryside, for example, it is sunny, full of colourful flowers, bushes, trees and lush grass. There is a river and distant mountains.
● Encourage children to notice man-made influences encroaching on this peaceful landscape, for example, a major road, a well and a rubbish dump. Talk about why the author might have included these by establishing the part they each play in the story. Contrast this peaceful environment with the dark lair of the lizard, full of evil shadows and stark walls.
● Discuss how walking into these environments might affect other senses, for example: the sound of bees buzzing, frogs croaking and beetles skittering along; the smell of fragrant flowers, sweet honey and fresh grass; the texture of slimy slugs, sticky honey and smooth hard ladybird wings. Contrast this with the dark lair of the lizard, with the smell of damp moss, rotten leaves, mouldy walls; the echoing sound of shadowy creatures scratching in crevices; the touch of a lizard skin and cold wet walls.
● Divide the board into two sections headed *Good* and *Evil* and ask children to think of sensory words to describe each one, following the above discussions.
● Invite children to go into groups and choose which of these settings they would like to create a picture about. Encourage them to concentrate on the landscape rather than the characters that live there at this stage.
● Show children the resources and encourage them to ask for additional materials they need.

Group work
● Provide large paper for the pictures (the back of a roll of wallpaper is ideal).
● Ask children to write sentences describing their finished picture, using words discussed and those they think of themselves. Remind children to say sentences aloud before writing, and then check by reading to confirm that they make sense. Include a picture title and stick the sentences to the bottom.

Review
● Bring groups together to discuss their pictures and explain why they chose that setting. Ask them to read their descriptive sentences aloud. Discuss how this will help children to find clues in book illustrations in their future reading.

Curriculum objectives
● To link what they read or hear to their own experiences.
● To say out loud what they are going to write about.

Resources
Superworm by Julia Donaldson; outdoor access to garden plot or somewhere with suitable hiding places, such as stones and long grass; 2 buttons; cork; toffee wrapper; plastic fork; card rectangles; black pens

2: Treasure hunting

Introduction
● Read the section of *Superworm* where Superworm tunnels to find treasure for Wizard Lizard. Write down what he finds and speculate on the treasure that Wizard Lizard expects. Discuss what will happen to Superworm if he fails.

Whole-class work
● Discuss the concept of a treasure hunt. Ask children to share past experiences of looking for treasure. Recall how these hunts usually involve searching for clues, for example, with a pirate's treasure map.
● Explain that the children are going to hide treasure outdoors and write clues.

Group work
● Divide into five groups and read the board list of Superworm's finds. Provide each group with one of these items to hide, for example, a cork.
● Suggest children choose a hiding place and write sentence cards to describe the route, for example: *Turn right as you leave the classroom. Walk forward three paces....* Encourage children to say sentences aloud before writing and check they make sense by reading. Remind them of the importance of putting their route instructions in the correct sequence.
● Allow one group at a time to hide their treasure, and supervise to ensure other groups' treasure is not retrieved!
● Ask groups to swap cards and try to find each other's treasure.

Review
● Bring groups together to check all treasure is found. Talk about how the sentence clues helped or hindered their searches.

Curriculum objectives
● To join words and join sentences with *and*.
● To use '-ing', '-ed', '-er' and '-est' where no change is needed in the spelling of root word.

Resources
Superworm by Julia Donaldson; photocopiable page 137 'Choosing words'

3: Choosing words

Introduction
● Recall the use of *and* to join words and sentences together. Use starter activity 13 'Captions and combinations' to revise this.
● Decide on pairs of words to describe *Superworm* characters or items and join them with *and*, for example, *blue and magic* to describe the lizard's flower.
● Remind children that these describing words are known as *adjectives*.
● Recall different word endings and how they are used, for example, *strongest, taller* and *small,* relating to comparative attributes, and *drowned* and *fastened* to denote the past tense.

Whole-class work
● Display photocopiable page 137 'Choosing words' and focus on the first section. Write down a sentence about Superworm using the given adjectives joined by the word *and*. Work through the rest of the sheet together.

Paired work
● Provide each child with the photocopiable sheet.
● Encourage reading sentences aloud to a partner before writing to check that they make sense, particularly when completing the second section.

> **Differentiation**
> ● Challenge more confident learners to write their own character sentences containing two or more adjectives joined by *and*.

Review
● Bring the class together and work through the photocopiable sheet on the board, asking pairs to read out their partners' variations.

Curriculum objectives
- To be encouraged to link what they read or hear read to their own experiences.
- To re-read books to build up their fluency and confidence in word reading.
- To check that the text makes sense to them as they read, and correct their inaccuracies.

Resources
Superworm by Julia Donaldson; children's setting pictures from lesson 1; backing paper in blue and brown; painting and collage materials

4: Underground overground

Introduction
- Recall the dinosaur display made in Autumn 1. Explain that they are going to create a similar wall display depicting the story of *Superworm*, adding descriptive labels and captions in the next lesson.
- Re-read the story, with pairs volunteering to read each page and others helping them with less familiar words. Invite everyone to join in with the repeated chant. Encourage children to link the ideas they have of the story setting with their own experiences of outdoor environments.

Whole-class work
- Show children the resources. Suggest backing the wall with blue to represent the landscape above ground and brown to represent underground.
- To support ideas for the underground section, display the image of Superworm at work tunnelling for treasure.

Group work
- Divide into mixed-ability groups, each allocated a different task, for example, paint and collage characters, create trees, add underground texture.
- Encourage children to be adventurous, checking through text and illustrations for support as they work (stress clean hands!).
- Gather the class together to discuss the display at various stages.

Review
- Discuss the display and talk about how re-reading the book and thinking about their outdoor experiences helped children to decide what to include.

Curriculum objectives
- To spell common exception words.
- To join words and join sentences with *and*.
- To re-read what they have written to check that it makes sense.

Resources
Superworm by Julia Donaldson; coloured pens; photocopiable page 'Extract from *Superworm*' from the CD-ROM; photographs of the dinosaur display created in Autumn 1; white paper

5: Labels and captions

Introduction
- Explore the finished display created in lesson 4, and the photographs of the dinosaur display from Autumn 1. Recall the information included in the dinosaur display and discuss what worked well.

Whole-class work
- Ask children to write their ideas for display annotations as a list on the board, for example, a sentence introducing each character, labels to identify creatures and plants, captions such as *Wizard Lizard's lair*.
- Read through the list of possible inclusions and choose the most popular.
- Divide these into separate headings and allocate group tasks.
- Recall recent work about using *and* as a joining word and suggest using this in captions, for example, *Brother snails and sister slugs, The black and grim crow.*
- Revise common exception words children are likely to use, such as *the, is, where, here, friends* and remind them to check spelling carefully with others.

Group work
- Suggest that they name each group table, for example, *label making, caption creation* and *character descriptions*. Display photocopiable page 'Extract from *Superworm*' from the CD-ROM for reference and provide access to the story.
- Ask children to read and check finished signs, labels and captions for accuracy before attaching them to the display.

> **Differentiation**
> - Support less confident learners with writing simple labels, such as *An ant and a bug.*

Review
- Bring the class together to discuss the success of their written information.

Week 3 lesson plans

This week a new book, *Monkey Puzzle*, is introduced and children predict and compare common features and events with other books by Julia Donaldson and Axel Scheffler. Focus is given to the significance of title and events before children move on to comparisons of characters in stories they have explored so far. Adjectives are used to describe their attributes. Children represent these favourite characters by making finger and glove puppets to use in re-enactments of events, using prompt sentences they have written themselves. Reading an instruction page helps to develop reading skills. Finally, children write book reviews about their favourite Julia Donaldson books, with focus on correct punctuation, word spacing and sentence structure.

Expected outcomes
● All children can discuss the characters in a story.
● Most children can retell a story using puppets.
● Some children can write a book review.

Curriculum objectives
● To predict what might happen on the basis of what has been read so far.
● To discuss the significance of the title and events.
● To listen to and discuss a wide range of poems, stories and non-fiction at a level beyond that at which they can read independently.

Resources
Monkey Puzzle by Julia Donaldson and Axel Scheffler (if children are already familiar with this story, substitute a less familiar Julia Donaldson/Axel Scheffler title and plan slightly modified lesson activities, introducing an image or object related to the title, for example, an image of a hermit crab for *Sharing a Shell*); another monkey story book by a different author with a different illustrator, for example, *I love you, little monkey* by Alan Durant and Katharine McEwen; media resource 'Monkey puzzle tree' on the CD-ROM

I: What a puzzle!

Introduction
● Ask the children to name books they have explored by Julia Donaldson with illustrations by Axel Scheffler.
● Invite individuals to identify their favourite from these titles and say why.

Whole-class work
● Hold up two books, *Monkey Puzzle*, and another about a similar character but by a different author and illustrator. Cover the names of the author and illustrator and ask children to identify the one written by Julia Donaldson. Encourage them to give reasons for their choices, the most popular probably being that they can tell by the illustrations. Point out that not all of Julia Donaldson's books have the same illustrator, for example, *Tyrannosaurus Drip*.
● Ask if the title gives them any clues. Probably not, as Julia Donaldson likes to write about animals. Question whether she could have written both books.
● Ask children to identify the book illustrated by Axel Scheffler. They should find this much easier. Talk about their reasons for choosing this book.
● Reveal the names of authors and illustrators and discuss what children have learned from this activity, for example, illustrators with a distinctive style are easy to identify, but we need to read a name or some words before we can identify an author.
● Read a page from each of the books, without revealing which one it is, and ask children if they can identify the story written by Julia Donaldson. Briefly recall what makes her style so memorable.
● Read the title, *Monkey Puzzle*, to the children and ask them to predict the story content.
● Display media resource 'Monkey puzzle tree' on the CD-ROM and ask why the tree has this name. Speculate that it would be a puzzle to any monkey trying to climb it.

Group work
● Leave the monkey puzzle image on display and divide into groups.
● Invite them to draw a monkey puzzle tree and write a caption explaining it.
● Suggest that they discuss the puzzle the monkey might face and how events might link to this puzzle. Ask them to consider other features that might occur, given their previous experiences of Julia Donaldson's writing, for example, rhyming words, a repeated phrase, following a predictable sequence.
● Invite them to convey their ideas in written sentences.

Review
● Bring the class together to share their monkey puzzle drawings and written predictions. Comment on their pictures and discuss how a clever title shares its name with this unusual tree. Read the story and discuss whether any of the group predictions came close to what actually happened. Discuss the significance of events in relation to building up a story sequence.

Curriculum objectives
● To discuss what they have written with the teacher or other children.
● To draw on what they already know or on background information and vocabulary provided by the teacher.
● To apply simple spelling rules and guidelines, as listed in Appendix 1.

Resources
Photocopiable page 138 'Character adjectives'; copies of Julia Donaldson books explored in previous lessons, including *Superworm* and *Tyrannosaurus Drip* by Julia Donaldson; pencils

2: Character adjectives

Introduction
● Recall previous lessons involving exploring Julia Donaldson's characters.
● Revise the meaning of *adjective*. Identify adjectives Julia Donaldson uses to describe her characters by referring to the books.

Whole-class work
● Display and read photocopiable page 138 'Character adjectives'.
● Work through the boxes for Superworm as an example.
● Begin by asking for words to describe Superworm's appearance.
● Gather ideas about Superworm's character by discussing his actions, for example, saving Baby toad, kindly cheering up bees, cleverly turning into a fishing-line. Ask children to come up with words to describe these characteristics, such as *brave, helpful, kind, clever, strong*.
● Explain that children should choose their own character from a Julia Donaldson story to write about in the last row of boxes.

Paired work
● Provide access to books for further ideas. Invite pairs of children to complete the photocopiable sheet. Suggest that they complete each character description on their own before discussing what they have written with their partner. Encourage them to support each other with spelling if necessary.

> **Differentiation**
> ● Challenge more confident learners to write extended character profiles.

Review
● Ask pairs to read their work and discuss their ideas with the class. Talk about how working with partners helps with new ideas and checking spelling.

Curriculum objectives
● To draw on what they already know or on background information and vocabulary provided by the teacher.
● To apply phonic knowledge and skills as the route to decode words.

Resources
Copies of Julia Donaldson books explored previously; photocopiable page 'Puppets from gloves' from the CD-ROM; old gloves (gardening gloves, if possible); buttons; sequins; wool; small collage materials; waterproof pens; PVA glue; fabric scraps

3: Puppets from gloves

Introduction
● Make finger puppets before the lesson. Display them and ask children to identify who they are. Talk about why they are called finger and glove puppets.
● Explain that the children are going to make their own puppets and invite them to suggest suitable characters they think they could make.

Whole-class work
● Display photocopiable page 'Puppets from gloves' from the CD-ROM and ask the children to read what they will need. Support with difficult words, such as *collage* and *materials*. Establish what these words mean by showing actual examples. Build up words together using previously taught GPCs.

Group work
● In mixed-ability groups, suggest that children choose a story or scene from a Julia Donaldson story to re-enact and consider character puppets they will need. Provide a selection of books you have explored for them to choose from.
● Ask them to allocate members of the group to a character or characters.
● Hint that children may like to start by drawing a picture of how their character will look, labelling the features.
● Support children as they create their puppets using the instructions.

Review
● Bring the class together to show their puppets and discuss how they made them. Talk about the importance of following instructions and allocating tasks when working in a group.

Curriculum objectives
● To listen to and discuss a range of poems, stories and non-fiction at a level beyond that at which they can read independently.
● To compose a sentence orally before writing it.
● To make inferences on the basis of what is being said and done.

Resources
Puppets made in lesson 3; copies of Julia Donaldson books children chose their puppet characters from; card

4: Retell the event

Introduction
● Discuss types of puppet and how they can be used to dramatise stories.
● Recall the puppets made yesterday and identify the stories they feature in.
● Suggest that children choose a key event from their chosen story and re-enact this using their puppets.
● Introduce the word *script* and explain how actors in film, theatre and television productions follow a written script until they know their lines.
● Suggest that, as time is limited, children might like to write short sentences on cards to outline the sequence of their event rather than a complete script. They can then use these as prompts along with the puppets.

Group work
● Ask children to return to the groups they were in to make their puppets.
● Suggest that they begin by composing their sentences on paper and then have a trial performance with the puppets.
● Provide access to books to use in their planning.
● After the first re-enactment, encourage them to modify their sentences in the light of discussion, then write the sentence on card ready for review time.

Review
● Ask groups to re-enact their story events with puppets and prompt cards. Invite class comments on choices and the way groups interpreted the events.

Curriculum objectives
● To begin to punctuate sentences using a capital letter and a full stop, question mark or exclamation mark.
● To leave spaces between words.
● To compose a sentence orally before writing it.
● To join words and join sentences using *and*.

Resources
Photocopiable page 139 'My favourite Julia Donaldson book'

5: Book review

Introduction
● Explain the meaning of *review*, as discussed in Autumn 1, and consider again why we might read reviews. Recall how reviews help us, for example, when deciding whether to read a particular book or buy a toy.
● Recall Julia Donaldson books you have explored and explain that the children are going to write reviews about their favourites from among them.

Whole-class work
● Display photocopiable page 139 'My favourite Julia Donaldson book' and tell children that they will use this to write their reviews.
● Read 'The setting' and ask children their opinions about a setting from a particular book. Write down a response as an example, emphasising the need to complete the whole sentence with correct punctuation.
● Explain that the children need to say what they really think, so they can choose from the two words, *like* and *dislike*.
● Children may have a number of ideas for each answer; remind them about joining words using *and*.

Independent work
● Supply each child with the photocopiable sheet to complete.
● Encourage children to compose their sentences orally before writing them, to check punctuation and to leave spaces between words.

> **Differentiation**
> ● Invite less confident learners to choose a favourite character, draw a picture and write a short sentence about this character.

Review
● Ask individuals to share their reviews with the class. Praise correct punctuation. Debate whether children will reconsider their own responses in the light of them.

Curriculum objectives
• To draw on what they already know or on background information and vocabulary provided by the teacher.
• To discuss the significance of the title and events.

Resources
Copies of Julia Donaldson books, including some titles not yet explored, with some not illustrated by Axel Scheffler; black card; scissors; white paper; coloured and black pens

Week 4 lesson plans

This week, children continue book-cover explorations with an amusing 'peephole' activity and an opportunity to design their own covers, choosing appropriate titles reflecting proposed events. They repeat memorable phrases from books explored and identify the characters who said these phrases. Alphabetical order is revised as children write title lists and use these to help to arrange books in a Julia Donaldson corner. They read and write Julia Donaldson and Axel Scheffler biographies using information provided. During this activity, using *and* to join sentences, writing appropriate word endings, and the grammar of word structure are revised. Finally, they use their biographies as support when they take part in hot-seat interviews.

1: Undercover detectives

Introduction
• Before the lesson, prepare a peephole by cutting a 2cm hole in large black card.
• Hold up some Julia Donaldson books that children have explored and discuss what they were able to discover from the covers.
• Introduce two contrasting less familiar titles, such as *Tabby McTat* and *The Troll*, and identify similarities and differences between these and the others.
• Hold up *The Troll* and ask if the illustrations are familiar. Identify the illustrator, David Roberts, and recall a more familiar title with his illustrations, *Tyrannosaurus Drip*. Read some of the text and comment on the choice of words. Ask children why this book is unlike the books they have looked at so far (the words do not have the same regular rhythm and rhyme patterns).
• Compare this book with *Tabby McTat*, which is likely to be more familiar to the children in the way it is illustrated and the language, rhyme and rhythm.

Whole-class work
• Hold up the peephole and explain how it will reveal just a tiny circle of a book cover.
• Demonstrate the effect by covering a book and holding it up. Show the children how the image seen will change as the peephole is moved around.
• Discuss how looking at part of something helps us to focus on tiny detail.

Group work
• Provide each group with a peephole card and several Julia Donaldson books.
• Invite them to take turns to hold the card over part of the cover while the others guess which book it is.
• Encourage them to discover which images and words make the book easier to identify, for example, the word *Room* or part of a cauldron (*Room on the Broom*) and which selections make it difficult, for example, the word *the*.
• Discuss this together and identify how including specific information, such as the title, author, illustrator and recognisable images of events or characters, help designers to create an informative book cover.

Paired work
• Divide into pairs to design an informative cover for an imaginary book.
• Suggest that they use their own names for the author and illustrator and make a list of characters and events to include on their cover.

> **Differentiation**
> • Challenge more confident learners to include blurb or quotes on their cover.

Review
• Bring the class together to discuss what they have learned about the most important features of book covers.

Curriculum objectives
● To recognise and join in with predictable phrases.
● To listen to and discuss a wide range of stories at a level beyond that at which they can read independently.
● To read accurately by blending unfamiliar words containing GPCs that have been taught.

Resources
Photocopiable page 140 'Who said that?'; a selection of Julia Donaldson books

2: Who said that?

Introduction
● Ask the children to recall some memorable repeated phrases from Julia Donaldson books, for example: *"He has terrible tusks and terrible claws, And terrible teeth in his terrible jaws."* (*The Gruffalo*). Repeat them together, commenting on rhyming words and alliteration. Discuss whether the words are said by specific character(s) or form part of the text.

Whole-class work
● Display and read photocopiable page 140 'Who said that?'.
● Read the words in the first box and decide who said them. If children say *Tyrannosaurus Rex*, ask them to read the words again and discuss their meaning. Talk about what Tyrannosaurus Rex would actually chant (*Up with hunting...*). Write the name of the identified character and book in the boxes.
● Speculate whether the words in the remaining boxes are said by one character or a group.

Paired work
● Provide pairs of children with the photocopiable sheet to complete. Ask them to discuss the quotes with one another before making a decision.

Differentiation
● Work with those who struggle with reading content. Provide pictures of the characters and read the words in the boxes. Ask them to hold up the correct picture to match the character.

Review
● Review the lesson activities and discuss how this has helped children to recall memorable phrases and characters.

Curriculum objectives
● To name the letters of the alphabet in order.
● To re-read what they have written to check that it makes sense.

Resources
A selection of books by Julia Donaldson; upper- and lower-case alphabet lists

3: The Julia Donaldson corner

Introduction
● Recall Julia Donaldson books explored and suggest making a display in a special Julia Donaldson corner where children can spend time browsing.
● Discuss other places to browse books, for example, a library or bookshop. Talk about how books are arranged in groups according to subject or author, and then in alphabetical order of title.

Whole-class work
● Recall alphabetical order activities, for example, creating dinosaur lists.
● Show children an upper- and a lower-case list of letters in alphabetical order.
● Hold up one of the books and write the title on the board. Confirm that titles usually start with a capital letter.

Group work
● Divide into groups of similar ability and provide a differentiated list of titles (not in alphabetical order) , for example, challenge more confident learners with a complete title list and others with fewer titles.
● Ask groups to write a revised list of their given titles in alphabetical order, and check that they make sense.

Review
● Invite the groups to read out their lists one at a time. Locate the books as they are read out to make it easy to arrange them in alphabetical order in the Julia Donaldson corner. Continue adding books from lists until all titles are in order. Check the final book arrangement.

Curriculum objectives
● To draw on what they already know or on background information and vocabulary provided by the teacher.
● To use '-ing', '-ed', '-er' and '-est' endings where no change is needed in the root of words.
● To learn the grammar for Year 1 in Appendix 2.

Resources
Photocopiable page 'Julia Donaldson' from the CD-ROM; photocopiable page 'Axel Scheffler facts' from the CD-ROM

4: Biographies

Introduction
● Recall previous work on adding the suffixes '-er', '-ing' and '-ed' and use starter activity 8 'Make me different' to revise how they are used.
● Introduce the word *biography*. Explain that this is an account of a person's life written by someone else. Consider how interesting it would be to know more about favourite authors and illustrators.

Whole-class work
● Display and read photocopiable page 'Julia Donaldson' from the CD-ROM. Discuss what she might have been like as a little girl.
● Continue through the whole page, explaining new vocabulary, such as *Children's Laureate*.
● Ask the children to find words ending in '-er' that describe what Julia and her husband can do, for example, *writer, performer, busker, player* and *singer*.
● Display photocopiable page 'Axel Scheffler facts' from the CD-ROM and explain that these are facts about Axel, but the endings have been missed from some of the words.
● Read through the facts, supporting children with any new vocabulary. Ask them to suggest the correct word ending, '-ing' or '-ed', at each stage.

Group work
● Divide into small groups, each with photocopiable page 'Axel Scheffler facts'.
● Encourage children to read the sentences aloud and discuss the endings.

Review
● Bring children together to share their answers. Discuss what they have learned about Julia Donaldson and Axel Scheffler.

Curriculum objectives
● To discuss what they have written with the teacher or other children.
● To re-read what they have written to check that it makes sense.

Resources
Children's completed 'Axel Scheffler facts' sheets from lesson 4; photocopiable page 'Julia Donaldson' from the CD-ROM; selection of Julia Donaldson and Axel Scheffler books

5: Hot-seat interviews

Introduction
● Recall discussions about biographies in lesson 4.
● Talk about how children have discovered facts about this author and illustrator.
● Display photocopiable page 'Julia Donaldson' from the CD-ROM and ask children what sort of questions they might like to put to Julia if they met her.
● Recall past experiences of hot-seating and explain that you would like children to take on the roles of Julia and Axel to be interviewed in the hot-seat.

Paired work
● Divide children into pairs and provide them with both photocopiable page 'Julia Donaldson' and their completed photocopiable page 'Axel Scheffler facts' for ideas about questions they would like to ask Julia and Axel. Also encourage the children to think of questions involving their favourite characters.
● Allow time for them to write down their questions, re-read them to check they make sense and practise them on one another. Remind children to consider how they might answer the questions if they are in the hot-seat.

Whole-class work
● Bring the class together and ask pairs to sit in the hot-seat as Julia and Axel. Invite another pair to ask them questions. Continue with different pairs.

Review
● Discuss the outcome of these interviews. Share new facts children have discovered about Julia and Axel.

Week 5 lesson plans

This week, children revisit discussions about the importance of illustration when they listen to a new Julia Donaldson story without illustrations. They identify recognisable features of this author's stories, such as rhyming text, and try to visualise the setting and characters. Inferences about the importance of illustration are made during this discussion. Children then revise the features of a good story. They focus on maintaining appropriate writing posture and correct letter formation as they plan and write their own stories, role-playing events and composing sentences orally first. Additional focus during these writing activities is on revising sentence sequencing and correct punctuation. Children create books from their written stories and read them aloud.

1: Features of a good story

Introduction
● Recall the Julia Donaldson stories read so far and talk about the work of some of the illustrators.
● Briefly remind children of the importance of illustrations.

Whole-class work
● Explain that you are going to read a story that children may not have heard before. Invite them to find somewhere comfortable to sit as they will be listening rather than looking at the book as you read. Recall previous work on visualising events in the *mind's eye* and suggest they close their eyes.
● Read your Julia Donaldson title without letting the class see the illustrations.
● Ask for their impressions of the story. Talk about features that identify Julia Donaldson as the possible author, such as rhyming couplets.
● Try to describe the characters and consider how difficult it is to visualise them if the type of creature is unfamiliar, for example, *Blob*, the purple anemone, and *Brush*, the bristleworm in *Sharing a Shell*.
● Display photocopiable page 'Extract from *Sharing a Shell*' from the CD-ROM (or a suitable page from your chosen book). Suggest that they take on the role of illustrators, working in groups to illustrate this page from the story.

Group work
● Leave the extract on the board and explain that children can tear tissue and glue it to the picture to create features and added texture.
● Suggest that children start by making a written list of what to include based on the displayed text, for example, the sea, three characters, a shell, a pool.
● Encourage them to be imaginative about probable additional features, such as rocks and sea creatures.

Whole-class work
● With the class, discuss similarities and differences in their interpretations.
● Reveal the illustration that accompanies the extract in the book. Again, comment on similarities and differences between this image and the children's pictures. How close were they in their interpretations of the characters? Did their settings resemble the one displayed?
● Speculate on who might have illustrated the book. Discuss illustrators of Julia Donaldson books that children have already explored and decide if these illustrations could have been created by one of them. Reveal the name *Lydia Monks* on the front of *Sharing a Shell* and encourage debate about the impact of her illustrations on the story.
● Read the story again, this time showing the illustrations as you read.

Review
● Bring the class together to recall previous discussion about the value of illustration in a good story.

Curriculum objectives
● To sit correctly at a table, holding a pencil comfortably and correctly.
● To form lower-case letters in the correct direction, starting and finishing in the right place.
● To form capital letters.

Resources
Photocopiable page 141 'Our story plan'

2: Planning a good story

Introduction
● Recall previous lessons involving creating story plans.
● Draw attention to good writing posture and letter formation. Emphasise that this needs to be consistent at all times.

Whole-class work
● Ask children to recall features of good stories and write these on the board, for example, interesting characters and settings.
● Discuss the significance of title and events.
● Identify the three story sections, *Beginning, Middle, End,* and write these down. Draw attention to correct capital and lower-case letter formation while writing, commenting on correct starting and finishing points and direction. Encourage children to suggest when capital letters are needed.
● Ask children to sit at tables, pick up a pencil and hold it up to demonstrate the correct grip. Invite them to demonstrate how to sit correctly when writing.

Paired work
● Divide children into pairs and ask them to discuss a possible story they would like to write, perhaps inspired by one of the Julia Donaldson stories you have explored recently. Suggest, for example, that they think of a further plot involving the evil Wizard Lizard or a new adventure for Monkey Puzzle.
● Provide each child with photocopiable page 141 'Our story plan' to complete.
● Praise correct posture and letter formation as they work.

> **Differentiation**
> ● Focus on correct posture and pencil grip as less confident learners draw an invented character. Write a sentence for them to complete about this character.

Review
● Gather the class to share their proposed story ideas. Praise effort with good posture and letter formation.

Curriculum objectives
● To compose a sentence orally before writing it.
● To sequence sentences to form short narratives.

Resources
Photocopiable page 141 'Our story plan'; the children's completed versions of this page

3: Performing events

Introduction
● Recall the story planning in lesson 2. Display photocopiable page 141 'Our story plan' and discuss the planning sequence.
● Explain that these plans will be used to support the writing of their events.

Whole-class work
● Ask children to recall the two main events they wrote about on their plan.
● Invite them to consider what their characters might do or say.
● Suggest that they try out their ideas through role play, for example, taking on the role of the main character in conversation with other characters.

Paired work
● Ask children to work with their partners from lesson 2 and provide them with their completed planning pages.
● Suggest that they take the first event they have written about, and act this out. Encourage them to experiment with dialogue.
● Once they are happy with character interaction and words used, ask them to compose a sequence of sentences orally before writing the event.

Review
● Bring the class together so that pairs of children can read one of their events aloud. Ask for comments on presentation and sequencing.

Curriculum objectives
● To sequence sentences to form short narratives.
● To begin to punctuate sentences using a capital letter and a full stop, question mark or exclamation mark.

Resources
The children's completed photocopiable sheets 'Our story plan' for reference; strong paper; coloured pens

4: Authors and illustrators

Introduction
● Recall the previous three lessons on producing a story.
● Discuss the roles of author and illustrator in creating a good story book.

Whole-class work
● Explain that pairs will use their written events to create small story books.
● Decide whether it is better for one child to write the text while another creates the illustrations, or for both to take turns to write and illustrate each section. Suggest that taking turns will provide them with equal chances.
● Ask the children to help to create a simple list of possible sections, for example, opening page, first event, second event and end page.

Paired work
● Explain that this activity will help to revise children's sentence formation and punctuation while they are writing.
● Suggest that they write down who will be writing or illustrating each page. Talk about the merits of completing the writing first.
● Provide necessary resources, and the children's completed plans and written events from lessons 2 and 3.

> **Differentiation**
> ● Ask less confident learners to illustrate their sentences from lesson 3 and arrange them in a sequence.

Review
● Bring the class together to share their completed pages. Encourage comments on sentence sequencing and good punctuation.

Curriculum objectives
● To discuss what they have written with the teacher or other children.
● To participate in discussion about what is read to them, taking turns and listening to what others say.

Resources
The children's completed photocopiable sheets 'Our story plan', event sentences (lesson 3) and stories (lesson 4); hole-punch; thin ribbon; coloured pens

5: Let's share stories

Introduction
● Recall the week's lessons and remind children how they developed initial plans, wrote and illustrated events and completed the story.
● Explain that the aim of this lesson is to complete their books by adding a cover and then sharing the whole process with others.

Whole-class work
● Outline the process of the children's book creation, from deciding upon characters and setting to introducing a sequence of events that developed into a satisfying plot.
● Talk about how they chose a suitable title and created effective illustrations.
● Recall previous book cover explorations. Ask for suggestions for essential features needed. Create a reference list of these on the board.

Paired work
● Provide the children with their completed pages from lesson 4, strong paper and coloured pens to design both front and back covers.
● Once finished, check covers over and suggest adding any missing aspects.
● Create a simple book by fastening the covers and inner pages together.
● Provide their previous planning pages and written events so that children can discuss the whole process during review time.

Review
● Bring the pairs into similar-ability groups of six so that they can explain how they arrived at their finished books and read their stories. Invite others to make constructive comments on what is read to them.

Curriculum objectives
● To recognise and join in with predictable phrases.
● To learn to appreciate rhymes and poems, and to recite some by heart.

Resources
The Gruffalo's Child by Julia Donaldson and Axel Scheffler; media resource 'The Gruffalo's Child song' on the CD-ROM; access to online video of Julia Donaldson and her husband singing 'The Gruffalo's Child song'; Julia Donaldson books already explored

Week 6 lesson plans

Children start and finish this week of rhyme and song exploration by learning a Julia Donaldson rhyme to sing or recite. They explore other songs she has written and find rhymes in books already explored. This involves identifying predictable phrases, finding rhyming words and joining them with *and*, and discussing alternative graphemes using correct letter names. Rhyme work continues with choosing missing rhyming words to fit into sentences from Julia Donaldson's books, and children read words of more than one syllable in these sentences. They have fun using instruments to beat rhythms in rhymes both known and invented. Finally, groups choose a favourite rhyming text or song to perform and write a short review.

1: The Gruffalo's Child song

Introduction
● Recall your recent explorations of Julia Donaldson books and ask the children to think of some of the memorable repeated lines.
● Remind them that Julia used to write songs to sing with her husband as they toured Europe as students. Explain that she has written lots of songs about stories such as *Sharing a Shell* and *The Gruffalo*.
● Visit the Julia Donaldson official website to hear clips of Julia singing these songs with her husband. Discuss which ones the children like best and why.

Whole-class work
● Read *The Gruffalo's Child* and invite comments about their favourite Julia Donaldson and Axel Scheffler features. Identify the repeated phrases.
● Display media resource 'The Gruffalo's Child song' on the CD-ROM and read the lyrics together.
● Look at the shape of the song and count the verses. Talk about the regular structure. Discuss what happens in each verse.
● Underline repeated phrases, such as *Aha! Oho!* and *Where can he be?*.
● Circle the rhyming words at the end of the first two lines in each verse.
● If possible, listen to and watch the video of Julia Donaldson and her husband singing the song. Play it again, and ask children to join in.

Group work
● Divide into six groups and allocate one of the verses to each group to learn.
● Encourage them to use different tones and expressions, for example, when asking a question or imitating the voice of a character, such as the snake hissing his way through the words or the owl hooting *Too-whit! Too-whoo!*
● Suggest that they add actions, for example, twisting and turning their bodies like a snake looking from side to side with narrow eyes like a sly fox.

Whole-class work
● Bring the class together to sing the song, initially with groups singing their verses and then as a whole class with groups leading the singing of their verse.
● Leave the words on display at first but then remove them for a final performance of the song.
● Recall the story events and characters and discuss how successfully Julia Donaldson has included them in a song.
● Suggest they perform a dramatisation of the story, in assembly or to another class. Ask individuals to mime the characters, using effective facial expression and bodily movements, while the rest of the class sing the song.

Review
● Ask the class whether they think that learning the words of a rhyme or song and then reciting or singing them, has helped them to appreciate the joy of rhyme and the value of repeated phrases in stories.

Curriculum objectives
● To use letter names to distinguish between alternative spellings of the same sound.
● To join words and join sentences using *and*.

Resources
The Snail and the Whale and *Room on the Broom*; photocopiable page 142 'Collecting rhymes'; scissors

2: Collecting rhymes

Introduction
● Read the titles of featured books together and identify the rhyming words.
● Explain that the words they will be exploring all come from these books.

Whole-class work
● Display photocopiable page 142 'Collecting rhymes'. Ask individuals to circle pairs of words that rhyme. Continue until all rhymes are circled.
● Underline *pool* and *school* and ask children to name the letters making the sound /oo/. Do the same with *sky* and *high*, asking children to name the letters 'y' and 'igh', (the graphemes that make the same /igh/ sound in *sky* and *high*).

Paired work
● Provide pairs with the photocopiable sheet and ask them to cut out the squares, find the rhyming words and arrange them in pairs in two rows, those whose phonemes use the same letters and those that use different letters.
● Suggest that they write phoneme pairs with the same letters on one piece of paper and those with different spelling on another, joining each pair of rhyming words with *and*, for example, *cat* and *hat*, *roar* and *shore*.

> **Differentiation**
> ● Create a differentiated page with GPCs already taught for less confident learners.

Review
● Gather the class together so that pairs can self-check their written pages as you work through the page on the board with them.

Curriculum objectives
● To read words of more than one syllable that contain taught GPCs.
● To use letter names to distinguish between alternative spellings of the same sound.

Resources
Photocopiable page 143 'Find the rhyming word'

3: Make it rhyme

Introduction
● Recall previous work involving matching rhyming words. Discuss how some phonemes have alternative graphemes. Think of examples together.

Whole-class work
● Display photocopiable page 143 'Find the rhyming word' and explain that the sentences are all from Julia Donaldson books.
● Read the first sentence. Identify which book it is from (*The Snail and the Whale*) and which event it is about. With this in mind, choose the correct word from the given alternatives.
● Use letter names as you discuss the spelling of alternative words. Identify the split digraph 'u-e' in *rule* and *mule*. Highlight words ending in '-ing' and clap the syllables. Find words of more than one syllable, such as *children, Disaster!*, and break them into separate syllables.
● Work through the remaining boxes. Pose questions to encourage reading of single words, for example, identifying the longest and the shortest word.

Independent work
● Provide each child with the photocopiable sheet to complete.

> **Differentiation**
> ● For less confident learners, use only taught GPCs and a choice of two contrasting words, for example: *Tabby McTat had a (dog/cat)*.

Review
● Bring the class together to discuss how they read the words by recognising GPCs and breaking them into separate syllables.

Curriculum objectives
● To recognise and join in with predictable phrases.
● To learn to appreciate rhymes and poems, and to recite some by heart.

Resources
Superworm by Julia Donaldson; photocopiable page 'Extract from *Superworm*' from the CD-ROM; photocopiable page 142 'Collecting rhymes' used in lesson 2 of this week; percussion instruments

4: Rhymes and chants

Introduction
● Recall when children tried chanting a verse from a *Superworm* extract.
● Remind them how they added percussion to their chant to emphasise the beat and increase their enjoyment.

Whole-class work
● Display and read photocopiable page 'Extract from *Superworm*' from the CD-ROM. Create the second verse chant again, clapping in time to the words.
● Turn to the page towards the end of the book that reads *Superworm, the swing! The slide! The hoola-hoop! The fairground ride!* Create a chant from these words, clapping as you speak. Do the same with the opposite page. Ask children to join in as they become familiar with the word sequence.

Paired work
● Provide children with photocopiable page 142 'Collecting rhymes'. Ask each pair to invent chants using pairs of rhyming words, for example: *The land by the sand! The snail on the whale! The sand on the land! The whale by the snail!*
● Supply percussion instruments so they can emphasise the rhythmic effect.

> **Differentiation**
> ● Support less confident learners by reading the words with them and helping them to invent short phrases.
> ● Challenge more confident learners to make up their own rhyming chants.

Review
● Bring the class together to share chants and make constructive comments on effective rhythm and choice of words.

Curriculum objectives
● To apply simple spelling rules and guidelines, as listed in Appendix 1.
● To use letter names to distinguish between alternative spellings of the same sound.
● To learn to appreciate rhymes and poems, and to recite some by heart.

Resources
Tabby McTat by Julia Donaldson; photocopiable page 'Tabby McTat's favourite song' from the CD-ROM; copies of Julia Donaldson books explored so far

5: Performing favourites

Introduction
● Recall the most memorable of Julia Donaldson's rhymes.
● Explain that children are going to learn a new rhyme.

Whole-class work
● Read *Tabby McTat* to the class and display photocopiable page 'Tabby McTat's favourite song' from the CD-ROM. Explore how Julia Donaldson repeats the sound of the words *Me, you* in the word *MEEE-EW*. Also look at *guitar* and *are* and ask children to use letter names to show the difference between the spellings.
● Ask children to read it with you, with some of the class clapping the rhythm while others emphasise the cat's mewing and purring. Discuss why this is the characters' favourite song.
● Repeat a few times, then hide the screen and see if they remember it.

Group work
● Invite groups to decide which of Julia Donaldson's songs and rhymes is their favourite. Explain this can be a short section of a rhyming text, poem or song.
● Once words have been chosen, ask children to decide why this particular selection is their favourite and write notes about it.
● Invite them to compose sentences that form a short review describing their chosen text. Encourage application of simple spelling rules.

Review
● Ask groups to recite their chosen favourites and read out their reviews.
● Discuss what they have learned about alternative spelling rules.

Curriculum objectives
● To begin to punctuate sentences using a capital letter and a full stop, question mark or exclamation mark.

Resources
Photocopiable page 'Start and finish the sentence' from the CD-ROM

Grammar and punctuation: Start and finish the sentence

Revise
● Recall previous lessons involving when to use capital letters and full stops. Explain that you would now like children to choose between adding a full stop, a question mark or an exclamation mark to the end of sentences.
● Display photocopiable page 'Start and finish the sentence' from the CD-ROM. Ask children to read the instructions with you to make sure that they understand what they have to do.
● Read the first sentence together and decide which of the words in brackets to use. Once children have chosen this, ask someone to underline it.
● Read the three given choices for punctuating the end of the sentence and decide which one to use. Establish that the sentence is a question before asking someone to write a question mark.
● Discuss when an exclamation mark is usually used, for example, to highlight a strong statement or something exciting. Ask children to find a sentence this applies to, for example, *Get out of my way!* Discuss reasons for choosing this.

Assess
● Provide each child with the photocopiable sheet to complete, asking them to read the sentence aloud before deciding on the punctuation mark.

Further practice
● Simplify or extend sentences according to children's reading levels.
● Challenge children to write sentences that demonstrate the use of the different punctuation marks explored.

Curriculum objectives
● To respond speedily with the correct sound for all 40+ phonemes, including, where applicable, alternative sounds for graphemes.
● To read accurately by blending sounds in unfamiliar words containing GPCs that have been taught.
● To use letter names to distinguish between alternative spellings of the same sound.

Resources
Interactive activity 'Finding rhymes' on the CD-ROM

Spelling: Finding rhymes

Revise
● Recall recent work on GPCs involving comparing rhyming words in Julia Donaldson books.
● Work through some examples on the board of words with regular and alternative graphemes, for example: *cross/boss, snail/whale.* Ask individuals to 'sound-talk' these words by breaking them down into separate phonemes, for example: /cr/ /o/ /ss/ and /sn/ /ai/ /l/.
● Display interactive activity 'Finding rhymes' on the CD-ROM and look at the first screen. Focus on the first word and invite someone to find the rhyming word and drag and drop it into the given box. Do the same with the remaining words, identifying sounds and the letters used to spell them.
● Work through the second screen in the same way, asking children to identify alternative spellings for the same sounds, and naming the letters used.
● Leave the third screen for children to tackle themselves.
● Discuss what children might like to type into the 'learning blog' at the end to highlight successes or difficulties.

Assess
● Provide children with access to the interactive activity and a computer.
● Observe individual responses and note difficulties identifying graphemes.

Further practice
● Provide children who need support with a simplified exercise based on taught GPCs.
● Challenge more confident learners to spell aloud and write a list of words to rhyme with the examples given.
● Use starter activity 6 'Clapping my meal'.

Curriculum objectives
● To respond speedily with the correct graphemes for all 40+ phonemes, including alternative sounds for phonemes.
● To read common exception words, noting unusual correspondence between spelling and sound where these occur in the word.
● To read words containing taught GPCs and '-s', '-es', '-ing', '-ed', '-er' and '-est' endings.
● To check that the text makes sense to them as they read and correct inaccurate reading.

Resources
Interactive activity 'Jumbled words' on the CD-ROM

Reading: Jumbled words

Revise

● Recall recent reading activities, including exploring book extracts and searching for rhymes and predictable phrases in Julia Donaldson's work.
● Talk about work involving revision of word endings, for example, creating plurals by adding '-s' and '-es', and using the past tense by adding '-ed' and '-ing' to words.
● Discuss work on punctuation of sentences, for example, adding full stops and capital letters, question marks and exclamation marks.
● Emphasise that, although the above exercises helped with their writing skills, they also improved their reading ability and their understanding of the sense of what they were reading.
● Write a jumbled sentence on the board, such as: *school today, When John arrived at he was late missed the bus because he had.*
● Read the sentence together and explain that it is a 'jumbled' sentence that must be sorted into the correct order so that it makes sense.
● Ask the children if there might be a clue to help them to decide how the sentence starts. Recall the use of capital letters and identify those in the sentence. Decide which one will start the sentence, arriving at the conclusion that it must be *When* because this word would not appear in the middle of a sentence with a capital letter.
● Read along from *When* until the words stop making sense at the word *at.* Decide what must follow this word. Continue in this way until the end of the sentence is reached, marked by the full stop. Check that all words have been used before reading the whole sentence to check that it makes sense.
● Spend time analysing the sentence, for example, identifying the common exception words *school, today, the,* and words ending in '-ed' (*arrived, missed*), establishing that the sentence is in the past tense.
● Display the first screen of the interactive activity 'Jumbled words' on the CD-ROM. Focus initially on the first jumbled sentence and follow the same stages of clue-finding as for your own sentence. Once children think they have identified the correct sentence, demonstrate how to join the two sentences by dragging the given line between them.
● Work through the second jumbled sentence, this time leaving children to identify clues and join the two boxes.
● Discuss what they might write in their learning blog when they have finished.
● Ask children to work through the screens with a partner initially so that they can discuss how they will look for clues, check that they are correct and fill in their learning blog.

Assess

● Provide each child with access to the interactive activity and ask them to complete it.
● Observe them as they work, and be ready to support with helpful hints about how to complete the activity, but not which sentences to choose.
● Remind them about filling in the learning blog.

Further practice

● If any children are struggling with the reading level of this work, include them in the discussion and reading of the interactive activity, supporting and encouraging them. However, create a different page for their assessment that invites children to read a very simple sentence and then discuss orally the correct word order (remember that it is reading ability that is being tested).
● Extend the activity to challenge children's reading skills by asking them to make sentences from more complex word cards and then arrange them in a jumble for a partner of similar ability to re-arrange.

Curriculum objectives
● To use the grammatical terminology in Appendix 2 in discussing their writing.
● To sequence sentences to form short narratives.
● To use '-ing', '-ed', '-er' and '-est' endings where no change is needed in the spelling of root words.
● To apply simple rules and guidelines, as listed in Appendix 1.

Resources
Superworm by Julia Donaldson; *The Gruffalo's child*; coloured pens

Writing: Superworm's child

Revise

● Read the stories of *The Gruffalo's Child* and *Superworm* and recall explorations into Julia Donaldson's books. Talk about the rhythmic elements.
● Explain that children are going to write their own stories about a new character, 'Superworm's Child', who will be developed from the characters in these two stories.
● Recall how a story follows a sequence of beginning, middle and end.
● Revise work on using connecting words and phrases, such as *At last, Then, After that* to help stories, and events within them, to flow.
● Ask children to consider story language explored previously and call out some suitable opening sentences, for example, *Once upon a time, Long, long ago, There was once a....* Talk about possible endings for the story. Most stories have a happy ending. Perhaps this story could end differently?
● Recall sentence writing and remind children about including word spaces and correct punctuation, such as full stops, capital letters, question marks and exclamation marks. Emphasise the need to use correct grammatical terminology when discussing their writing. Recall the use of appropriate endings to denote past tense and remind children to be aware of this.

Assess

● Write the title *Superworm's Child* on the board and invite children to speculate about what this character might look like. Ask them to visualise this character in their 'mind's eye', allowing their imaginative ideas to wander freely. Encourage them to be adventurous, so that they do not simply recreate a miniature Superworm. Suggest exciting alternatives, such as a worm with wings, rainbow swirling skin or flapping ears.
● Consider the direction the story might take, for example, when Superworm's Child discovers a magic power. Decide how this power might dictate possible events, for example, flying to rescue trapped bees or hearing distressed creatures howling over great distances. Perhaps the story has frightening elements, or a problem for Superworm's Child to solve?
● Divide into groups so that children can discuss this new character and the stories they propose to write. Encourage them to decide whether they think they would like Superworm's Child to be a boy or a girl and to draw pictures of him/her. Encourage children to make notes of interesting suggestions before bringing them together as a class to share ideas.
● Write a list on the board, with the children's help, to remind them of things they need to include in their story, for example, title, at least three sentences to cover the beginning, middle and end, capital letters, full stops, word spaces. For more confident learners, include question marks and exclamation marks, as well as dialogue with speech marks.
● Ask the children to write a story about Superworm's Child that has at least three sentences representing the beginning, middle and end.
● Invite children to read their finished stories to partners and discuss features such as imaginative language, strong sequence and sentence structure.
● Choose stories at random to discuss with the class. Draw attention to and give praise for correct sentence punctuation, appropriate spelling of word endings and exception words.

Further practice

● Support those who have difficulty by encouraging them to make Superworm and his child from play dough and use them to re-enact a simple story. Model appropriate voices and dialogue as you move the characters around. Help the children to compose and write three simple sentences about the story that emerges. Use correct terminology relating to sentence structure as you draw attention to the completed writing.
● Challenge more confident learners to write stories involving two or more favourite characters, for example, Cinderella, Jack and the three bears.

Clever contractions

- Read the sentence in each box.
- Find the contraction together.
- Circle this word.

"To find that treasure down below,
I'll feed you to my hungry crow."

Not to panic – all is fine…
It's SUPERWORM, the fishing-line!

The wizard wakes. "This isn't funny!"

"I'm wrapped in leaves and stuck with honey."

I can find and read words with contractions in a
sentence.

How did you do?

■ SCHOLASTIC
www.scholastic.co.uk

Choosing words

■ Write a sentence about each character. Use *and* to join the adjectives.

Name of character	Adjectives	
Superworm	super-long super-strong	
Wizard Lizard	wicked cruel	
Crow	black hungry	
Baby toad	careless silly	

■ Choose the correct words to go in the gaps in the sentences.

strong stronger strongest
feel feeling felt
drown drowned drowning

Superworm is the _____ worm of all.

The bees are _____ bored today.

Beetle is _____ in the well.

I can use *and* to join words and choose the correct word so that the sentence makes sense.

How did you do?

Character adjectives

- Write words to describe how these characters look.
- Write words to describe what they are like.
- You can choose a character for the last row.

My name	My appearance	My character
Superworm		
Little monkey		
Tyrannosaurus Drip		

I can use adjectives to describe a character.

How did you do?

Name: _____   Date: _____

My favourite Julia Donaldson book

■ Complete the sentences about your favourite book by Julia Donaldson.

Title: _____

The setting: I (like or dislike) _____ the setting because

_____

The main character: I (like or dislike) _____ the main character because

_____

_____

The events: My favourite event is _____

_____

The rhymes: The rhymes are _____

The illustrations: The illustrations are _____

_____

I rate this book

I can complete sentences about my favourite book.

How did you do?

Who said that?

- Read the words in the boxes.
- Which book are they from and who said them?

"Down with hunting!" and he hooted, "Down with war!" "Down with bellyfuls of duckbill dinosaur!"	
Book:	Character:

"Superworm is super-long. Superworm is super-strong. Watch him wiggle! See him squirm! Hip, hip, hooray for SUPERWORM!"	
Book:	Characters:

"I've lost my mum!"	
Book:	Character:

"Buzz off! – THAT'S MY WITCH!"	
Book:	Character:

I can read the words spoken by a character and say which book they came from.

How did you do?

PHOTOCOPIABLE

Name: _____   Date: _____

Our story plan

■ Use this page to plan a story with your partner. Remember to hold the pencil correctly and form letters correctly as you write.

Title: _____

Main character: _____

Setting: _____

Beginning Write down words you are going to use to begin your story.
Middle Write about two of the main events in your story. 1. 2.
End Write down what happens at the end.

I can hold a pencil correctly and form letters correctly when I write.

How did you do?

Name: _____   Date: _____

Collecting rhymes

■ Cut out the cards and match the rhyming words.

snail	broom	feast	cat
shriek	wind	sky	pool
wand	waves	hat	bird
roar	beak	whale	beast
high	grinned	caves	pond
school	furred	shore	room

Find the rhyming word

- Read each sentence.
- Choose the correct rhyming word from the box on the right.
- Write it in the correct place to finish the sentence.

These are the children, running from school,

Fetching the firemen, digging a _____ .

rule
mule
pool

"I am a dog, as keen as can be. Is there room on the

broom for a dog like _____ ?"

he
me
key

"Hush, little monkey, don't you _____

I'll help you find her," said Butterfly.

fry
try
cry

This is the tale of a tiny snail

And a great big, grey-blue humpback _____ .

wail
whale
nail

Tabby McTat was a home-loving _____ .

hat
cat
rat

Help! Disaster! Baby toad

Has hopped on to a major _____ .

rode
rowed
road

I can choose the correct word so that the sentence
rhymes and makes sense.

How did you do?

Animals

This half-term's animal theme is introduced through the popular story *Handa's Surprise*. Children explore characters, setting and events, and learn more about the featured animals and fruits. African animals are compared with those that live in Britain. Children write animal stories based on Handa's encounters, but set in their locality. They read, learn, recite and write animal poems using the knowledge and vocabulary gleaned from earlier activities. Prior learning is embedded and new learning opportunities introduced.

Expected prior learning
- Understand the meaning of the term plot.
- Know what is meant by a question mark and an exclamation mark.
- Can use describing words and '-er' and '-est' suffixes.

Overview of progression
- Children become more familiar with a popular story and learn to sequence the plot in order.
- They research non-fiction books and learn new vocabulary, before including these words in their own sentences.
- They take on the role of animal characters, moving and exhibiting body language and sounds. Work on adjectives encourages children to add details of character traits to their writing.
- They embed previous understanding of suffixes as they use these to denote past and present tenses and plurals.
- They learn to classify members of the animal kingdom, identify animals and write about them with confidence.
- Children adapt a well-known story, and incorporate ideas from poems and rhyming words into their own poetry.

Creative context
- The children express their ideas creatively using paint and collage, drama, small-world and role play.
- Children enhance their scientific knowledge of the way that the animal kingdom is classified, which links to science.
- Aspects of order and sequence are included in activities involving ordering of animals and sequencing story events; children create a class pictogram, which all links to maths.

Preparation
The book focussed on in this chapter is *Handa's Surprise* by Eileen Browne.

You will also need:
Percussion instruments; flat basket; examples of fruit from the story; coloured pens; scissors; strips of white paper; large sheets of paper; glue sticks; sticky tape; building blocks or cardboard boxes; card strips; examples of cartoon strips; internet access; small-world animals; non-fiction books about African animals, Africa and the animal kingdom; globe; atlases; sand tray; fabric with African designs; cameras; camouflage fabric; binoculars; safari hat; African safari holiday brochures; magnifying glasses; clipboards; small-world models and books about British animals; materials to create a display about animals; animal poetry books;

On the CD-ROM you will find:
Media resources 'Handa's Surprise book cover', 'Extract from *Handa's Surprise*'; interactive activities 'Question or not?', 'Caption choices', 'Choose the label', 'Favourite animals', 'Recount frame', 'Rhymes and patterns', 'Finding rhymes', 'Down on the farm', 'Identifying the senses'; photocopiable pages 'Handa's fruit', 'African animals' 'Outline map of Africa', 'Animal factsheet', 'On the Ning Nang Nong', 'Fun facts (1)', 'Fun facts (2)

MSCHOLASTIC

Chapter at a glance

An overview of the chapter. For curriculum objective codes, please see pages 8–10.

Week	Lesson	Curriculum objectives	Summary of activities	Outcomes
1	1	RC: 1, 9, 10, 11	Explore cover and read story. Predict happenings. Discuss significance of title and events. Consider Handa's thoughts at the end. Make inferences.	• Can discuss key stories, significance of title and events. • Can make predictions based on clues and make inferences about what is said and done.
	2	RWR: 3 WC: 9	Read accurately and explore effect of punctuation. Change punctuation and discuss effect.	• Can read accurately given text. • Can punctuate sentences with capital letter and full stop, question mark or exclamation mark.
	3	RWR: 1, 2, 4 WT: 9 WC: 12	Read fruit and character names using phonic knowledge. Read common exception words. Apply spelling rules. Use grammatical terminology.	• Can use phonic knowledge and skills to read given words and apply spelling rules. • Can read exception words. • Can use grammatical terminology.
	4	WT: 14 WC: 3, 12	Revise beginning, middle and end. Order pictures from the story. Number them. Retell the story using pictures.	• Can sequence sentences to form narrative. • Can order pictures and digits correctly. • Can retell a story in sequence.
	5	WT: 14 WC: 2, 3	Create a storyboard to summarise the story. Compose sentences orally. Sequence sentences and number them.	• Can compose sentences orally and sequence them to form narrative. • Can form digits.
2	1	RC: 10, 12 WC: 9	Explore animals in story and discuss role. Link to fruits they stole. Make inferences, and punctuate sentences correctly.	• Can discuss a story and the role of animals. • Can make inferences based on what others say. • Can write sentences with correct punctuation.
	2	RC: 12 WT: 12 WC: 10	Discuss what is read and how to describe animal features. Write descriptive captions for animals using I.	• Can write sentence captions beginning with I to name and describe animals.
	3	RC: 10 WC: 10	Find out how animals move and eat. Mime animal movements. Get in role using I when talking.	• Can make inferences during discussions about animals. • Can use capital letter for the pronoun I.
	4	WT: 12, 15 WC: 9	Revise handwriting families. Write speech bubble sentences for animals with correct punctuation and letter formation.	• Can understand handwriting families. • Can write sentences with correct punctuation and letter formation.
	5	RC: 10, 12	Take part in dramatisation of events. Take part in discussion and make inferences based on outcome of this.	• Can take part in a discussion about dramatisation of events and make inferences based on what is said and done.
3	1	RWR: 9 RC: 7	Search books, internet, globes, atlases and maps to discover more about Africa. Share discoveries with the class.	• Can build confidence in word reading through exploring non-fiction books. • Can research to collate facts about Africa.
	2	RWR: 9 RC: 7	Create animal fact-finder folders using previous knowledge and information. Re-read books from earlier research.	• Can re-read previous texts during research. • Can draw on previous knowledge and information provided by teacher.
	3	WT: 8 WC: 9	Order animals and write words with correct endings in sentences. Compose sentences orally before writing them. Use correct punctuation.	• Can use correct endings in comparative words. • Can write these in sentences, using full stops and capital letters. • Can compose orally first.
	4	WT: 8 WC: 9	Read sentences and change the ending of word by adding '-ing'. Make up sentences using this ending. Focus on correct punctuation.	• Can use '-ing' endings to complete sentences and in new sentences. • Can use capital letter and full stop, question mark or exclamation mark.
	5	RC: 7 WC: 2, 9	Create African game lodge role play. Display written information. Compose captions and sentences orally first.	• Can use knowledge from research. • Can punctuate sentences correctly and compose them orally and discuss them before writing.
4	1	RC: 2 WT: 9	Explore animals in the local area. Learn meaning of key categories and put animals under these headings. Spell names.	• Can link what they read about animals to own experiences of animals. • Can apply spelling rules names of animals.
	2	RC: 2 WT: 6 WC: 12	Categorise own pets using chart. Create pet pictogram. Write sentences about the results.	• Can help to create a pictogram. • Can use spelling rules for plurals in sentences.
	3	RC: 2 WT: 9	Walk to look for wildlife. Make links between what they have read and their experiences. Log sightings on clipboards.	• Can write and label finds using spelling rules and guidelines. • Can link the experience with what they have read.
	4	WT: 8 WC: 2, 3, 11	Write recount of walk and findings. Use '-ed' and '-ing' endings.	• Can write a recount in sequence. • Can use '-ed' and '-ing' endings.
	5	WT: 9 WC: 4	Create a display with work from the week with labels, signs and captions. Apply spelling rules and guidelines.	• Can apply spelling rules and guidelines when making signs, labels and captions. • Can re-read to check writing makes sense.

Chapter at a glance

Week	Lesson	Curriculum objectives	Summary of activities	Outcomes
5	1	RC: 2 WC: 2, 4	Set up areas displaying wild, pet and farm animals. Write informative sentences about them. Compose orally and re-read.	• Can link what they read to experiences of animals. • Can re-read sentences to check sense.
	2	RC: 2 WT: 1 WC: 1	Plan characters for story similar to *Handa's Surprise* set in this country linking to own experiences. Write using taught phonemes.	• Can say aloud what they plan to write. • Can use taught phonemes.
	3	RC: 2 WT: 1 WC: 1	Plan events and animals for story, linking to own experiences using role play. Write using taught phonemes.	• Can link what is read to own experiences when planning. • Can use taught phonemes.
	4	WC: 2, 3, 9	Write drafts. Focus on sequencing sentences with beginning, middle, end and using correct punctuation.	• Can compose orally before writing. • Can sequence sentences to form a narrative. • Can punctuate correctly.
	5	RC: 12 WC: 3, 4, 5	Finish stories. Check for sense. Read a story to the class and discuss reactions. Listen to other stories and discuss.	• Can check finished work for sense by re-reading. • Can participate in a discussion about what is read to them.
6	1	RWR: 6, 9 RC: 5	Learn an animal poem and recite it. Explore poetry books to find and read animal poems. Identify key features.	• Can re-read books and read poems aloud to develop confidence and fluency. • Can appreciate poems and learn one to recite.
	2	RWR: 6, 9	Search poetry books and read adjectives to describe animals. Write a list of animals and adjectives. Create animal/adjective combinations.	• Can read poems to build confidence and fluency. • Can identify adjectives and use them in their own animal descriptions.
	3	WT: 1 WC: 2	Recall African animals and use adjectives from previous reading in poems about them. Compose orally before writing.	• Can write poems, composing sentences orally before writing. • Can use words containing taught GPCs.
	4	WT: 1, 9 WC: 2	Explore rhyming words and write poems associated with farm animals. Compose orally before writing, use taught phonemes and apply spelling rules.	• Can compose sentences orally before writing poems. • Can confidently use words with taught phonemes. • Can apply spelling rules and guidelines.
	5	RC: 5 WC: 6	Create farmyard display and showcase favourite poems, both read and composed, by reading them out.	• Can appreciate rhymes and recite some. • Can read aloud clearly enough to be heard by peers and teacher.

Background knowledge

Present tense: Verbs in the present tense are used to talk about now.

Tense: The choice between verb forms that is normally used to indicate time (although tense and time do not always match up).

■ SCHOLASTIC

Week 1 lesson plans

This week the animal theme of the chapter is introduced through *Handa's Surprise*. Children explore the cover and read the story, predicting happenings and discussing the significance of the title and events. They make inferences about Handa's thoughts during various story events. Children revise punctuation and discuss the effect of changing punctuation marks. They use grammatical terminology and apply spelling rules as they write. Reading skills are enhanced by reading fruit names, and common exception words, using existing phonic knowledge. Sequencing sentences to form a narrative with a beginning, middle and end is supported as children order and number pictures, and use them to retell the story. Finally, they summarise the story through storyboards or story-maps.

1: *Handa's Surprise*

Introduction
- Display media resource 'Handa's Surprise book cover' on the CD-ROM. Ask children to read the title and name the author. Explain that Eileen Browne also illustrated this book. Discuss how the advantage of both writing and illustrating a book is that the characters and setting are just as you imagine them.
- Discuss the cover image and decide who the character might be. Ask what she is carrying and whether these are familiar fruits. Invite children to identify the bird in the background. Explain that the colours and the patterns around the edges of the cover are African designs. Given the clues they can see, where do they think the story might be set?

Whole-class work
- Read the short story outline on the back cover to the children and ask them to speculate on what might happen. Remind them of the title and read the blurb again while children listen for the word *surprise*. Ask if they think that this is the surprise referred to in the title.
- Read the story to the children, pausing at significant points to ask them to predict what might happen next, for example, as the zebra watches Handa walking by. After a few animals have taken fruits, ask children if they can predict the pattern of the rest of the story. Will Handa have any fruit left?
- Talk about how Handa's thoughts are written as if she is saying them aloud, and ask how we know they are questions in her head. Find the words *thought Handa* to confirm this. Read the last page again and look at Handa's puzzled expression. Explain that children will discuss this further in groups.
- Ask children if they ever have questions in their heads, for example, as they wonder what will be for lunch or who they will play with outside.

Group work
- Write three questions on the board for children to respond to:
  - *What questions does Handa ask herself as she walks along?*
  - *What might she be thinking at the end of the story?*
  - *What questions do you ask yourself?*
- Ask children to discuss their responses to the first two questions and write their agreed answers in sentences.
- Ask individuals to complete question three, writing a sentence starting with the personal pronoun *I*.
- Promote taking turns to listen and speak and encourage children to make their own inferences taking into account the ideas of others in the group.

Review
- Ask groups and individuals to read out their sentence responses. Use this evidence to assess their ability to understand the story, make predictions based on clues in the book, and inferences based on what is said.

Curriculum objectives
● To read accurately by blending sounds in unfamiliar words containing GPCs that have been taught.
● To begin to punctuate sentences with a capital letter and a full stop, question mark or exclamation mark.

Resources
Handa's Surprise by Eileen Browne; interactive activity 'Question or not?' on the CD-ROM; media resource 'Extract from *Handa's Surprise*' on the CD-ROM; percussion instruments

2: Changing punctuation

Introduction
● Read *Handa's Surprise* together, blending sounds in unfamiliar words.
● Recall Handa's questioning thoughts, and identify the question marks.
● Display media resource 'Extract from *Handa's Surprise*' on the CD-ROM. Highlight the exclamation marks. Note use of capital letters and italics for complete words. Underline the question mark.
● Read the sentence in unison, saying the word *tangerines* as an excited response to a surprise in the first line and as a surprised question in the second. Comment on how punctuation affects the way these words are interpreted.

Whole-class work
● Suggest changing punctuation to see if this alters the implied meaning, for example, swapping question marks with exclamation marks so that Handa questions Akeyo for being surprised.
● Try moving the italics and capital letters to stress different words, for example, stressing *favourite* and *surprise*.
● Highlight unusual punctuation in the rest of the book, such as the ellipsis. Discuss the use of the apostrophe to contract *she will* to *she'll*.

Independent work
● Invite individuals to revise use of question marks by completing interactive activity 'Question or not?' on the CD-ROM.

Review
● Discuss the lesson's activities together and comment on how they have helped understanding of the use of punctuation.

Curriculum objectives
● To apply phonic knowledge and skills as the route to decode words.
● To apply spelling rules and guidelines as listed in Appendix 1.
● To use the grammatical terminology in Appendix 2 in discussing their writing.
● To read common exception words, noting unusual correspondence between spelling and sound where these occur in the word.
● To respond speedily with the correct sound to graphemes for all 40+ phonemes, including, where applicable, alternative sounds for graphemes.

Resources
Handa's Surprise by Eileen Browne; flat basket; examples of fruits featured in the story (or photocopiable page 'Handa's fruit' from the CD-ROM); coloured pens

3: Reading skills

Introduction
● If possible, arrange a basket of fruit like Handa's and sit around it (alternatively, display photocopiable page 'Handa's fruit' from the CD-ROM).
● Read *Handa's Surprise*, pausing for children to identify each fruit.
● If you have the fruit, pass around examples for children to feel and smell.

Whole-class work
● Invite children to use existing phonic skills to read words on the board.
● Start with basic letter-sounding in words such as *banana*. Discuss the pronunciation of words ending in 'o', such as *mango* and *avocado*.
● Split longer words into separate ones to assist reading, for example: *pine/apple*, *passion/-fruit*.
● Explain that the 'g' in *orange* is pronounced /j/. Recall familiar words with this pronunciation, such as *large*, *giraffe*, *giant*.
● Identify some common exception words from the book and write these down, for example, *she*, *the*, *friend*, *said*. Discuss unusual correspondences.

Paired work
● Suggest that pairs write a sentence each about a story event, using words from the board and their own. Invite them to illustrate their sentences.
● Encourage them to use grammatical terminology when discussing and composing sentences (*word*, *sentence*, *capital letter*, *full stop*), and to apply spelling rules (see Appendix 1) when writing them.

Review
● Enjoy sampling the fruits together. Ask pairs to share sentences. Discuss how the activities have helped children's reading and writing skills.

4: Handa's journey

Introduction
● Revise *beginning*, *middle* and *end* as you re-read *Handa's Surprise*. Discuss what happens at the beginning and end of this story, and identify events that define the outcome. Consider whether this might be one event, for example, when the goat butts the tree, or several involving all of the creatures.

Whole-class work
● Display photocopiable page 168 'All in order'. Explain that the pictures will be used alongside children's written sentences to retell the story.
● Demonstrate how children can create their own sequence called *Handa's journey* by taping or sticking pictures and written sentences to individual blocks, small boxes or a strip of card, and arranging them in order, with each sentence following its picture.
● Talk through the pictures together and invite suggestions about what to write about each one.

Paired work
● Divide into pairs, each child with the photocopiable sheet to cut out.
● Suggest that they discuss and agree order before writing the digits.
● Encourage them to compose their sentences orally, and to use grammatical terminology (such as *sentence, capital letter, full stop, exclamation mark*) when discussing them with a partner, before writing them on paper strips.

Review
● Bring the class together to retell the story using their versions of *Handa's journey*. Discuss how the activity helped them to retell it in the correct sequence.

Curriculum objectives
● To sequence sentences to form short narratives.
● To form digits 0 to 9.
● To use grammatical terminology in Appendix 2 when discussing their writing.

Resources
Handa's Surprise by Eileen Browne; photocopiable page 168 'All in order'; scissors; strips of white paper; large sheets of paper; glue sticks; sticky tape; building blocks or small boxes; card strips

5: Storyboard strips

Introduction
● Recall creating *Handa's journey* during the previous lesson and discuss how this helped children to follow the story sequence.
● Recall previous work on storyboards and story maps (Autumn 1) and how these helped children to sequence story events.

Whole-class work
● Discuss different ways of creating storyboards and consider which ones might work best with this story.
● Explore some pages from a suitable comic with cartoon strip stories and discuss what is included in them, such as speech bubbles and captions. Look for similar images on internet search engines.
● Discuss the idea of Handa going on a journey to visit Akeyo and consider drawing a map or path for this, introducing the animals as they appear along the route. Sentences could then be added in boxes.
● Suggest that children go into groups to create a plan of *Handa's Surprise* together using their preferred method of storyboard or story map.

Group work
● Remind individual groups about the need to compose sentences orally and then write them in sequence to tell the story. Ask them to number the sentences in story order.

Review
● Invite groups of children to show their work and read their sentences in order to the class. Encourage comments on interpretations, accuracy of sentence order and numbering.

Curriculum objectives
● To compose a sentence orally before writing it.
● To sequence sentences to form short narratives.
● To form digits 0 to 9.

Resources
Handa's Surprise by Eileen Browne; large sheets of paper; coloured and black pens; examples of cartoon strips from suitable comics; access to the internet

Curriculum objectives
• To participate in discussion about what is read to them, taking turns and listening to what others say.
• To make inferences on the basis of what is being said and done.
• To begin to punctuate sentences using a capital letter and a full stop, question mark or exclamation mark.

Resources
Handa's Surprise by Eileen Browne; photocopiable pages 'African animals' and 'Handa's fruit' from the CD-ROM; small-world models of animals from the story; real or imitation fruits representing those from the story (use pictures from CD-ROM if these are unavailable); two open baskets similar to Handa's; large rectangular pieces of white card; coloured and black pens

Week 2 lesson plans

This week, children focus on the animals in the story. They discuss the roles of animals, take turns to speak and listen to others, and make inferences based on what is said. They revise punctuation by writing sentences describing animal features using the personal pronoun *I*. Children explore how the animals might move and eat, using clues from illustrations and by getting into role to mime their actions. Handwriting families are revised using 'air writing' and by focusing on correct formation when writing thought-bubble sentences. Finally, children role-play scenarios depicting what might happen when animals take the fruit home to their families or partners. Inferences are made based on group discussion and class observation of scenarios.

1: African animals

Introduction
• Recall the story *Handa's Surprise*. Explain that this week's lessons will focus on animals. Invite children to recall the names of the animals in the story.

Whole-class work
• Arrange the model animals in one basket and leave the other basket empty. Keep the fruits, or fruit pictures, in a box beside you. Ask the children to sit in a circle around the baskets.
• Read the story, using the props to help children make links between the animals and the fruit they took.
• Invite a child to put seven fruits in the basket as the story begins and leave it on the floor beside the animal basket.
• Ask children to take the appropriate animal and fruit out of the baskets as the story progresses and stand them side by side on the carpet.
• As each animal is taken from the basket, invite the children to name it. If they have doubts, turn to the double-page spread at the back of the book depicting all of the animals with their names underneath.
• Draw columns on the board headed *Animal* and *Fruit*. Invite the children to help to write the names of the first animal and fruit in the correct columns. Continue with different children until all animals are linked to fruits.
• Focus on spelling these words, recalling fruit spellings from week 1, and following the same approach for animal words. Make links, for example, recall the soft 'g' in *orange* and link this to the initial sound of *giraffe*.

Group work
• Provide each group with photocopiable pages 'African animals' and 'Handa's fruit' from the CD-ROM to cut out.
• Explain that you would like them to make cards linking the animal to the fruit they took. They can do this by sticking the animal and fruit pictures on a piece of card and then writing a sentence underneath.
• Ask them to use the word *and* in a sentence about how the goat is linked to the tangerine, for example: *The goat hit the tree and the tangerines fell off.*
• Praise and recall correct punctuation as children write.

Differentiation
• Ask those needing support to write a simple sentence, using the words on the board to help them, for example: *This is a monkey.*
• Model appropriate sentences before challenging more confident learners to follow your example, such as: *The monkey leaned out of the tree and grabbed a banana from Handa's basket.*

Review
• Ask groups to arrange their cards in order and use them to retell the story.
• Discuss how class and group conversations helped during the activities.

2: Animal adjectives

Curriculum objectives
● To participate in discussion about what is read to them, taking turns and listening to what others say.
● To use a capital letter for names of people, places, the days of the week, and the personal pronoun I.
● To begin to form lower-case letters in the correct direction, starting and finishing in the right place.

Resources
Handa's Surprise by Eileen Browne; photocopiable page 'African animals' from the CD-ROM; black pens; non-fiction books about African animals, for example, *Planet Earth: Animals of Africa* by Lisa Ryan-Herndon; internet access

Introduction
● Read *Handa's Surprise*. Ask the children what they can tell about the animals from reading the words.
● Discuss other ways of finding out about them, such as non-fiction books, watching wildlife television programmes and searching the internet.

Whole-class work
● Display photocopiable page 'African animals' from the CD-ROM and focus on one animal at a time. Identify each animal and say its name. Ask children to think of adjectives to describe this animal, using the name as well, for example, *orange-coated monkey, curious ostrich, long-tongued giraffe.*
● Explain that you are creating a large page for each animal with a picture in the centre and children's descriptive sentences around it.
● Give an example of the sentence structure to follow, for example, *I am a grumpy goat.*
● Revise how to use the personal pronoun *I* and to form lower-case letters correctly, using example sentences.

Paired work
● Allocate an equal number of pairs to each animal.
● Provide non-fiction books featuring the animals, and access to appropriate internet sites. Encourage children to use these resources to expand their ideas.
● Ask children to discuss their findings and to write a sentence each from the animal's point of view, beginning *I am a...* .

Review
● Ask pairs to stick their sentences onto the prepared pages. Read the finished pages and discuss the adjectives. Praise good letter formation.

3: Animal movements

Curriculum objectives
● To make inferences on the basis of what is being said and done.
● To use a capital letter for names of people, places, the days of the week, and the personal pronoun I.

Resources
Handa's Surprise by Eileen Browne; photocopiable page 'African animals' from the CD-ROM

Introduction
● Read *Handa's Surprise* and display photocopiable page 'African animals' from the CD-ROM.
● Discuss how these animals might move and eat. Look for clues in the images.

Whole-class work
● Focus on one animal, for example, the monkey. Invite children to comment on illustration clues, for example, it climbs a tree and jumps among branches. Discuss whether it would peel the banana or eat it whole. Use children's past experiences of monkeys at the zoo or on television to help.
● Explore other creatures. How does the goat manage to shake the tree?

Group work
● Divide into same-ability groups of eight and ask them to role play an animal.
● Take turns to role play the animal moving and eating while others make constructive comments based on book evidence or previous knowledge.
● Ask individuals to write sentences using *I* to describe how their animal moves and eats, for example: *I am a parrot and I fly through the sky. I pick up fruit in my curved beak.* Encourage less confident learners to compose sentences orally.
● Encourage children to say their sentences to the group for comments, before repeating their role play.

Review
● Bring the class together to watch role plays and comment on accuracy. Praise appropriate use of *I*.

Curriculum objectives
● To understand which letters belong to which handwriting families.
● To begin to punctuate sentences using a capital letter and a full stop, question mark or exclamation mark.
● To begin to form lower-case letters in the correct direction, starting and finishing in the right place.

Resources
Handa's Surprise, photocopiable page 'African animals' from the CD-ROM; thought-bubble shapes cut from white paper large enough for children to write a sentence in and stick beside animal images; large sheets of coloured paper; glue sticks

4: Handwriting families

Introduction
● Remind children of handwriting families. Recall work on this (Autumn 1).
● Write large letters that involve strokes that go down and off in another direction, for example, 'j', 'l', 't'. Draw these in the air together.
● Repeat with letters that go down and retrace upwards ('r', 'b', 'h'), that go anticlockwise round ('c', 'g', 's'), and that zigzag ('w', 'z', 'v').
● Save this for paired work.

Whole-class work
● Ask children to name the animals from *Handa's Surprise*. Write these in lower-case letters on the board. Read them together. Choose an animal and invite children to draw the letters in the air as you say them.
● Ask children to recall speech and thought bubbles in stories and cartoon strips and discuss their purpose.
● Decide how Handa's thoughts and the animals' thoughts might read if they were in thought bubbles.

Paired work
● Provide same-ability pairs with blank thought bubbles, and animal images from photocopiable page 'African animals' from the CD-ROM to cut out and stick to a large sheet of coloured paper.
● Ask them to write sentences in the bubbles describing the animals' thoughts.
● Encourage correct letter formation. Stick the bubbles alongside the animals.

Review
● Ask pairs to share their thought bubbles with the class. Encourage discussion about the way drawing 'air' letters helps handwriting.

Curriculum objectives
● To participate in discussion about what is read to them, taking turns and listening to what others say.
● To make inferences on the basis of what is being said and done.

Resources
Handa's Surprise by Eileen Browne; small pieces of paper for the names of the featured animals; a small box

5: Animal reactions

Introduction
● Read *Handa's Surprise* and recall explorations of the animals, including movement role play and speculating on their thoughts using speech bubbles.

Whole-class work
● Focus on animal illustrations in the book and consider whether these creatures live alone, in pairs or with a family.
● Discuss whether there might be babies, young and old animals within these families who cannot search for food as efficiently.
● Talk about how the family members or partners feel, for example, as the giraffe brings a fine juicy pineapple home to share.

Group work
● Ask children to divide into groups, with each group representing the family of one of the featured animals.
● Write the animals' names on pieces of paper and invite each group to pull a name from a box. This will be the family they represent.
● Ask the group members to allocate family roles and role play a short scene of events that take place when the leader of the family brings home the fruit.
● Encourage children to modify actions and dialogue after trying ideas out and discussing what works best.

Review
● Ask groups to perform their short scenes. Invite observers to comment positively on the interpretations and make inferences about the animal characters from them.

Week 3 lesson plans

Children start the week by collating facts about Africa from information provided by the teacher, such as books, the internet, globes, atlases and maps. Groups assemble their discoveries in animal fact-finder folders. Children then order model animals by height and size, using words with the correct endings to describe these animals in sentences. Sentences are composed orally before writing, and focus is on correct punctuation, revising use of capital letters and full stops. Children rewrite sentences, changing the ending of words by adding '-ing'. Finally, they have fun gathering together the week's discoveries and using them in a role-play African game lodge. Their written information is displayed inside the lodge, on walls, tables and suspended from netting.

Expected outcomes
● All children can use describing words to provide detail.
● Most children can use some suffixes.
● Some children can effectively introduce new information and vocabulary into their written work.

Curriculum objectives
● To re-read books to build up their fluency and confidence in word reading.
● To draw on what they already know or on background information and vocabulary provided by the teacher.

Resources
Handa's Surprise by Eileen Browne; non-fiction books about Africa, for example, *We all went on safari: A counting journey through Tanzania* by Laurie Krebs & Julia Cairns, *Africa (Pull Ahead Continents)* by Madeline Donaldson; photocopiable page 'Outline map of Africa' on the CD-ROM; globe; atlases; sand tray; small-world African animals; fabric with African designs; internet access; scissors; glue sticks

I: Discover Africa

Introduction
● Before the lesson, set up an 'African research' area containing resources where groups of children can visit to collate facts. Possible areas to include might be: computer access to video and sound clips; book titles; globes and atlases; a sand tray used as an African landscape with small-world wildlife.
● Read *Handa's Surprise* and recall initial discussions about the country it is set in (week 1). Encourage the children to share facts they know about Africa or have gleaned from the book.
● Suggest that it will help their understanding of the story if they learn more about this continent, and the people and animals that live there.

Whole-class work
● Hold up the globe and show children where their school is located. Demonstrate the journey from the school to Africa, travelling in a straight line. Discuss the position of Africa at the other side of the world, close to the equator where it is very hot. Define *equator* as an imaginary circle around the Earth.
● Ask children to think of some sources of information that they might search in their discoveries of Africa, for example, non-fiction books, maps, globes, atlases and internet sites.
● Discuss the type of information we can discover from maps, such as the location of the place we are researching. Explain that some maps also show the features of the landscape, such as seas, rivers and mountain ranges.
● Consider information to be found in books, such as how people live and the wildlife to be found. Invite suggestions about what we might discover on the internet that we cannot find in the above resources, for example, sound clips and films of wildlife, and examples of the music of the area.

Group work
● Invite groups to visit the 'African research' areas in turn to explore the resources and make notes about things that interest them.
● Supply children with large sheets of white paper, glue, scissors, and black and coloured pens to create a montage of individual drawings and writing related to the information gathered.
● Suggest creating an interesting title for the sheet.

Differentiation
● Encourage those requiring support to identify resources of interest and explore these with them. Invite them to draw a picture and scribe a sentence with them.

Review
● Invite groups to share montages, and ask individuals to explain their contributions. Ask children to introduce vocabulary they have learned and comment on difficulties or successes in reading these words. Discuss the role of the research areas in increasing their knowledge of Africa.

Curriculum objectives
● To re-read books to build up their fluency and confidence in word reading.
● To draw on what they already know or on background information and vocabulary provided by the teacher.

Resources
Books about African animals as used in week 1; access to relevant internet sites; photocopiable page 'African animals' from the CD-ROM; interactive activities 'Caption choices' and 'Choose the label' on the CD-ROM; card folders for each group; glue sticks; coloured pens; scissors; small box

2: Fact finders

Introduction
● Recall lessons involving finding out about the animals in *Handa's Surprise*.
● Explain that children will spend the rest of the week compiling animal information to display in an 'African game lodge'.

Whole-class work
● Display interactive activity 'Caption choices' on the CD-ROM and choose the most appropriate caption for each image. Emphasise that children should be precise in the information they provide in their captions.
● Work through interactive activity 'Choose the label' on the CD-ROM to establish the difference between a label and a list. Discuss when children might use labels in their prepared information, and when a list would be appropriate, for example, a labelled animal drawing or a descriptive word list.

Group work
● Ask each group to select an animal to research from names in a box.
● Supply each group with a folder. Cut out images from photocopiable page 'African animals' from the CD-ROM and ask children to stick them on their folder and to create sentences, drawings and African designs to go inside it.
● Encourage groups to share their proposed work according to expertise, for example, searching internet sites, drawing pictures, writing captions.

Review
● Ask groups to share their folder contents and discuss their research methods.
● Talk about how working as a team helps everyone to learn more.

Curriculum objectives
● To add prefixes and suffixes using '-ing', '-ed', '-er' and '-est' where no change is needed in the spelling of root words.
● To begin to punctuate sentences using a capital letter and a full stop, question mark or exclamation mark.

Resources
Photocopiable page 169 'Order the animals'; small-world African animals that display three different sizes or heights, such as a male, female and baby giraffe; scissors; glue sticks

3: Order the animals

Introduction
● Recall activities involving ordering items according to size and height.
● Write *tall, taller* and *tallest* on the board and discuss how the meaning of the word *tall* changes by adding '-er' and '-est'. Use starter activity 8 'Make me different' to remind children about changing word endings.

Whole-class work
● Ask the class to sit around some small-world African animals. Hold up the largest of three small monkeys and make a statement about it, for example, *This monkey is small.* Can they find two smaller monkeys? Invite children to choose another three of the same animal to make comparative sentences about.
● Display and read photocopiable page 169 'Order the animals'.
● Look at the first row and decide on a word that can be used to describe all three images, on its own or by adding '-er' or '-est' to the end.
● Think of sentences to describe each image using these words.

Paired work
● Provide each pair with the photocopiable sheet to cut out and glue under their sentences. Remind them about composing sentences orally before writing and then checking their punctuation.

Differentiation
● For pairs struggling, provide partially completed sentences to add word endings to.

Review
● Bring the class together to show finished work and read their sentences.
● Discuss how the lesson has helped with revising word endings and sentence punctuation.

Curriculum objectives
- To use '-ing', '-ed', '-er' and '-est' where no change is needed in the spelling of root words.
- To begin to punctuate sentences using a capital letter and a full stop, question mark or exclamation mark.

Resources
Photocopiable page 170 'Animal descriptions'

4: Animal descriptions

Introduction
- Recall previous activities involving changing word endings.
- Discuss what can happen when word endings are changed. Write *I help my Dad at home* on the board and compose new sentences by adding different endings to *help*, for example: *I am my Dad's helper; I like helping my Dad; My big brother helps me.*

Whole-class work
- Display photocopiable page 170 'Animal descriptions'. Read the instructions and the sentence in the first box. Discuss the meaning of *hunter*. Invite children to decide which word to add to the second sentence so that it makes sense (*hunting*). Identify any letters removed or added.
- Explain that the children will work with partners to complete the page so that they can discuss words before writing them.
- Remind them to add a full stop to complete each sentence.

Paired work
- Provide pairs with the photocopiable sheet. Allow time for discussion.
- When they have finished their own page, ask them to read their partner's sentences to check that they make sense and include the full stop.

Independent work
- Invite individuals to compose sentences about what other animals like doing, using words ending in '-ing', supporting with spelling if necessary.
- Emphasise correct punctuation.

Review
- Complete 'Animal descriptions' on the board for self-checking. Ask children to read their own sentences and comments on correct use of word endings.

Curriculum objectives
- To draw on what they already know, or on background information and vocabulary provided by the teacher.
- To begin to punctuate sentences using a capital letter and a full stop, question mark or exclamation mark.
- To compose a sentence orally before writing it.

Resources
Photocopiable page 'African animals' from the CD-ROM; group folders of information (from lesson 2); African montages and written work completed in lessons 1 to 4; camouflage fabric or net; cameras; binoculars; safari hats and other role-play resources related to observing wild animals; African safari holiday brochures; card

5: African game lodge

Introduction
- Recall the week's work involving gathering information on African animals.
- Explore brochures about African safari holidays and talk about how tourists watch wild animals from game lodges or vehicles.
- Suggest creating a role-play game lodge where tourists can discover information about wildlife while they are waiting to observe them.

Whole-class work
- Set up the game lodge either indoors or outdoors, using camouflage fabric draped over the chosen area. Leave gaps where tourists can watch animals.
- Discuss the type of information that could be displayed, for example, fact folders on a table, montages and maps on the wall, information sheets in files.

Group work
- Arrange children into the same groups they were in during lesson 2.
- Invite them to create some card sentences, using photocopiable page 'African animals' from the CD-ROM, about ways to spot the featured animal, for example: *Try to find the zebra in the long grass.* Suggest composing orally before writing and remind them of correct punctuation.
- Suspend these cards as mobiles from the lodge netting.

Review
- Ask individuals to visit the lodge in role as tourists and comment on the information and the way it is presented.

Curriculum objectives
● To be encouraged to link what they read or hear to their own experiences.
● To apply simple spelling rules and guidelines as listed in Appendix 1.

Resources
Photocopiable page 'Animal factsheet' from the CD-ROM; non-fiction books about the animal kingdom

Week 4 lesson plans

This week the children learn key animal categories and put animals under these headings. They link what they read about animals to experiences of local wildlife and pets. Spelling rules are applied as they write the names of animals and create a pet pictogram. They write sentences about the results, focusing on using grammatical terms when discussing them. Children enjoy a walk to find wild animals, creating labelled drawings, writing about their discoveries and taking photographs. On return, they write recounts of their walk. Focus is on revising '-ed' and '-ing' endings when writing in the past tense, sequencing sentences and composing them orally before writing. Finally, children create an interactive display showcasing the week's work.

1: Local animals

Introduction
● Prepare a column chart prior to the lesson, using the headings from the photocopiable page 'Animal factsheet' from the CD-ROM.
● Recall *Handa's Surprise* and invite children to list the animals appearing in it. Enquire if they have seen any of these animals in real life, and where this was.
● Question why we never see giraffes or elephants in our fields and talk about some of the animals that we do see.

Whole-class work
● Explain that scientists decided to sort the animals that live on this planet into different categories. Define the word *category* as a group of things sharing common features. Talk about how the children are already familiar with most of these but that there are some new words to learn as well.
● Display photocopiable page 'Animal factsheet' from the CD-ROM and read the word *Vertebrates* together. Explain that these animals have a backbone. Ask them to repeat the word. Read *Invertebrates* (on the second page) and explain that these animals do not have a backbone. Ask children to repeat the two words and notice the similarity in spelling.
● Read through each category, and the key features of the animals within it. Discuss wording that children find unfamiliar, for example, *warm-blooded* and *cold-blooded*, and talk about what these expressions mean. Consider terms such as *ear holes*. Describe how birds and reptiles do not have visible ears, simply small holes on the side of their heads. Check understanding of words such as *gills*. Talk about amphibians who breathe with lungs and gills at different stages in their life cycle.
● Ask children to think of examples for each category.
● Display the chart that you have prepared and explain that this is designed so that children can list the animals they know under the correct headings. Write examples they gave for the factsheet under the headings as examples.

Group work
● Provide each group with a chart to fill in and the factsheets to check animal features and categories.
● Ensure easy access to books about animals for further examples.
● When children are ready to write down an animal ask them to discuss the spelling with others and remember the simple rules and guidelines.

> **Differentiation**
> ● Challenge confident learners to find more unusual animals in books, such as the hyena or wallaby, and discuss which category they belong to.

Review
● Bring the class together to discuss what they have learned about animal categories. Revisit any words children found particularly difficult to spell.

Curriculum objectives
● To be encouraged to link what they read or hear to their own experiences.
● To use the spelling rule for adding '-s' or '-es' as the plural marker for nouns and the third-person singular marker for verbs.
● To use the grammatical terminology in Appendix 2 in discussing their writing.

Resources
Pre-cut pictures of pets taken from photocopiable page 171 'Common pets'; interactive activity 'Favourite animals' on the CD-ROM; glue sticks; tape; coloured pens; building blocks; large sheet of paper

2: Our pets

Introduction
● Recall comparisons between African wild animals and local wild animals.
● Introduce the term *domesticated* for animals that live with us.

Whole-class work
● Invite children into a circle to discuss their pets and name the different types.
● Tape a pre-cut picture of each type of pet to a block. Arrange these in a line.
● Invite each child to put a block on the appropriate picture block(s) to represent their pet(s).
● Count how many blocks are above each picture block and analyse results, encouraging children to identify which pet is most common.
● Explain that this information can be represented another way, introducing the words *table*, *graph* and *pictogram*.
● Display interactive activity 'Favourite animals' on the CD-ROM.
● Go through each screen, asking individuals to tick the appropriate boxes.

Paired work
● Provide pictures from photocopiable page 171 'Common pets' and ask children to colour their favourite animal or their own pet and add their names.
● Invite them to stick the finished pictures on the prepared pictogram in the correct column(s) (create the pictogram before the lesson).
● Suggest partners discuss facts they find interesting on the finished pictogram and write a sentence about one of them such as: *There are four hamsters; There are more dogs than cats*. Remind them of plural endings and encourage use of grammatical terminology in discussion (*sentence, full stop, plural, singular*).

Review
● Bring children together to read their sentences and consider how they reflect their understanding of the pictogram results.

Curriculum objectives
● To apply simple spelling rules and guidelines, as listed in Appendix 1.
● To be encouraged to link what they read or hear to their own experiences.

Resources
Plan a short walk in a local area; interactive activity 'Choose the label' on the CD-ROM; books linking with probable wildlife to look for on the proposed walk, for example, *The RSPB First Book of* series, including *Birds, Butterflies and Moths, Minibeasts, Mammals, Pondlife, Seashore*; clipboards; magnifying glasses; cameras

3: Out in the wild

Introduction
● Recall animal categories previously explored.
● Tell children that you are going for a walk and describe the environment, for example, woods, allotments, seashore, school garden. Draw attention to non-fiction books available to give children more idea of what they might see.
● Discuss resources to record finds, such as paper, clipboards and cameras.

Whole-class work
● Consider labelling drawings or creating animal lists during the walk. Work through interactive activity 'Choose the label' on the CD-ROM again to revise the terms *list* and *label*. Suggest that labelling drawings will help with recall back in the classroom. Similarly, a list might be a quick way of logging them.

Group work
● Work in groups during the walk so that adults can support those who have difficulties recording, and children can discuss discoveries with one another.
● Provide a camera for each group and take turns to take photographs.
● Remind children to respect the environment and wildlife.
● On return, ask groups to collate information and complete their notes.

Review
● Bring groups together to show their pictures and read out interesting notes. Decide on the most unusual animals seen, and contrast with the most common. Display photographs taken and identify the animals.

Curriculum objectives
● To compose a sentence orally before writing it.
● To sequence sentences to form a narrative.
● To use '-ing', '-ed', '-er' and '-est' where no change is needed in the spelling of root words.
● To learn the grammar for Year 1 in Appendix 2.

Resources
Interactive activity 'Recount frame' on the CD-ROM; children's written work from lesson 3; photocopiable page 172 'Plan a recount'

4: My walk

Introduction
● Recall yesterday's walk and the information collected.
● Explain that children are going to write a *recount* of what happened (define this term as an account of an event or experience). Ask children to decide whether it should be written in the present tense, because it is happening now, or in the past tense, because it has already happened. Recall the grammar of word structure when writing words about things that happened in the past, for example, adding '-ed' (*walked, climbed*).

Whole-class work
● Display interactive activity 'Recount frame' on the CD-ROM.
● Work through the words with question marks and ask the children to add appropriate words in the columns, for example, *When? - yesterday morning*.
● Explain that they should write three sentences in a sequence to recount the walk. Invite them to suggest appropriate connecting words to include, for example, *First, After that, Then*.

Paired work
● Leave the interactive activity displayed for reference.
● Provide photocopiable page 172 'Plan a recount' and their walk notes.
● Remind individuals to first compose sentences orally and discuss them.
● Support with spelling when necessary.

Review
● Bring children together to read their individual recounts. Discuss the most interesting and praise use of correct grammar and tense.

Curriculum objectives
● To apply simple spelling rules and guidelines as listed in Appendix 1.
● To re-read what they have written to check that it makes sense.

Resources
Children's written work from lessons 1 to 4, including pictograms and clipboard notes; previously explored books about animals of this country and photographs taken in lesson 3; green fabric; backing paper reflecting colours of the environment of the walk; table; small-world models of pets and local wildlife; pet accessories; pet leaflets from a local vets practice

5: Find out more

Introduction
● Recall previous lessons this week involving wild and domesticated animals children are familiar with.
● Suggest collecting together completed work and resources used in these lessons to create a display reflecting children's learning.

Whole-class work
● Discuss previous displays children have created, and the value of making them interactive with resources to explore and handle.
● Draw a labelled diagram on the board of how the wall display might look, for example, with a background reflecting the colours children noticed during their walk, and written work mounted on this.
● Discuss possible items to put on the table, for example, model animals, pet artefacts, a block pictogram.

Group work
● Allocate the preparation of different display sections to groups, for example, helping with mounting written work and photographs, assembling resources.
● All groups should write signs, lists and captions linked to the section of the display they have worked on, apply spelling rules and checking sense by re-reading, for example, background builders could create an attractive title and table planners could create card questions about resources.
● Allow time to check the display and make modifications.

Review
● Observe the display and discuss whether creating it has helped children to realise new learning they have achieved over the course of the week.

Week 5 lesson plans

This week, children continue exploring British animals by setting up classroom areas displaying wild, pet and farm animals. They extend learning by adding informative signs, captions and sentences. As they research facts and write these, they link what they read to their own experiences, compose sentences orally and re-read them to check sense. This leads into three lessons linking *Handa's Surprise* with writing similar stories set in this country. Groups of children plan characters, setting and events, and draft a story. They use taught phonemes correctly, revise sentence sequencing and use correct punctuation. Finally, individuals write their own stories based on notes made in groups, and read them to the class for comments.

1: British animals

Introduction
● Recall discussions about local animals and explain that children are going to widen their research to include all British animals.
● Invite children to suggest where these animals might be found, for example, living wild, as pets or on farms.

Whole-class work
● Recall the benefits of using interactive displays to convey information. Suggest creating three displays about wild animals, farm animals and pets.
● Talk about how labels, signs, captions, questions and informative sentences create additional learning opportunities.
● Display interactive activity 'Caption choices' on the CD-ROM and work through it to revise the need to be precise in information provided in captions.

Group work
● Divide the class into three large groups, each one to research and create the display for a chosen animal group. Find out if any group has a particular preference as to which group they research.
● Ask each group to begin by deciding how to create the background for their display using familiar resources from around the school, for example, borrow a farm layout mat from a younger class, or use a builder's tray to create a countryside. Suggest using a table for pet accessories and artefacts.
● Begin to set out the displays. Support with ideas, such as making an undulating farm landscape in a builder's tray using crumpled paper draped in green fabric and use real twigs pressed into lumps of dough for trees.
● Arrange the appropriate animals on the displays and stand the books alongside. Use lots of fabric drapes to make the displays attractive.
● Suggest dividing into two smaller groups with each one responsible for either sentences and labels, or signs and captions.
● Invite those writing sentences and labels to explore the display and decide where they could be useful. Discuss the importance of informative sentences and decide whether to write these in mini-booklets or to use folded card.
● Repeat these stages with the groups writing signs and captions. Talk about how they will create these, for example, using card folded in the centre so that it stands up, or cut out as a cloud and suspended above the display.
● Ask groups to compose their captions or sentences orally first and then to re-read them to check for sense. Encourage them to include some questions.

> **Differentiation**
> ● Support children by helping them to use words with familiar GPCs for their sentences.

Review
● Gather the class together to discuss things that have worked well and those that could be improved. Talk about what kind of interaction introduced new learning opportunities.

Expected outcomes
● All children can sequence sentences to form short narratives.
● Most children can adapt a familiar story into one of their own.
● Some children can include new vocabulary they read or hear read in their own stories.

Curriculum objectives
● To be encouraged to link what they read or hear to their own experiences.
● To re-read what they have written to check that it makes sense.
● To compose a sentence orally before writing it.

Resources
Interactive activity 'Caption choices' on the CD-ROM; small-world models and books about British wild animals, pets and farm animals; farm layout mat; table; pet accessories and leaflets; builder's tray; green fabric; model trees; other resources for displays decided by children

2: Planning a story (1) – setting and characters

Introduction
● Read *Handa's Surprise* and recall where it is set.
● Ask the children why the same things could not happen in this country, making reference to the setting and animals.

Whole-class work
● Explain they are going to write a similar story but set in their local area.
● Discuss possible settings; in the countryside, or a large town.
● Decide how the role of the main character would be affected, for example, would she still be a girl and would she carry a basket on her head?
● Talk about the fruits in the basket. They could be the same, but perhaps she would pick raspberries from her garden or pick apples from a tree.

Group work
● Ask groups to choose two character names, the type of setting and the kind of fruits in the basket, ready for further planning next lesson.
● Suggest that they write three headings, *Characters, Setting* and *Fruit,* and make notes under these. Ask them to discuss their ideas aloud before writing.
● Encourage the children to sound-talk any words they are unsure of spelling, breaking the words down into separate phonemes before they attempt to spell them.

Review
● Gather the class together to share character and setting ideas. Praise effort in making good links with *Handa's Surprise* and using correct spelling.

3: Planning a story (2) – events

Introduction
● Recall the story characters, fruits and settings from the previous lesson.
● Explain that these will be used to support planning of events that will happen in their own versions of *Handa's Surprise.*

Whole-class work
● Name the animals involved in *Handa's Surprise.* Recall previous discussions about likely animals Handa would encounter in Britain, such as dogs or cats.
● Suggest including another surprise turn of events in the story, for example, the animals putting something into Handa's basket in exchange for the fruit. Discuss what these items might be, for example, a dog might leave a ball.

Group work
● Ask groups to write *Animals* or *Events* at the top of separate sheets of paper and make notes of their ideas on these.
● If they plan to have additional items in the story they should write them on another sheet, for example, *ball - dog.*
● Remind them about sound-talking to help them spell any tricky words.
● Suggest they take the first or main event they have written about and act this out by taking on character and animal role(s). Encourage experimentation with dialogue and animal sound effects.
● Continue through the list of events until all group members are happy.

Review
● Invite groups of children to perform their stories. Decide on the most interesting version of *Handa's Surprise* with constructive comments on characters, setting and events.

Curriculum objectives
● To sequence sentences to form short narratives.
● To compose a sentence orally before writing it.
● To punctuate sentences using a capital letter and a full stop, question mark or exclamation mark.

Resources
Children's notes from lessons 2 and 3; photocopiable page 173 'Plan our story'

4: Write a draft

Introduction
● Recall the previous two lessons on story planning. Explain that the next stage is to start drafting the story.

Whole-class work
● Display photocopiable page 173 'Plan our story' and ask children to recall completing a similar page last term. Read the instructions and revise possible opening and closing words.

Group work
● Arrange the children into the same groups as in lessons 2 and 3. Provide completed notes from these lessons and the photocopiable sheets.
● Ask children to complete these pages together so that they can compose sentences orally and discuss them before working alone.

Independent work
● Invite individuals to write a story draft by expanding on the planning page they have completed, choosing an alternative title if they wish.
● Remind them that it is now their own story, rather than a group story.
● Praise good spelling and punctuation as you observe them working.

> **Differentiation**
> ● Encourage less confident learners to compose three sentences orally and then support them while they write it.

Review
● Bring the groups together to read examples of their story planning pages and look at how the individual drafts have developed from these. Encourage comments on choice of words, interesting new ideas and good sequencing.

Curriculum objectives
● To sequence sentences to form short narratives.
● To re-read what they have written to check that it makes sense.
● To discuss what they have written with the teacher or other children.
● To participate in discussion about what is read to them, taking turns and listening to what others say.

Resources
Children's completed photocopiable page 173 'Plan our story' and other notes made throughout the week; white and coloured paper; coloured pens

5: Listen to my story

Introduction
● Recall the week's lessons. Remind children how they started by reading *Handa's Surprise*, and then wrote new stories set in this country.

Whole-class work
● Discuss the story writing process, working in groups to decide characters, setting and sequence of events, and finally completing individual story drafts.
● Discuss the significance of a strong title. Ask some individuals to share theirs and comment on the most striking.
● Encourage children to remember comments during the review session at the end of the last lesson and perhaps modify their stories to reflect these.

Independent work
● Provide the children with their completed planning pages from the previous lesson, and the selection of writing resources to choose from.
● Ask them to write their story in full on colourful paper, making any changes in the light of review comments.
● Suggest that children make their story look attractive by decorating around the writing with a striking design or some relevant illustrations.
● Once finished, ask them to re-read their story to check it makes sense.

Review
● Bring the class together so that they can read their stories aloud and take part in discussions about their own story and the stories of others.

Week 6 lesson plans

Children start the week learning and reciting the nonsense poem, 'On the Ning Nang Nong' by Spike Milligan. They extend appreciation of rhyme and poetry by searching poetry books for interesting animal poems. They then look for suitable adjectives to describe these animals. Focus is on building confidence by re-reading words of more than one syllable containing taught GPCs. Children use the adjectives they discover to write poems about African animals and British farm animals. All poetry writing activities focus on composing sentences orally, using taught phonemes and applying spelling rules. Finally, children recite their own poems and their favourite poems to the class, focusing on clear reading. These poems are then displayed in a farmyard poetry area.

1: 'On the Ning Nang Nong'

Introduction
● Recall lessons involving listening to poems and discussing their key features.
● Explain that children will finish their exploration of animals by exploring poems about them, starting by learning a nonsense poem.

Whole-class work
● Recall poems and rhyming words that children have enjoyed together, such as nursery rhymes and rhyming chants from *Tyrannosaurus Drip*, *Superworm* and *Tabby McTat*. Discuss the pleasure of reciting these to an audience.
● Display photocopiable page 'On the Ning Nang Nong' from the CD-ROM and explain that this is a nonsense poem written by a man who had a great sense of fun, Spike Milligan. Explain that, when he recited this poem, the words were always changing so no one really knows the exact words of the original.
● Read the poem, tackling unusual and nonsense words using taught GPCs.
● Invite comments about key features, such as rhyming words, use of punctuation and capital letters to denote how the reader should express the words, and point out the definite shape to the whole poem.
● Identify ways in which we can tell that the poet had a sense of the ridiculous, for example, in the way he plays with the nonsense words *Ning Nang Nong*, moving them around so that they rhyme with different words.
● Discuss nonsense aspects, such as teapots going *jibber, jabber, joo!*, cows going *Bong!* and mice going *Clang!*
● Read the poem again, this time with added emphasis on nonsense words and words that represent sounds.
● Divide the poem into convenient sections by underlining lines 3, 6, 9, 11, 13, 15, 17 and writing the numbers 1 to 7 between each one. Read each section as one verse and then pause before reading the next.

Group work
● Divide into groups of seven and provide each group with the photocopiable sheet. Suggest they underline and number the sections as on the board.
● Go around each group allocating one of the sections to each child to learn.
● Encourage the groups to practise reciting the poem, with children reading their own lines. Suggest that they add appropriate expression and actions, for example, acting like a monkey and shouting *Boo*, wrinkling a nose like a mouse and squeaking a high-pitched *Clang*, swaying like a tree, waving branches and uttering a throaty *Ping*. Suggest that everyone makes their noises in unison at the end of the poem to denote the noisy place that it is.

Review
● Bring the groups together to perform their version of the poem and discuss the most effective interpretation. Ask whether they think that learning the words of a poem, and reciting them together, has helped them with appreciating the joy of rhyme.

Curriculum objectives
● To re-read books to build up their fluency and confidence in reading.
● To read words of more than one syllable that contain taught GPCs.

Resources
A selection of animal poetry books, for example, Giles Andreae's books including *Rumble in the Jungle, Commotion in the Ocean, Farmyard Hullabaloo!* (Orchard), *The Friendly Octopus and Other Poems About Animals* by Brian Moses (2010, Wayland), *My First Oxford Book of Animal Poems* by John Foster (2001, OUP); photocopiable page 174 'Finding animal words and adjectives'; whiteboard

2: Animals and adjectives

Introduction
● Explain that children are going to search poems to find adjectives that are used to describe animals.

Whole-class work
● Display and read photocopiable page 174 'Finding animal words and adjectives', commenting on familiar GPCs and tackling difficult words together.
● Read the list of adjectives and ask individuals to identify rhyming words and circle them. Continue until only the word *sad* is left without a rhyming word. Emphasise that poems do not have to rhyme every time.

Group work
● Provide groups with the photocopiable sheet and ask them to choose a book of animal poems to look through.
● Encourage them to write names of new animals on their list first and follow this by finding adjectives to add (they do not have to be in any order).
● Once children are satisfied with their lists they can begin thinking of linking descriptive words to create animal characters. Suggest they choose three different animals from the list and work with a partner within the group.

> **Differentiation**
> ● Support the less confident by creating a differentiated page with fewer words using GPCs already taught. Ask them to pair an animal with an adjective, such as *a sad dog*.

Review
● Invite groups to share their adjective/animal character combinations with the class. Ask for comments on those that are most effective and why.

Curriculum objectives
● To compose a sentence orally before writing it.
● To spell words containing each of the 40+ phonemes already taught.

Resources
Handa's Surprise by Eileen Browne; interactive activity 'Rhymes and patterns' on the CD-ROM; children's adjective lists and paired words (from lesson 2) and their African animal sentences using adjectives (from week 2, lesson2); poetry and fiction books with poems or rhyming text about African animals, for example, *We're Going on a Lion Hunt* by David Axtell; stories by Mwenye Hadithi to highlight adjectives in alliterative titles, such as *Cross Crocodile, Lazy Lion, Hot Hippo, Hungry Hyena, Baby Baboon*

3: African animal poems

Introduction
● Recall lesson 2 when children searched for animal adjectives, and remind them of work on African animal adjectives in week 2.
● Explain that children are going to write poems about African animals.

Whole-class work
● List the animals the children discovered when researching Africa.
● Display a book by Mwenye Hadith, or invent your own alliterative title. Ask children if they notice the rhythmic pattern the adjective creates, for example, *cross crocodile, lazy lion*. Discuss how this creates an animal character.
● Display *Four Little Speckled Frogs* on the interactive activity 'Rhymes and patterns' on the CD-ROM. Suggest writing an African animal number rhyme using adjectives with the same initial sound.
● Start with four and work downwards, for example: *Four lazy lions feeling tired and grumpy, Three cross camels looking really humpy.*

Paired work
● Provide same-ability pairs with access to previous written work and a selection of books. Suggest that they use these resources, and their own ideas, to write an African animal poem.
● Remind them to compose sentences orally before writing them down.
● Encourage them to sound-talk difficult words to help them with spelling.
● Stress that their poems need not always rhyme.

Review
● As a class share poems and discuss the stages in the writing process.

Curriculum objectives
• To compose a sentence orally before writing it.
• To spell words containing each of the 40+ phonemes already taught.
• To apply simple spelling rules and guidelines, as listed in Appendix 1.

Resources
Poetry books containing poems about farm animals, for example, *Farmyard Hullabaloo!* By Giles Andreae; interactive activities 'Finding rhymes' and 'Down on the farm' on the CD-ROM

4: Down on the farm

Introduction
• Recall the week's focus on wild animal poetry, particularly African.
• Explain that children will be working with partners to compose a farm animal poem today.

Whole-class work
• Display interactive activity 'Finding rhymes' on the CD-ROM and recall identifying the rhyming words. Complete this again for revision.
• Display interactive activity 'Down on the farm' on the CD-ROM and read the instructions and text. Draw attention to known phonemes and discuss spelling rules that apply.
• Invite children to drag and drop the correct words into the boxes. Read the poem together to check that it makes sense. Close the screen.

Paired work
• Provide pairs with access to interactive activity 'Down on the farm' to complete together before they begin to plan their poem.
• Encourage them to make lists of farm animals and words to link with them. Stress that these words do not necessarily have to rhyme. Recall the value of alliteration, for example, *shy sheep*. Encourage children to say proposed sentences orally, and to apply spelling rules as they write them.

> **Differentiation**
> • Help less confident learners to think of rhymes and alliterative adjectives to include.
> • Challenge more confident learners to compose a verse about each farm animal.

Review
• Bring the class together to share their poems. Discuss words used and the spelling rules that apply to them.

Curriculum objectives
• To read aloud their writing clearly enough to be heard by their peers and teacher.
• To learn to appreciate rhymes and poems, and to recite some by heart.

Resources
Small-world farm animals and farm mat; children's farm poems from lesson 4; farm-animal poetry books used in lesson 4

5: Farmyard poetry

Introduction
• Create a farmyard table with two display boards (one for children's poems and one for other poems they like).
• Introduce the display area and explain that the children's poems will be displayed here once they have read them to create a farmyard poetry area.
• Explain that the display will be a combination of favourite rhymes that the children have read, and those they have written.

Whole-class work
• Read some favourite farm animal poems from poetry books, encouraging children to suggest some they have enjoyed.
• Ask children to recite suitable nursery rhymes.

Paired work
• Invite the same pairs as in lesson 4 to choose a favourite poem to recite, as well as their own poem. Suggest that they write these down if they cannot remember them by heart. Encourage them to practise before deciding who will read each poem. Gather the class and invite pairs to stand next to the farm layout to recite their poems, or read them if necessary.
• Ask children to illustrate or mount their poems. Attach these to the board.

Review
• Bring the class together to discuss the poetry reading, making positive comments about loud clear voices and the actual poems read.

Curriculum objectives
● To begin to punctuate sentences using a capital letter and a full stop, question mark or exclamation mark.

Resources
Prepared text

Grammar and punctuation: Punctuate the sentences

Revise
● Before the lesson, type up a poem but miss out all the punctuation.
● Recall previous lessons involving correct use of punctuation.
● Explain that someone has typed something but forgotten to add punctuation so that there are no complete sentences.
● Ask the children to recall different punctuation that might be needed to create separate sentences. Invite examples of sentences that end in a question mark. Talk about when an exclamation mark is usually used, for example, to highlight a strong statement or something exciting.
● Revise when capital letters are needed, for example, to start sentences, for names, places and days of the week, and the personal pronoun *I*. You could use starter activity 3 'Names and addresses' to reinforce this.
● Read your prepared text without pausing to mark sentences. Invite the children to describe the effect this has. Is it easy to understand what the passage is about?

Assess
● Provide each child with a copy of your text and ask them to rewrite it, this time including punctuation. Remind them to include their names.

Further practice
● Simplify or extend sentences and text length according to the reading levels of those involved.
● Challenge children to follow this with additional sentences of their own that demonstrate the use of the punctuation marks explored.

Curriculum objectives
● To respond speedily with the correct sound for all 40+ phonemes, including, where applicable, alternative sounds for graphemes.
● To read accurately by blending sounds in unfamiliar words containing GPCs that have been taught.
● To use letter names to distinguish between alternative spellings of the same sound.

Resources
Photocopiable page 175 'Choose the word'

Spelling: Choose the word

Revise
● Recall recent work on GPCs when reading poems and researching non-fiction books.
● Work through some animal-linked examples of words with regular and alternative graphemes, for example: *bird/herd, snail/whale*. Ask individuals to 'sound-talk' these words.
● Display photocopiable page 175 'Choose the word' and read the instructions together.
● Invite children to find the eight animals that appear in *Handa's Surprise*. Underline these and revise by reading them again.
● Focus on the first sentence and read it together. Ask children to read the words in the box alongside, explaining that one of them is a nonsense word. Identify this and then read the other two words, identifying the phonemes and the letters used to spell them. Decide which word should be written in the sentence and then think of a sentence using the remaining word in context.

Assess
● Provide children with the photocopiable sheet to complete.
● Note individual difficulties reading GPCs and nonsense words.

Further practice
● Provide children needing support with a simplified exercise based on two taught GPCs. Do not include nonsense words.
● Challenge more confident learners to think of a new fact about each animal and write this as a sentence, focusing on correct spelling of phonemes.

Curriculum objectives
● To apply phonic knowledge and skills as the route to decode words.
● To read accurately by blending sounds in unfamiliar words containing GPCs that have been taught.
● To respond speedily with the correct graphemes for all 40+ phonemes, including alternative sounds for phonemes.
● To check that the text makes sense to them as they read and correct inaccurate reading.

Resources
Photocopiable pages 'Fun facts (1)' and 'Fun facts (2)' (differentiated) from the CD-ROM; prepared sets of cut-out images of animals taken from photocopiable page 'African animals' from the CD-ROM; large sheets of paper; glue sticks

Reading: Identify the animal

Revise

● Recall previous activities involving African animals, from identifying those that appear in *Handa's Surprise* at the start of the chapter to writing poems about them in the last lesson.

● Display photocopiable page 'African animals' from the CD-ROM and identify the animals pictured. Recall the part they play in Handa's story and how children know that they are plant eaters. Invite children to recall any extra facts discovered about the animals during their research using books and the internet.

● Display photocopiable page 'Fun facts (1)' from the CD-ROM and explain that these are a few interesting facts about three of the animals. Some of these facts will be familiar and others new to the children.

● Before starting the task, spend time revising children's phonic knowledge and skills, for example, break longer words down into separate words, such as *with-out, toe-nails*. Ask children to search the photocopiable sheet to find words with '-est', '-ing', and '-er' endings. Circle these and ask children to read them aloud. Run a finger along the letters as you do so. Follow this by checking plurals to see whether they end in '-s' or '-es', again, reading these aloud and following the letters.

● Discuss how sentences are punctuated, pointing out the use of full stops and capital letters. Explain the use of the hyphen and ask children why they think the sentence ending in *plate* has an exclamation mark. Emphasise that, although exploring punctuation helps their writing skills, it will also improve their reading ability and their understanding.

● Draw attention to the words on both sheets that demonstrate familiar GPCs, including those with alternative sounds for graphemes, such as: *height/ size/hide/eye, brown/house*. Point out nouns that are split by a consonant in *size, hide, whole* (split digraphs).

● Ask the children to start by reading the facts about the first animal and deciding which one it is from photocopiable page 'African animals' from the CD-ROM. Once they are sure of their decisions they should cut out an image of this animal and glue it at the top of a sheet of paper before sticking the fact sheet underneath it. Then they should write the name of the animal they have identified and decorate the page with suitable illustrations. They will need to do this for all three animals on the fact sheets.

Assess

● Provide each child with photocopiable pages 'Fun facts (1)' and 'African animals' from the CD-ROM, and access to paper, scissors, coloured pens and glue sticks to complete the task.

● Observe them as they work, and be ready to support with helpful hints about how to apply their phonic knowledge and skills to decode words.

● Remind them about writing their name and the name of the animal they have identified on the page.

Further practice

● Include all children in the discussion and reading of photocopiable pages 'Fun facts (1)' from the CD-ROM, supporting and encouraging them in their attempts to break down words, identify endings and look for punctuation clues. However, provide any children who are struggling with the reading level of these fact pages with the differentiated version, photocopiable page 'Fun facts (2)' from the CD-ROM for their assessment. This presents children with simplified sentences.

● Challenge children's reading skills by asking them to find fun facts in non-fiction books and use these to create new and more complex word cards about the remaining animals from *Handa's Surprise*, so that you have a complete set of fact cards to accompany the book. Invite them to choose partners of similar ability to read the new facts and identify the animals.

■SCHOLASTIC

Curriculum objectives

- To compose a sentence orally before writing it.
- To spell words containing each of the 40+ phonemes already taught.
- To begin to punctuate sentences using a capital letter and a full stop, question mark or exclamation mark.
- To re-read what they have written to check that it makes sense.

Resources

Interactive activity 'Identifying the senses' on the CD-ROM; children's photographs, notes and recounts from their walk (week 4); coloured pens

Writing: A sensory walk

Revise

- Recall previous work on animal poems. Ask the children to recite favourites.
- Discuss children's own poems about African animals and farm animals. Talk about how interesting adjectives brought the animals to life.
- Recall the walk taken earlier in the term and some of the wildlife observed.
- Invite children to close their eyes while you take them back to the walk in their imaginations. Begin by asking what they can smell. Perhaps they are aware of the dampness rising from the ground or the wild garlic in the undergrowth? Ask them about pleasant smells like flowers and unpleasant ones like rotting leaves.
- Tell them to imagine that you pause to enjoy a break, sitting in groups to share drinks and snacks. Discuss the nice tastes and those that they disliked.
- As you continue on your way, ask children to describe sounds, such as scampering creatures or swishing branches.
- Invite the children to imagine that they stop and touch something nearby, for example, stretching to rub fingers along the trunk of a tree.
- Finally, ask about animals the children can see, their appearance and what they are doing.
- Instruct the children to open their eyes and say what they enjoyed about their 'sensory walk'. Explain that they are going to write a poem about this walk, bringing in all of the senses.
- Display interactive activity 'Identifying the senses' on the CD-ROM and explain that this will help children to focus on their senses before writing.
- Look at the image of a market on a busy day and talk about what children can see and what they might hear and smell.
- Display the activity screen and read the names of the senses. Read the words underneath and invite individuals to drag and drop them into boxes.
- Focus on and recall sentence writing. Remind children about correct punctuation, such as full stops, capital letters, question marks and exclamation marks. Talk about breaking words down into separate sounds to help children spell them correctly. Emphasise the need to compose sentences orally before writing them and to re-read what they have written to check that it makes sense.

Assess

- Provide children with their written work and photographs relating to their walk and encourage them to refer to these when planning their poems.
- Suggest that they write headings for the five senses and begin by writing possible words underneath them. Recall that the term has focused on animals and that the walk was to record animals in the area. Emphasise that children should focus on this when writing their poem.
- Encourage them to be adventurous in their choice of adjectives and suggest that they use the 'mind's eye' technique to recall exactly what they observed.
- Divide into pairs so children can discuss some of the words that they intend to include in their poem, particularly adjectives referring to the senses.
- Choose poems at random to discuss with the class. Draw attention to and give praise for correct sentence punctuation and appropriate spelling of words.

Further practice

- Support those who have difficulty by encouraging them to think of words to describe one of the animals that they saw on the walk, for example, *woodlouse: hard, lots of legs, grey, busy, hiding, shiny*. Help them to pair these words and write simple sentences, for example, *A woodlouse is grey and hard; A woodlouse is shy and busy; A woodlouse runs on lots of legs*. Focus on simple punctuation and re-reading for sense.
- Challenge more confident learners to write separate verses for the beginning, middle and end of the walk, or for each animal seen. Encourage use of alliterative adjectives, such as *wandering woodlouse*.

All in order

- Cut out the pictures.
- Place the pictures in order and number each box in story order.

■ SCHOLASTIC
www.scholastic.co.uk

Name: _____ Date: _____

Order the animals

■ Cut out the pictures.
■ Stick them on paper in order.
■ Write a sentence underneath each one.

Name: _____   Date: _____

Animal descriptions

- Read the first sentence.
- Add a word ending with '-ing' to finish the second sentence.

A lion is a hunter.

A lion likes _____

A monkey is a jumper.

A monkey likes _____

A parrot can fly.

A parrot likes _____

A zebra can gallop.

A zebra likes _____

An ostrich is a fast runner.

An ostrich likes _____

A giraffe can stretch.

A giraffe likes _____

A goat can butt.

A goat likes _____

I can change the ending of a word so
that the sentence makes sense.

How did you do?

PHOTOCOPIABLE ■SCHOLASTIC www.scholastic.co.uk

Name: _____   Date: _____

Common pets

■ Cut out the pictures to use on a pictogram.

Plan a recount

- Use this page to plan your recount.
- Write notes in the boxes.
- Then write three sentences to use in your recount.

When?	
Who?	
What?	
Where?	
How?	

1. _____

_____

2. _____

_____

3. _____

_____

I can make notes and write sentences
for a recount.

How did you do?

PHOTOCOPIABLE   SCHOLASTIC
www.scholastic.co.uk

Plan our story

- Use this page to finish your group story plan.
- Make sure your sentences are in sequence and check your punctuation.

Title: _____

Main characters: _____

Setting: _____

Beginning: Write a sentence for the beginning of your story.

_____

_____

Middle: Write sentences for two of the events in your story.

1. _____

_____

2. _____

_____

End: Write a sentence to end your story.

_____

I can write a sequence of sentences and punctuate them correctly.

How did you do?

Name: _____   Date: _____

Finding animal words and adjectives

- Read these words from animal poems.
- Find some more animal words and adjectives in poems.
- Write them in the correct boxes on the page.
- Use them to help you write an animal poem.

Animals	My animals	Adjectives	My adjectives
dog		snappy	
snail		lumpy	
bat		bold	
frog		small	
giraffe		tall	
monkey		sad	
elephant		happy	
crocodile		old	
worm		grumpy	

I can find animal names and adjectives in a poem
and write them under the correct heading.

How did you do?

Choose the word

- Read these facts about the animals in *Handa's Surprise*.
- Choose the word with the correct spelling so that the sentence makes sense.

A monkey uses its long _____ to hang on to a tree.

| tale |
| tail |
| tayle |

An ostrich has two _____ and one claw on each foot.

| toes |
| tows |
| tose |

A zebra lives in a _____ with other zebras.

| heard |
| herd |
| hurd |

An elephant does not eat _____ .

| meet |
| meat |
| mete |

A giraffe has very big _____ .

| feat |
| feet |
| fete |

An antelope has a _____ of twisted horns.

| pear |
| per |
| pair |

A parrot often has _____, red and yellow and feathers.

| blew |
| bloo |
| blue |

A _____ is the name for a noise made by a goat.

| bleet |
| blete |
| bleat |

I can choose the word with the correct spelling to complete the sentences.

How did you do?

Sea and coast

This half-term's sea and coast theme begins with children exploring coastal settings and sharing activities based on *The Lighthouse Keeper's Lunch* by Ronda and David Armitage, including learning new vocabulary, playing word games, writing menus and inventing recipes. They read, learn, recite and enjoy water poems, creating music and inventive sound effects. Exploring *The Rainbow Fish* by Marcus Pfister involves children in discussing emotional dilemmas, and learning about underwater settings, particularly coral reefs. The final week consolidates learning through writing tasks related to forthcoming summer holidays. Prior learning is embedded and new learning opportunities introduced.

Expected prior learning
- Developing processes for learning new words.
- Know what recipes are.
- Begin to recognise adjectives and use them in written work, with correct endings.
- Familiar with features of information texts, recounts and stories.

Overview of progression
- Children encounter a wealth of new vocabulary in both fiction and non-fiction books and take part in activities to ensure they understand meanings clearly. They can then use these words in appropriate contexts in their writing.
- They know how to write the days of the week in the correct order.
- Work on adjectives ensures that children use them increasingly in written work.
- They begin to use the prefix 'un-' appropriately.
- Class, group and partner discussions relating to personal experiences enable children to recall events using all of their senses, and this helps them to write more descriptive poems of their own.
- As children become engaged in stories, they absorb ideas and then use their imaginations more effectively in their own creative writing.
- They understand how to check their writing by re-reading and are able to correct initial inaccuracies.

Creative context
- Children express ideas creatively using paint and collage, drama, music, small-world and role play.
- Children enhance their knowledge of coastal features, which links to geography.
- Children understand some different habitats, such as a coral reef, and some of the properties of water and light, which links to science.
- Aspects of order and sequence are included in activities involving days of the week, the passing of time and story events, which links to maths.

Preparation
The main two texts are *The Lighthouse Keeper's Lunch* by Ronda and David Armitage and *The Rainbow Fish* by Marcus Pfister.

You will also need:
A map of Britain; pictures of lighthouses; card; materials for a pulley; individual whiteboards and pens; materials for setting models; coloured pens; scissors; glue sticks; examples of diaries; cookery books; collage materials; biscuits and icing materials; wellington boots; non-fiction books about water, the coast and coral reefs; materials to make rainbows; streamers; paper raindrops; percussion instruments; shells and models of underwater creatures; seaside items.

On the CD-ROM you will find:
Media resources 'Water sounds and images', 'Tropical fish', 'Mystery image'; interactive activity 'Recount frame'; photocopiable pages 'Water', 'Puddle Play', 'Extract from *The Troll*'

Chapter at a glance

An overview of the chapter. For curriculum objective codes, please see pages 8–10.

Week	Lesson	Curriculum objectives	Summary of activities	Outcomes
1	1	RC: 2, 7, 13	Discuss experiences of the coast. Read and learn new vocabulary from *The Lighthouse Keeper's Lunch* and use it in sentences.	• Can discuss new vocabulary read and link to own experiences and use words in sentences.
	2	RC: 3, 6, 10, 11 WC: 2	Read and enjoy *The Lighthouse Keeper's Lunch*. Predict what might happen based on what is read. Identify vocabulary learned. Write sentences.	• Can predict what might happen based on what has been read. • Can compose sentences orally before writing.
	3	RWR: 3 WT: 9 WC: 2	Groups create pulleys with string and baskets. Move words from one end to the other. Make sentences with the words.	• Can read words and write applying spelling rules and guidelines. • Can compose sentences orally before writing.
	4	RC: 2, 3, 12	Create a model setting with lighthouse and cottage. Discuss resources needed. Link to own experiences.	• Can make links between story and own experiences. • Can participate in discussion.
	5	WT: 3, 9, 10 WC10	Order sentences. Write days of the week on cards and match with sentences. Write dictated sentence.	• Can write days of the week using capital letters. • Can write dictated sentence correctly.
2	1	RC: 3, 7 WT: 3 WC: 10	Revise story. Explore food eaten. Write Mr Grinling's diary detailing food. Use capitals for days of the week. Write in order.	• Can show familiarity with a story. • Can write days of the week in order with capital letters.
	2	WT: 14 WC: 10	Devise lunch list of ten numbered dishes for Mr Grinling to choose from. Use capital letters for days of the week.	• Can write days of the week using capital letters. • Can form digits from 0 to 9.
	3	RC: 7 WC: 2	Create 'mean mixtures' to put in sandwiches to warn off seagulls. Write recipe. Enjoy practical mixing and making model sandwiches.	• Can write recipe, composing sentences orally first. • Can use previous knowledge and background information.
	4	RC: 7 WT: 14 WC: 2	Write recipe for lighthouse sandwiches using template provided. Compose sentences orally first. Number instructions.	• Can write sentences, composed orally first. • Can form digits 0 to 9 in instructions.
	5	RWR: 3 RC: 7	Decorate biscuits to create iced sea biscuits. Taste in role as Mr Grinling. Pretend to eat mustard sandwiches as seagulls.	• Can blend sounds accurately. • Can follow instructions and attempt to read instructions themselves.
3	1	RC: 1, 5 WT: 5	Enjoy listening to and learning to recite water poems. Express personal opinions. Use letter names for alternative GPCs.	• Can listen to poems and discuss, sharing opinions. • Can use letter names for alternative GPCs.
	2	RC: 1, 2	Listen to books about water and explore water sounds. Make rainbows in trickling water and bubbles.	• Can listen to non-fiction read by teacher about properties of water. • Can link to own experiences and experiments.
	3	WC: 1, 2	Explore photographs of water and listen to water-related music and sound effects. Compose sentences of their impressions.	• Can compose sentences about water orally before writing. • Can discuss proposed writing with a partner.
	4	RC: 5 WT: 5	Invent rhyme strings for water poems, move to words and add sound effects. Write down using letter names when spelling.	• Can appreciate rhymes and recite by heart. • Can use letter names to distinguish spelling of rhyming words.
	5	RC: 2, 5	Link what they have read to experiences. Put on a performance, reciting, using percussion, dance and reading work.	• Can appreciate rhymes and poems and recite some in a performance. • Can link what they read to own experiences.
4	1	RC: 1, 2	Recall lighthouse setting. Compare with possible underwater settings. Explore non-fiction books. Create imaginary images.	• Can link reading of non-fiction books to own experiences. • Can discuss what is read to them.
	2	RC: 1, 2	Read, share and enjoy *The Rainbow Fish*. Discuss and link to own experiences.	• Can link reading of a story to own experiences and discuss what is read to them.
	3	RWR: 7 WC: 9	Identify contractions in book. Revise punctuation referring to book for examples.	• Can understand role of apostrophe in contractions. • Can apply punctuation in written work.
	4	RC: 1, 2 WT: 7 WC: 11	Discuss a character and revise use of prefix 'un-'. Take part in conscience alley, linking story problem to own experiences.	• Can listen, discuss and link story event to own experiences. • Can use prefix 'un-' and understand its effect.
	5	WT: 7 WC: 3, 11	Plan and write underwater narrative. Use adjectives with prefix 'un-' to define key attribute of character. Learn grammar while writing.	• Can sequence sentences to form a story. • Can use 'un-' prefix in relation to character and develop a story from this adjective.

Chapter at a glance

Week	Lesson	Curriculum objectives	Summary of activities	Outcomes
5	1	RC: 1, 7	Explore coral-reef setting in *The Rainbow Fish*. Learn about coral reefs from non-fiction, images and artefacts.	• Can use previous knowledge and teacher information to learn about coral reefs. • Can discuss non-fiction texts that are beyond own reading level.
	2	WC: 3, 4	Learn names of creatures that inhabit coral reefs. Research these and write sentences about them. Re-read for sense.	• Can write a sequence of sentences about a coral reef creature. • Can re-read to check that they make sense.
	3	WC: 4, 5, 6	Design a group poster, writing individual sentences and re-reading for sense. Read poster aloud to class and discuss.	• Can write individual sentences on poster and re-read for sense. • Can read writing aloud clearly and discuss.
	4	WC: 4, 5, 6	Design poster in pairs about previously researched creature. Read aloud writing clearly to class and discuss.	• Can write individual sentences on poster and re-read for sense. • Can read writing aloud clearly and discuss.
	5	RC: 2 WC: 4, 5	Create 'Coral reef discovery area'. Link the reading of the story and facts to experiences. Re-read writing for sense. Hold discussions.	• Can link fiction and non-fiction reading to own experiences. • Can re-read written work to check for sense.
6	1	WT: 8 WC: 8, 9, 12	Write seaside visit recount. Revise sentence grammar, including punctuation, using *and*, and past-tense endings.	• Can write recount, punctuating sentences, using *and*, and forming correct word endings to denote past tense.
	2	WT: 1, 5, 6 WC: 8	Sort seaside items into hoops. Write sentences about pairs of items (*and*). Involves reading and writing taught phonemes and plurals.	• Can join words with *and*. • Can read and write taught phonemes and distinguish alternative spellings. • Can apply spelling rules for plural markers.
	3	WT: 2, 7 WC: 11	Write words with/without prefix 'un-' on flags. Insert them into correct sandcastles. Use common exception words.	• Can use prefix 'un-' appropriately. • Can use common exception words.
	4	WC: 4, 7, 9, 10	Write a seaside story based on lesson 1's recount events. Punctuate, leave finger spaces and check writing for sense.	• Can use capitals correctly in a story. • Can punctuate accurately and leave spaces between words. • Can re-read to check for sense.
	5	WT: 2, 3 WC: 10	Write calendar entries for an ideal holiday week outlining each day's events. Revise spelling of common exception words.	• Can write days of the week in order with capital letters. • Can begin to write about future events. • Can spell common exception words.

Background knowledge

Future: Reference to future time can be marked in a number of different ways. All of these involve the use of a present tense verb. The future is referred to in this chapter when children write about what they plan to do in the coming holidays.

Week 1 lesson plans

The sea and coast theme for this half-term is introduced through children's shared experiences and by listening to *The Lighthouse Keeper's Lunch* by Ronda and David Armitage. The rich story vocabulary is explored and children use new words in sentences to demonstrate their understanding. They predict story events based on what is read, and identify vocabulary learned. A story-related word game using a simple pulley to transport words in baskets supports reading and sentence sequencing. Children become more familiar with the setting by creating a model, complete with lighthouse and cottage. Focus is on participating in discussion, taking turns and listening. Finally, children order sentences reflecting events and write the days of the week on cards to link with these events.

Expected outcomes
● All children can predict what might happen on the basis of what has been read so far.
● Most children can write the days of the week.
● Some children can learn new vocabulary and use it appropriately both orally and in their writing.

Curriculum objectives
● To explain clearly their understanding of what is read to them.
● To be encouraged to link what they read or hear read to their own experiences.
● To draw on what they already know or on background information and vocabulary provided by the teacher.

Resources
The Lighthouse Keeper's Lunch by Ronda and David Armitage; a map of Britain; pictures of lighthouses; photocopiable page 200 'New words'

1: Down by the sea

Introduction
● Explain that the children will be exploring the sea and coast.
● Display a large map of Great Britain and invite children to point out the sea and coastline. Explain that this is an island surrounded by sea. Make a list of natural coastal features, such as sandy bays, cliffs and rocks.

Whole-class work
● Ask children to share experiences of visiting the coast. If possible, identify and circle coastal places they have been to on the map. Talk about things they enjoyed during these visits, for example, splashing in the sea, searching for sea creatures with nets in rock pools, or sharing picnics on the sand.
● Explain that the story children will be exploring for the next two weeks is about a lighthouse. Spend time exploring some pictures of lighthouses. Talk about what they look like, their key features and why they are there.
● Hold up *The Lighthouse Keeper's Lunch* and explain that some of the words in the story might be new to them. Suggest that children become familiar with some of these words before reading the story.
● Display photocopiable page 200 'New words'. Explain what the words *adjective* and *verb* mean before continuing.
● Read the adjective, *scrumptious*, together, breaking it into syllables and tackling the '-ious' ending. Ask if children have heard of this word before. Read the definition and invite children to suggest sentences using this word.
● Continue in this way through the rest of the page. If children have difficulty making up sentences, provide them with an example.

Paired work
● Provide pairs of children with the photocopiable sheet to complete.
● Suggest they choose one or two new words from the page and make up a sentence of their own for each word.
● Ask the pairs to carefully read the word and its meaning together.
● Encourage lots of discussion and remind them to compose their sentences orally before writing them down. Promote taking turns to listen and speak, and encourage individuals to take into account the ideas of their partners.

Differentiation
● Provide less confident learners words from the story such as *napkin* and *herring*. Discuss these with them, saying the words in sentences to give a clear meaning.
● Challenge more confident learners with other new words from the story, such as *varmints, shanties, great gusto, racked their brains* and *lackaday* and ask them to put these words into sentences.

Review
● Bring children together and invite pairs to read their sentences.

Curriculum objectives
● To predict what might happen on the basis of what has been read so far.
● To make inferences on the basis of what is being said and done.
● To become very familiar with key stories, fairy stories and traditional tales, retelling them and considering their particular characteristics.
● To compose a sentence orally before writing it.
● To discuss word meanings, linking new meanings to those already known.

Resources
The Lighthouse Keeper's Lunch by Ronda and David Armitage; photocopiable page 200 'New words'

2: *The Lighthouse Keeper's Lunch*

Introduction
● Recall the previous discussions about lighthouses and coastal features.
● Display photocopiable page 200 'New words' and ask children which words they particularly like or remember. Leave it on display.

Whole-class work
● Show the children the front cover of *The Lighthouse Keeper's Lunch* and read the title together. Discuss the term lighthouse keeper, referring to other occupations, such as zookeeper, to clarify this. Ask questions to encourage children to predict what the story might be about.
● Read the story, pausing at intervals to predict what might happen next, for example, deciding what terrible thing happened when Mrs Grinling sent the basket down the wire on Monday, or predicting the ingenious plan.
● Pause after reading new vocabulary to discuss meaning, checking the displayed photocopiable page.

Paired work
● Invite pairs to practise using some of the new vocabulary in context by composing sentences to link with the story events. Suggest that they do this orally before writing sentences down to share during review time.

> **Differentiation**
> ● Support less confident learners as they compose sentences using the alternative words from lesson 1.

Review
● Bring the class together to discuss what they liked/disliked about the story and share their sentences.

Curriculum objectives
● To compose a sentence orally before writing it.
● To apply simple spelling rules and guidelines, as listed in Appendix 1.
● To read accurately by blending sounds in unfamiliar words containing GPCs that have been taught.

Resources
The Lighthouse Keeper's Lunch by Ronda and David Armitage; small squares of white card; string; cotton reels; sticky tape; small baskets; individual whiteboards; small strips of paper

3: Pulleys and baskets

Introduction
● Revisit the pages in the book where ropes, baskets and pulley are illustrated.
● Suggest using a similar idea in a game.

Whole-class work
● Thread a cotton reel onto string. Tape a basket to it. Ask two children to hold a length of string. Invite one child to lift the string so that the cotton reel slides to the other, who slides it back again.
● Explain that the game is to pass words from one group to another in the basket and arrange them into a sentence. This is written on paper, rolled up and returned in the basket. The group that returns the correct sentence first is the winner.
● Provide a sample sentence, for example: *Once there was a lighthouse keeper called Mr Grinling.*

Group work
● Pair similar-ability groups on adjacent tables and provide resources needed.
● Ask them to write their sentence words on separate cards and assemble them in order to check they make sense before putting them in the basket.
● Suggest children compose sentences orally first.
● Support children with sentence composition and word spelling.

Review
● Gather the class to talk about successes or difficulties encountered.
● Discuss how the activity helped revise and improve reading and writing skills.

4: A model setting

Introduction
- Read *The Lighthouse Keeper's Lunch* and explore the first double page depicting the lighthouse, rocky shore, cliffs and cottage.
- Discuss whether this is a strong story setting.

Whole-class work
- Suggest that children create a setting model to help to retell the story.
- Discuss where this could be located, for example, in a sand or builder's tray, on a carpet or on a table. Talk about the merits of each location, for example, sand could be included in a builder's tray, a table draped in grey fabric alongside the carpet could form cliffs, and items could be taped to a table top.
- Once location is decided, list possible creations on the board, for example, a cottage made from bricks, a string pulley, a plastic bottle 'lighthouse' weighted with sand and lit by a winking torch, a fabric or crumpled tissue sea.

Group work
- Allocate separate tasks to the groups, for example building the cottage, making the lighthouse and erecting a pulley.
- Suggest that they discuss their ideas before gathering resources they need. Encourage them to discuss and modify any initial decisions they make about suitable materials which then prove inadequate in practice.

Review
- Gather the class to retell the story together using the setting and props. Discuss how this re-enactment helps them to recall events.

Curriculum objectives
- To be encouraged to link what they read or hear read to their own experiences.
- To become very familiar with key stories, fairy stories and traditional tales, retelling them and considering their particular characteristics.
- To participate in discussion about what is read to them, taking turns and listening to what others say.

Resources
The Lighthouse Keeper's Lunch by Ronda and David Armitage; coloured and white paper and card; lengths of fabric; recycled materials such as boxes and cartons; paint; PVA glue; sticky tape; small-world equipment, including boats, characters, animals and birds; string; construction bricks; shells and stones; sand

5: All in order

Introduction
- Read *The Lighthouse Keeper's Lunch*. Focus on what happens each day, and reinforce this, as they will need to remember the order of events.

Whole-class work
- Dictate a sentence about a story event for children to write on their whiteboards, for example, *Mrs Grinling put the lunch in the basket*. When children have finished, write it on the board and read it together for self-checking.
- Ask children to write the days of the week on their whiteboards and check spelling and punctuation with an adjacent child.
- Display photocopiable page 201 'Tell the story' and read the sentences. Ask what children notice about their order.
- Explain that pairs of children will be making days of the week cards and arranging their sentences next to them in the correct order.
- Read the instructions, clarifying that the empty box is to write about Sunday's events, as this is not mentioned in the story.

Paired work
- Supply pairs with the resources they need, including the photocopiable sheet, to create days of the week and sentence cards.
- Remind them about using capital letters correctly.
- Once they have completed their card sets, ask them to match them in the correct order.

Review
- Ask pairs to self-check their work as you go through the sentences.
- Share some sentences about Sunday.

Curriculum objectives
- To use a capital letter for names of people, places, the days of the week, and the personal pronoun *I*.
- To spell the days of the week.
- To write from memory simple sentences dictated by the teacher that include words using the GPCs and common exception words taught so far.
- To apply simple spelling rules and guidelines, as listed in Appendix 1.

Resources
The Lighthouse Keeper's Lunch by Ronda and David Armitage; individual whiteboards; photocopiable page 201 'Tell the story'; card squares; coloured and black pens; scissors; glue sticks

Expected outcomes
- All children can form digits 0 to 9.
- Most children can use describing words in their sentences.
- Some children can write an accurate sequence of instructions.

Curriculum objectives
- To draw on what they already know or on background information and vocabulary provided by the teacher.
- To become very familiar with key stories, fairy stories and traditional tales, retelling them and considering their particular characteristics.
- To spell the days of the week.
- To use a capital letter for the days of the week.

Resources
The Lighthouse Keeper's Lunch by Ronda and David Armitage; children's story ordering cards made from photocopiable page 201 'Tell the story' (week 1, lesson 5); examples of diaries such as office diaries, page-a-day and week-to-view; photocopiable page 202 'Mr Grinling's diary'

Week 2 lesson plans

This week, children familiarise themselves with food mentioned in *The Lighthouse Keeper's Lunch*. They write Mr Grinling's diary page, detailing his lunch each day, and follow this by devising a list of numbered lunch dishes for him to choose from. Focus is on using capital letters and forming digits. Children invent 'mean mixtures' to put in sandwiches to warn off seagulls, and enjoy messy mixing to make models of these. Recipes for lighthouse sandwiches are written, with focus on composing sentences orally and numbering instructions. Finally, children create iced sea biscuits, with focus on reading instructions. Role play encourages their understanding of feelings as Mr Grinling enjoys his iced biscuits and the seagulls eat mustard sandwiches.

1: Mr Grinling's diary

Introduction
- Recall *The Lighthouse Keeper's Lunch* and cards children made to order the story and match with the days of the week.
- Explain that children will be referring to these to help them complete a page of Mr Grinling's diary.
- Share their experiences of diaries, for example, they may have noticed a parent writing an appointment in one.
- Discuss how some people keep more detailed diaries of daily events.
- Pass around the diaries and discuss their probable purposes.

Whole-class work
- Find story evidence to reflect how much Mr Grinling likes food, for example, the delicious lunches he enjoys and his wide smile as he prepares to tackle his leisurely meal on the final page.
- Suggest that he might keep a record of his lunches in a diary to remind him of what Mrs Grinling prepared and what he received.
- Display and read photocopiable page 202 'Mr Grinling's diary'. Talk about which day it should start on. As Sunday is not mentioned in the story, the children can put this at the beginning or end as they choose. Discuss what he may have enjoyed for his lunch that day, recalling their ideas from the cards.
- Read the list of helpful words together and discuss why *Hamish* and *napkin* are included. Talk about the part they play in the story events.
- Encourage children to include expressive words and correct punctuation.

Paired work
- Ask children to work in pairs to support one another with sentence ideas, using their cards from the previous lesson to help. Do not give them their days of the week cards as the aim is to get them to write these independently.
- Invite them to fill in the photocopiable sheet individually. If children are struggling to fit their sentences into the spaces, suggest they use the sheet to make notes and provide additional paper for them to write their diary.
- Suggest they use the word *and*, or write separate sentences, when they have more than one dish to include in a day.

> **Differentiation**
> - Ask those needing support to fill in the days in the small column in order, supporting with spelling, and to draw a picture of Mr Grinling's lunch, or lack of it.

Review
- Invite children to read their diaries to the rest of the class for comment. Praise and recall correct spelling and punctuation.
- Discuss how creating a diary has helped children memorise the sequence of story events.

■ SCHOLASTIC

Curriculum objectives
• To use a capital letter for names of people, places, the days of the week, and the personal pronoun *I*.
• To form digits 0 to 9.

Resources
The Lighthouse Keeper's Lunch by Ronda and David Armitage; a selection of cookery books with clear photographs and simple step-by-step instructions for dishes, for example, *Children's Step-by-Step Cookbook* by Angela Wilkes, *Children's First Cookbook: Have Fun in the Kitchen* by Annabel Karmel; large sheets of paper; black pens; glue sticks

2: Mr Grinling's menu

Introduction
• Recall previous lessons involving Mr Grinling's lunches. Ask the children if they think Mrs Grinling decides what to put in the basket, or whether she discusses this with Mr Grinling.
• Show the cookbooks and share some of the photographs.

Whole-class work
• Explain that Mrs Grinling is going away next week and needs someone to prepare Mr Grinling's lunches.
• Suggest that groups of children come up with seven lunch dishes each.

Group work
• Ask groups to look through cookery books, or invent their own dishes.
• Invite them to write the title of each dish with a picture and description.
• Once they have done this, they can arrange the dishes in the order they think they should be eaten on a large sheet of paper, write the corresponding day beside each one and number them accordingly.
• Hang the finished sheets along the wall and invite a staff member to pose as Mr Grinling and come and choose his favourite menu.

Review
• Invite the class to discuss the menu selections and comment on which one they think Mr Grinling would prefer and why. Praise accurate number formation and use of capitals.

Curriculum objectives
• To compose a sentence orally before writing it.
• To draw on what they already know or on background information and vocabulary provided by the teacher.

Resources
The Lighthouse Keeper's Lunch by Ronda and David Armitage; coloured paper and pens; paint, PVA glue; collage items such as seeds, grains, twigs, pasta; thick card or vinyl flooring cut into sandwich shapes

3: Mean mixtures

Introduction
• Read *The Lighthouse Keeper's Lunch*. Discuss how the Grinlings stopped the seagulls eating their food.
• Ask children what they know about mustard. Look for clues in the seagull illustrations and the sounds the seagulls make.

Whole-class work
• Suggest that children invent 'mean mixture' sandwich fillings to warn off seagulls. Emphasise what not to use, as no one wants sick seagulls!
• Talk about tastes children really dislike, such as sour fruit or salty soup. Write these on the board. List individual dislikes, such as eggs, fish and sprouts.
• Discuss what seagulls might dislike.

Group work
• Suggest that groups invent their own 'mean mixture' for the sandwiches, listing ingredients and composing sentences orally before writing, for example, *Our mean mixture is made with rotten sprouts and sour plums.*
• Have fun making model sandwiches, mixing gooey potions of paint thickened with PVA glue to represent the described filling, and adding texture with seeds, grains and twigs. Spread the mixture thinly on the cut sandwich shapes and leave to dry.
• Create a display of the sandwiches with the children's written sentences.
• Add some painted seagulls with speech bubbles reading YUK! UGH! AAAK!
• Entitle the display *Mean mixtures*.

Review
• Bring the class together to discuss the resulting display and comment on the most successful ideas.

Curriculum objectives
● To compose a sentence orally before writing it.
● To draw on what they already know or on background information and vocabulary provided by the teacher.
● To form digits 0 to 9.

Resources
The Lighthouse Keeper's Lunch by Ronda and David Armitage; photocopiable page 203 'A lighthouse sandwich recipe'

4: Lighthouse sandwiches

Introduction
● Talk about sandwiches the children have enjoyed and their favourite fillings. Ask questions to encourage more detailed responses, for example, about the type and colour of bread they prefer.

Whole-class work
● Explore the lighthouse sandwich picture in *The Lighthouse Keeper's Lunch*. Try to decide what is inside it. Draw attention to the layers and colours. Point out that some ingredients look like salad items, and perhaps there is some cheese.
● Focus on the sandwich title and consider the reason for this. Maybe Mr Grinling only has this sandwich when he is at the lighthouse? Discuss possible ingredients for a sandwich named *lighthouse*. Perhaps it has a coastal link, such as fish, crab, prawns, tuna or salmon.
● Discuss savoury spreads, such as salad cream and mayonnaise, and sweet spreads such as jam and honey. Consider peanut butter or chopped egg.
● Display photocopiable page 203 'A lighthouse sandwich recipe'. Read the instructions together so that children understand what to do.

Paired work
● Provide same-ability pairs with the photocopiable sheet and suggest they discuss their ideas before completing it individually.
● Encourage focus on numbering the stages of sandwich making.

Review
● Ask children to share their sandwich recipes with the class. Encourage discussion about the most interesting and those with the easiest instructions.

Curriculum objectives
● To draw on what they already know or on background information and vocabulary provided by the teacher.
● To read accurately by blending sounds in unfamiliar words containing GPCs that have been taught.

Resources
The Lighthouse Keeper's Lunch by Ronda and David Armitage; icing sugar; hard round biscuits suitable for icing; utensils for mixing and piping icing; card circles; coloured pens; model 'mean mixture' sandwiches made for display in lesson 3

5: Contrasting reactions

Introduction
● Read *The Lighthouse Keeper's Lunch* and explore the picture of iced sea biscuits. Identify the iced images of an anchor, lighthouse and ship. Explain the meaning of *anchor*. Ask children to suggest other sea images that could be iced onto biscuits.
● Encourage the children to think how tasty these biscuits would be. Then turn to the page depicting the seagulls eating the mustard sandwiches and discuss how unpleasant these would taste. Read the sounds they are making together and have fun making these sounds, squawking and flapping imaginary wings.

Whole-class work
● Show the packet of icing sugar and utensils. Ask if children have made icing at home. Explain that they are going to decorate iced sea biscuits.

Group work
● Divide children into groups, with one group at a time making and icing their biscuits while others practise their icing designs on card circles.
● Once completed, suggest they pretend to be seagulls eating their 'mean mixture' sandwiches, or Mr Grinling tucking into delicious iced sea biscuits.
● Work at the icing table, encouraging children to read and follow instructions on the icing packet.

Review
● Ask the class to sit in their groups in a large circle pretending to be seagulls eating the model 'mean mixture' sandwiches.
● Put their own biscuits in front of them to enjoy, this time contrasting their body language to that of satisfied and contented Mr Grinling.

Week 3 lesson plans

This week children explore water-themed poetry. They listen to poems and learn to recite one together. The poems are discussed, and opinions shared. Non-fiction books introduce water experiments involving light and sound, and practical explorations follow, with children creating rainbows and water sounds. Photographs, music and sound effects encourage a creative approach to their learning, and children compose sentences describing their impressions of these. They follow this by inventing rhyme strings for water poems, adding body movements and sound effects, with focus on using letter names to distinguish spelling of rhyming words. Finally, children link these experiences by putting on a performance involving reciting poems, using percussion, dancing and movement, and reading written work.

Expected outcomes
- All children can link what they read or hear read to their own experiences.
- Most children can write poems based on experiences.
- Some children can effectively introduce music, movement and sound to enhance their poetry.

Curriculum objectives
- To listen to and discuss a wide range of poems, stories and non-fiction at a level beyond that at which they can read independently.
- To learn to appreciate rhymes and poems, and to recite some by heart.
- To use letter names to distinguish between alternative spellings of the same sound.

Resources
Photocopiable page 207 'Raindrops'; photocopiable pages 'Water' and 'Puddle Play' from the CD-ROM; wellington boots

1: Water poems

Introduction
- Remind children of this half-term's sea theme. Explain that they are going to explore and learn some new poems about water.
- Invite them to recall poems and rhymes they know about water, such as 'Rain, rain, go away!' and 'Dr Foster went to Gloucester'. Recite them together.

Whole-class work
- Read 'Water' by Meish Goldish, on photocopiable page 'Water' from the CD-ROM, explaining the meaning of the word *faucet* before you begin. Suggest that they close their eyes as they listen to the words so that pictures can form in their 'mind's eye'. Pause after each rhyming couplet so that children can fully absorb and imagine the words they have heard.
- Ask the children to open their eyes and share initial reactions to the poem. What did they particularly like or dislike about it? What sort of images popped into their minds? Did the poem help them to recall any facts about water, for example, where we find it or how it moves?
- Display the poem and ask children to circle the rhyming words. Talk about the pattern they make. Identify those rhymes with alternative graphemes, and use letter names to distinguish between them.
- Explain unfamiliar vocabulary, such as *creek* and *lagoon*.
- Underline words that describe the movement of water, such as *drip-drip*, *rushing*, *raining down*, *gushing*.
- Display and read photocopiable page 'Puddle Play' from the CD-ROM, imagining you are playing in puddles. If possible, go outside in the rain wearing wellingtons (or create puddles by pouring water on the ground), encouraging children to look into puddles to see reflections. Talk about what the poet means by *under my feet are trees and clouds*.
- Try saying the poem together, inventing actions to match the words.
- Display and read photocopiable page 207 'Raindrops'. Discuss its shape and why the poet has presented it like this.
- Read it once more, this time paying attention to the way words are pronounced, for example, *slip down* (slow sliding voice), *splashing* (emphasis on the first syllable), *thunder-crashing* (emphasising *crashing* with a clap).

Group work
- Provide groups of four with photocopiable page 'Water' and ask them to learn the poem. Suggest that they split the lines between them, for example, with three children learning four lines each, and one learning two.
- Once they are ready, suggest that they practise reciting the whole poem.

Review
- Bring the groups together to recite their poems.
- Finish with the whole class reciting together. Share views on favourite poems from the three they have explored.

Curriculum objectives
● To listen to and discuss a wide range of poems, stories and non-fiction at a level beyond that at which they can read independently.
● To be encouraged to link what they read or hear read to their own experiences.

Resources
Non-fiction books about water, for example, *Science Experiments with Water* by Sam Rosenfeld, *Experiments with water (One-Stop Science)* by Angela Royston; bubble liquid; glasses; small mirror; torch; water tray; lengths of narrow plastic pipe; straws; pouring containers; clipboards

2: Rainbows and reflections

Introduction
● Recall the water poems children enjoyed in the previous lesson. Explain that they are going to discover some of the amazing things water can do.
● Share relevant pages in non-fiction books about creating sound and light effects using water.

Whole-class work
● Ask children if they know how a rainbow is formed and discuss their responses before reading a clear explanation in a non-fiction book.
● Demonstrate how to create a classroom rainbow. Fill a glass almost to the top with water and rest a small mirror at an angle inside. Darken the room and shine a torch onto the mirror. Look around to find the rainbow. Try moving the torch beam to see what happens.
● Discuss how raindrops create the same effect when sunlight shines on them.

Group work
● Set up outdoor areas to visit where groups can make rainbows.
● Set up sound-making areas where groups can create interesting sounds by pouring water from different heights onto varying surfaces, blowing air through pipes in a water tray, and creating chimes with a row of glasses filled with varying amounts of water.

Review
● Invite children to share their observation notes and discuss their discoveries.

Curriculum objectives
● To compose a sentence orally before writing it.
● To say out loud what they are going to write about.

Resources
Media resource 'Water sounds and images' on the CD-ROM; blue ribbons, streamers or chiffon; raindrop shapes cut out of paper

3: Impressions of water

Introduction
● Take children into the hall. Explain that artists, poets, photographers and composers often experience water in unusual ways that enable them to create powerful impressions to alter our emotions.

Whole-class work
● Ask children to close their eyes and listen to some music. Open 'Water sounds and images' on the CD-ROM and play *Air* from Handel's *Water Music*. Invite comments on how it makes them feel and explain that it represents calm water. Ask them to open their eyes and to look at the calm water image on the first screen. Encourage children to decide whether the music reflects this image.
● Repeat with *Scene by the Brook* from Beethoven's *Symphony No. 6 'The Pastoral'*, displaying the second screen on the media resource. Clarify the meaning of 'brook'. Ask children to imagine water burbling as it passes small stones.
● Listen to the dramatic *Play of the waves* from Debussy's *La Mer*. Imagine watching tremendous waves crashing on shore as you explore music and the third screen of the media resource together.
● Invite children to create dance movements to accompany the music.

Paired work
● Invite pairs to listen to the sound effects that accompany the media resource images. Explain the types of water they represent.
● Suggest they divide a piece of paper into three and make notes about how these sounds make them feel, and the pictures that come into their minds.
● Ask them to write three short sentences on raindrop shapes describing the different water conditions, composing and discussing them first.

Review
● Invite the class to read their sentences and discuss words used.

4: Sounds and movements

Introduction
● Display photocopiable page 207 'Raindrops' and read it again. Comment on regular spelling of rhyming words, such as *drip, slip, splishing, splashing*.
● Display photocopiable page 'Water' and comment on alternative spellings of the same sound, for example: *creek/leak, lake/break*.
● Ask children to use letter names to distinguish between these spellings.

Whole-class work
● Make up a short rhyming string, for example, *plip, plop, slip, slop* and invite the children to say it with you.
● Display the image of waves on the third screen of media resource 'Water sounds and images' on the CD-ROM. Make up a short string to depict the wave crashing on shore, such as *swoosh, CRASH! splosh, SMASH!* Follow this with a string depicting the wave retreating, *TUMBLE, rattle, STUMBLE, prattle*. Put the two together and invite children to recite them.
● Try adding percussion, for example, cymbals or drums for crashing waves and maracas or rainmakers for retreating waves.

Group work
● Invite groups to invent short water poems, using xylophone, chime-bars or coconut-shell accompaniments.
● Suggest that they write their poems down, presenting them in effective ways, for example, in a wave shape.

Review
● Encourage the class to read their poems and discuss the effect that adding sound effects had on their appreciation of rhymes.

5: Enhancing poems

Introduction
● Talk about how exploring water creatively, using sound effects, photographs, music, percussion and dance, has helped children to express their ideas and inspired them to want to discover more, both about poetry and about water.

Whole-class work
● Suggest putting on a performance for assembly to demonstrate the different directions their explorations have taken them.
● Write a possible list of items with quirky titles to include in the performance programme, for example: *Raindrop Recollections, Super Sounds* (using percussion effects), *Dreams and Dancing* (free movement to water music).

Group work
● Ask groups to practise one of the events on the programme.
● Ensure that each group has access to the appropriate resources needed for their performance. Be ready to find additional items if requested.
● Once the groups are ready, invite them to perform to the class.
● Encourage constructive comments about how events could be improved.

Paired work
● Encourage pairs to design official programmes. Use all designs equally, photocopying the number you need.

Review
● Put on the planned performance to the invited audience and discuss successes and items for improvement afterwards.

Curriculum objectives
● To be encouraged to link what they read or hear to their own experiences.
● To listen to and discuss a wide range of poems, stories and non-fiction at a level beyond that at which they can read independently.

Resources
The Lighthouse Keeper's Lunch by Ronda and David Armitage; non-fiction books about coastal and underwater environments, for example, *Seaside Nature* by Paul Humphrey and *At the Seaside: Look What I Found!* by Paul Humphrey, *Under the Sea* by Alastair Smith, *Under the Sea Little Facts* by Ruth Owen; a diagram depicting above and below the water (water cycle diagrams are ideal); large sheets of coloured paper; coloured pens; collage items; tissue; PVA glue

Week 4 lesson plans

Children start the week by recalling the coastal setting of *The Lighthouse Keeper's Lunch* and contrasting this with possible underwater settings for the next story. They explore non-fiction books for ideas for their pictures of imaginary underwater settings. *The Rainbow Fish* is introduced and enjoyed, with focus on contractions in the text, revision of punctuation and learning the grammar of word structure. Children discuss the main character and use the prefix 'un-' to describe some of his negative characteristics. Taking part in conscience alley helps them to link a story problem to their own experiences. Finally, they plan and write their own short story set underwater, using adjectives with prefix 'un-' to describe their characters.

1: Watery settings

Introduction
● Recall *The Lighthouse Keeper's Lunch* and share images that show the setting.
● Talk about the key features of a rocky coastal setting, such as cliffs, rocks and rock pools, based on previous reading and own experiences. Ask individuals to suggest one of these and write it on the board under the heading, *Coastal features*.
● Discuss possible plants and animals to be found there, again recalling previous experiences. Write these under *Coastal plants and creatures*.
● Consider whether coasts look the same throughout the world, using evidence from past experiences, such as holidays, and facts learned from books and the internet. Consider the different wildlife to be found in extremely contrasting environments, such as the Arctic coast and the Mediterranean.
● Based on comments during these discussions, read passages from the chosen non-fiction books and explore any pictures of environmental features.

Whole-class work
● Explain that children are going to take their explorations from along the coast to discovering what is beneath the waves in preparation for sharing a story that is set under the sea.
● Invite speculations about what this might be like, asking questions about possible story features, such as hidden caves and deep dark areas.
● Talk about the creatures and plants to be found there. Question whether they will be the same in all waters, or whether sealife varies according to whether the sea is shallow and warm or deep and icy.
● Show children the books depicting underwater scenes and read a short passage linked to their interests that you know will attract them.
● Talk about the pictures and range of sealife to be found.
● Suggest that children create group pictures contrasting the coastal setting for *The Lighthouse Keeper's Lunch* above the waves and the imagined environment below the waves where the story they are going to share is set.
● Show some diagrammatic representations of this in books, for example, with the surface of the sea indicated as a wavy line and the coastal rocks above continuing to the seabed.

Group work
● Suggest that mixed-ability groups begin by exploring books and drawing a diagram of how their picture will look. Ask them to annotate this with colours and labels to show the materials they will use.
● Encourage children to be adventurous and to use their ideas freely. Remind them that their picture represents a story setting rather than real features.

Review
● Bring the class together to discuss what they have learned about using their own experiences and finding information in non-fiction books.

Curriculum objectives
● To be encouraged to link what they read or hear to their own experiences.
● To listen to and discuss a wide range of poems, stories and non-fiction at a level beyond that at which they can read independently.

Resources
The Rainbow Fish by Marcus Pfister; media resource 'Tropical fish' on the CD-ROM

2: *The Rainbow Fish*

Introduction
● Recall the previous lesson's discussion about the underwater setting.
● Explore the cover of *The Rainbow Fish* and read the title. Discuss the appearance of the fish and ask whether the children have ever seen such a brightly coloured fish in the sea around our coast.
● Introduce the term *tropical fish*, and explain the meaning of *tropical*.
● Display media resource 'Tropical fish' on the CD-ROM as a clue to where the story is set.

Whole-class work
● Read the story aloud, pausing to share the illustrations and ask children to name the creatures and plants.
● Stop at significant points to encourage children to predict what happens next, for example: *Do you think the Rainbow Fish will give the little blue fish one of his scales? Why did the other fish turn away from the Rainbow Fish?*
● Discuss the characters and pose relevant questions. Ask: *Why was the Rainbow Fish so lonely? What did the wise octopus advise the Rainbow Fish to do about this?*

Paired work
● Invite pairs to share initial impressions of the story and make notes to feed back at review time.
● Encourage them to note what they like or dislike about the setting, characters and events, and to consider the importance of the illustrations.

Review
● Bring children together to share their opinions and discuss the story further.

Curriculum objectives
● To read words with contractions and understand that the apostrophe represents the omitted letter(s).
● To begin to punctuate sentences using a capital letter and a full stop, question mark or exclamation mark.

Resources
The Rainbow Fish by Marcus Pfister; photocopiable page 204 'Revising punctuation'

3: Contractions and punctuation

Introduction
● Recall previous lessons involving contractions and the purpose of the apostrophe. Discuss how contractions are used in everyday speech and when writing in a relaxed style.
● On the board, write sentences with and without contractions, for example: *After lunch we'll be going outside; If it rains we will stay in.* Invite children to identify the contractions and discuss which letters have been replaced.

Whole-class work
● Re-read *The Rainbow Fish*, this time drawing attention to contractions. Read the sentence: *Why doesn't anybody like me?* Say it as it is written and then repeat without the contraction. Discuss what happens to the sense of the sentence.
● Locate question marks in the story and revise their use.
● Do the same with exclamation marks, for example: *Come and play with us!*

Paired work
● Provide pairs with photocopiable page 204 'Revising punctuation'.
● Remind them that the sentences could end with a full stop, a question mark or an exclamation mark.
● Suggest that they discuss the page and their proposed responses before completing it individually.

Review
● Reassemble the class. Display the page on the board and go through it together, asking pairs to check each other's work.

Curriculum objectives
● To be encouraged to link what they read or hear read to their own experiences.
● To listen to and discuss a wide range of poems, stories and non-fiction at a level beyond that at which they can read independently.
● To use the prefix 'un-'.
● To learn the grammar for Year 1 in Appendix 2.

Resources
The Rainbow Fish by Marcus Pfister

4: Conscience alley

Introduction
● Read *The Rainbow Fish* again, focusing on the main character.
● Ask the children to think of words to describe him, for example, *proud, lonely, unhappy, selfish*. Remind them that these are known as *adjectives* and discuss why these words are applicable.
● Draw attention to the word *unhappy*. Recall the use of the prefix 'un-' to create a word meaning the opposite of the original, for example, *kind/unkind*. Use starter activity 9 'Add my prefix' to revise this, if necessary.
● Write adjectives that start with 'un-' on the board, such as: *unhappy, unkind, unselfish, unfair, unlucky, unhealthy, unfit, unusual, unpopular*.
● Ask children to highlight words that could apply to the Rainbow Fish.

Whole-class work
● Discuss why the Rainbow Fish is lonely and unhappy. Talk about his dilemma about not knowing whether to share his special scales.
● Set up conscience alley with half the class persuading the Rainbow Fish to share his scales, and the other half opposite persuading him to keep them.
● Take on the role of the Rainbow Fish and walk between the lines, listening to their persuasive comments.
● Once you arrive at the end, sit in the hot-seat to be questioned and reach your conclusion.
● Invite class comments about your response and what they would have done.

Review
● Bring children together to discuss whether this is a useful way to solve a problem, and the benefits of considering both sides of a dilemma.

Curriculum objectives
● To sequence sentences to form short narratives.
● To learn the grammar for Year 1 in Appendix 2.
● To use the prefix 'un-'.

Resources
The Rainbow Fish by Marcus Pfister

5: Underwater stories

Introduction
● Recall *The Rainbow Fish*, and how you explored the prefix 'un-'.
● Write the adjectives used in the last lesson on the board.
● Explain that you would like children to invent sea creature characters that these adjectives could apply to, such as: *The unlucky octopus; The unusual whale*.

Whole-class work
● Suggest children write an underwater story featuring a character described by one of the adjectives on the board.
● Revise the features of a good story, such as strong characters, appropriate language, an interesting setting and exciting events. Recall the need for a definite beginning, middle and end.

Paired work
● Encourage children to discuss character ideas and features for their underwater setting with a partner.
● Consider possible dilemmas for their main characters, influenced by their choices of 'un-' adjectives, for example, an unkind character might have something happen and realise the effect this unkindness has on others.
● Ask children to write at least three sentences with illustrations. Support less confident pairs with this where necessary.

Review
● Invite children to read their stories to the class giving reasons for their choice of character adjectives.
● Discuss how explorations into *The Rainbow Fish* and *The Lighthouse Keeper's Lunch* have influenced their ideas for stories with a water connection.

Week 5 lesson plans

Following explorations of *The Rainbow Fish*, children use their previous knowledge, teacher information, non-fiction books, images and artefacts to discover more about coral reefs. They learn the names of the creatures that live there through their own research. Focus is on writing a sequence of sentences about one of these creatures, and re-reading to check that their writing makes sense. Groups of children design Rainbow Fish posters, and read these aloud to the class, and pairs of children design posters about the creatures they researched earlier. Both posters involve sentence writing. Finally, all work is showcased as children create a coral reef discovery area in the classroom, involving the revision of label, sign, caption and sentence writing.

Expected outcomes
● All children can use non-fiction books to discover information.
● Most children can check their writing and improve it.
● Some children can effectively introduce new vocabulary and facts they have learned into their written work.

Curriculum objectives
● To listen to and discuss a wide range of poems, stories and non-fiction at a level beyond that at which they can read independently.
● To draw on what they already know or on background information and vocabulary provided by the teacher.

Resources
The Rainbow Fish by Marcus Pfister; media resources 'Mystery image' and 'Tropical fish' on the CD-ROM; books about coral reefs, for example, *Coral Reef: Around the Clock with the Animals of the Ocean* by Caroline Bingham, *Coral Reef (What Can I See?)*; real or imitation coral (obtainable from pet shops); shells; models of coral reef animals, such as clown fish, crabs, shrimps and turtles; wild and domesticated animal models; real items associated with a coral reef, such as natural sponge and cuttlefish bone; everyday items, such as a spoon and pencil; drawstring bag; creative media, such as paint, collage, clay, recycled materials

1: The coral reef

Introduction
● Read *The Rainbow Fish* and look closely at the images of the setting. Explain that this is a special habitat called a *coral reef*, and ask children to share anything they already know about the term.
● Display the media resource 'Mystery image' on the CD-ROM. With the aid of short non-fiction passages read aloud, explain how a coral reef is formed over a very long time, emphasising that it is a growing, changing structure.
● Talk about how the colourful plant-like structures are actually deposits made by the hard outside skeletons of tiny creatures. Clarify the meaning of *outside skeleton* with reference to the children's *inside skeleton*.
● Compare the different tropical fish in *The Rainbow Fish* illustrations. Explore images of these colourful fish in media resource 'Tropical fish' on the CD-ROM.
● Ask children to name other creatures in *The Rainbow Fish*, such as *anemone, snail, starfish, crab, octopus* and *lobster*.
● Compare the attractive coral variations in *The Rainbow Fish*, non-fiction books and the media resource 'Mystery image' on the CD-ROM.

Whole-class work
● Ask the children to move into a circle.
● Put some model coral-reef creatures and real items, along with wild animal models and everyday items, into a drawstring bag.
● Play a game involving taking something out and deciding whether it would be found in a coral reef. Help children with unusual items and extend their knowledge with interesting facts.
● Arrange the coral-reef items on a table to use for reference in their work.
● Suggest that children represent the knowledge they are collecting together about coral reefs by making a group picture or model.
● Run through a few ideas for techniques, for example, creating an underwater scene in a box with clay models, or sticking shiny materials onto a painted picture to represent the reflections of the shimmering fish.

Group work
● Divide children into groups.
● Arrange reference books on a table adjacent to the coral-reef items from the bag game. Suggest that one child from each group handle these with clean hands, passing on information and showing images to individuals.
● Observe children as they are working, supporting with facts and suggestions, such as making shoals of tiny shiny fish with cellophane on card.
● Allow time for groups to visit one another's coral reefs before review time.

Review
● Gather the class to discuss things they have learned about coral reefs through exploring books, images, playing games and listening to explanations.
● Discuss how working creatively together to represent new words and facts helps to clarify them in an exciting way.

Curriculum objectives
● To sequence sentences to form short narratives.
● To re-read what they have written to check that it makes sense.

Resources
Books about coral reefs used in lesson 1; media resources 'Tropical fish' and 'Mystery image' on the CD-ROM; small-world models of coral-reef creatures

2: Life on a coral reef

Introduction
● Ask children to share information they remember from lesson 1, and to say which facts they found particularly interesting.

Whole-class work
● Ask children to name as many coral-reef creatures as they can. Write them in a list on the board as they say each one.
● Once they have exhausted suggestions, add any obvious missing ones.
● Your list should include at least twenty examples, such as: *clown fish, crab, shrimp, cuttlefish, sea turtle, sea anemone, puffer fish, shark, eel, sea snake, octopus, parrotfish, jellyfish, sponges, starfish, shrimp, lobster, snail, clam, ray.*
● Write these on strips of paper and put them in a box.

Paired work
● Invite pairs of children to pick two names each from the box to research using available resources (write some names more than once if necessary so that you have enough for everybody).
● Write these questions on the board: *What does this creature look like? What does it eat? What is the most interesting fact you could find about it?*
● Ask children to answer the questions about each creature, writing their sentences in the correct order.
● Remind them to re-read sentences to check they make sense.

Review
● Invite the pairs to read their sentences to the class. Praise good sequencing and interesting content.

Curriculum objectives
● To re-read what they have written to check that it makes sense.
● To read aloud their writing clearly enough to be heard by their peers and the teacher.
● To discuss what they have written with the teacher or other children.

Resources
The Rainbow Fish by Marcus Pfister; coral reef books; media resource 'Mystery image' on the CD-ROM; real or online examples of posters; children's sentences about coral reef creatures from lesson 2; large sheets of coloured paper; shiny collage materials such as sequins, cellophane, foil; PVA glue; coloured pens

3: Rainbow Fish posters

Introduction
● Explore the cover of *The Rainbow Fish*. Ask children to share their knowledge about where the Rainbow Fish lives, and the creatures that also live there.

Whole-class work
● Examine real or online examples of posters used for decoration, advertising (theatre performance) and learning (bones of the body).
● Explain that you would like children to create Rainbow Fish posters. These could fall into any of the categories above, for example, a decorative wall poster, an advertisement for the book or a factual poster about rainbow fish.

Group work
● Divide into six same-ability groups, with two creating decorative posters, two advertising the book, and two presenting facts about rainbow fish. Link the type of poster with the group's overall learning level.
● Ask less confident learners to create a decorative poster. Help them to write a lively sentence along the top.
● Invite two groups to write and sequence sentences for the poster along the lines of a book blurb.
● Challenge more confident learners to research real rainbow fish and create a factual poster with well-sequenced information.
● Encourage re-reading of sentences to check sense.

Review
● Invite groups to show their posters, read the accompanying sentences and discuss content with the class. Praise clear reading.

4: Informative posters

Introduction
● Recall the lessons on coral reefs and the creatures who inhabit them.
● Explain that pairs of children are going to create informative posters about the two creatures they investigated in lesson 2.

Whole-class work
● Discuss the informative rainbow-fish posters created in the last lesson and invite children to talk about their content.
● Observe some images of educational posters, and talk about key features, such as drawings, photographs, labels and informative text.

Paired work
● In the same pairs as lesson 2 provide children with their previous written work. Show them the books and other resources they can refer to.
● Suggest that they each choose one of the creatures they researched, and design an informative poster about it.
● Ask children to discuss their ideas first before working alone.
● Once they have finished, ask them to re-read their sentences to their partners to check they make sense.

Differentiation
● Encourage less confident learners to create a poster by writing their sentence about a coral reef creature from lesson 2 alongside a picture of it.

Review
● Bring the pairs together to show their posters and read the sentences. Encourage discussion about content and presentation. Praise clear reading.

5: Coral reef discovery area

Introduction
● Remind children how they started the week by re-reading *The Rainbow Fish* before researching life in the coral reef where it is set.

Whole-class work
● Ask children about interesting facts they have learned.
● Recall previous occasions when children created interactive areas to showcase a week's work. Discuss how they served as a springboard for further research and imaginative writing.
● Suggest creating a coral reef discovery area. Discuss dramatic ways of making this eye-catching, for example, enclosing it with blue sparkling fabric.
● As before, identify tasks to be done, such as creation of labels, captions and signs for all wall and table displays. Divide tasks between groups of children.

Group work
● Ensure that each group undertakes a task, for example:
   ● Mount posters and write signs and captions for these ready for display.
   ● Arrange a table of labelled 'real' models and artefacts with children's underwater models and factual sentences alongside.
   ● Put some water into a tray and create a miniature coral reef with artefacts and models.
   ● Organise books and access to media resources on the CD-ROM.
● Ask groups to re-read written signs and captions to check they make sense.

Review
● Gather the class to discuss the area and what they have learned.

Curriculum objectives
● To begin to punctuate sentences using a capital letter and a full stop, question mark or exclamation mark.
● To join words and join sentences using *and*.
● To use '-ing', '-ed', '-er' and '-est' where no change is needed in the spelling of root words.
● To use the grammatical terminology in Appendix 2 in discussing their writing.

Resources
If possible, photographs taken on a recent class seaside visit; items used on seaside trip, such as rucksacks, buckets, spades, towels; memory joggers, such as shells, pebbles, toy boat, kite, flip-flops, ball; interactive activity 'Recount frame' on the CD-ROM; photocopiable page 172 'Plan a recount'

Week 6 lesson plans

This week, children consolidate the year's learning through seaside-related activities. They write recounts of seaside visits, revising sentence structure and using grammatical terminology in discussion. They revise taught phonemes and plurals as they enjoy sorting seaside items into hoops and writing sentences about them, and revise the prefix 'un-' by writing words with and without this prefix on seaside flags before using them in sentences. Reference to the seaside visit recount provides ideas for children's adventure stories, and anticipation of the coming holiday supports written outlines of what they plan to do. Focus is on writing the days of the week in order, using letter names to distinguish alternative GPCs and recognising common exception words.

1: A seaside visit

Introduction

● Recall writing a class walk recount (Summer 1). Explain that children are going to write a seaside visit recount, ideally of an actual visit taken by the class or children's families. If there are any children who have never been to the seaside, dramatise a class seaside visit. Ensure that each event in the dramatisation is clearly sequenced for children to remember.
● Remind children that a recount is an account of an event or experience that has taken place and should be written in the past tense.

Whole-class work

● Show the seaside visit photographs (or suitable pictures linked to such a visit, such as a bucket and spade, ice-cream). Ask children to display them in a timeline. Discuss which photograph came *first, next, last* and so on.
● Invite children to get their seaside items and go outside, or into the hall. Explain that they are going to relive the visit again.
● Ask questions using appropriate language to denote time sequence, such as *What was the first thing we did? I think we did something else before that!*
● Go through the visit together, miming events. Pause occasionally to hold up a memory jogger, such as the boat, to remind children about boats seen at sea and toy boats.
● Sit on towels to discuss the visit replay. Remind children that a recount is a true account and so they should not introduce imaginary events.
● Return indoors and display interactive activity 'Recount frame' on the CD-ROM, explaining that this will help them to plan their recount.
● Work through questions and ask children to add appropriate words in the boxes, for example: *When? – last Wednesday; Who? – the whole class/my family*.
● Revise important aspects of sentence writing, for example, punctuating with a capital letter and full stop, question mark or exclamation mark. Talk about using *and* to join words and sentences, but emphasise that this should not be a long list, such as, *We played and had an ice-cream and dug a hole and...*
● Write some examples using '-ed' to change words from present to past tense, for example, *We climbed up sand dunes*. Discuss other word endings, such as, *I ran fast, Sam ran faster but Anna was the fastest*.

Paired work

● Leave interactive activity 'Recount frame' displayed for reference and provide children with photocopiable page 172 'Plan a recount'.
● Remind individuals to discuss sentences with their partners before writing.
● Encourage children to use terms such as *sentence, question mark, capital letter* and *plural* when discussing their writing.

Review

● Invite the class to read their recounts. Use grammatical terminology when praising effective sentence structure.

Curriculum objectives
• To join words and join sentences using *and*.
• To spell words containing each of the 40+ phonemes already taught.
• To use letter names to distinguish between alternative spellings of the same sound.
• To use the spelling rule for adding '-s' or '-es' as the plural marker for nouns and the third-person singular marker for verbs.

Resources
Selection of seaside items (or photographs of items) that can be bought, found or seen, for example, bucket, shell and boat; 3 hoops; drawstring bag

2: Seaside sentences

Introduction
• Write three columns on separate sheets of paper: *Things you might buy at the beach*; *Things you might find on the seashore*; *Things you might see in the sea*.
• Write the captions on the board and read them together.
• Ask children to circle words containing the phoneme /igh/, and underline words containing the alternative graphemes 'ea' and 'ee'.

Whole-class work
• Put the captions inside separate hoops, and the seaside items in a bag.
• Invite children pull an item out of the bag and decide which hoop to put it in.
• Once the items are allocated, ask children to compose sentences using the captions and hoop items as prompts.
• Encourage children to use plural endings by asking them to make up a sentence about seeing, finding or buying more than one of the items.

Paired work
• Ask pairs to compose sentences orally and discuss spelling before writing. Emphasise the need to include some plurals.

> **Differentiation**
> • Encourage less confident learners to write down two items and join them with *and*.
> • Challenge more confident pairs to combine their sentences, for example, *On the beach I found a piece of seaweed and a shell, and at the shop I bought two ice-creams and a kite*.

Review
• Invite pairs to read their sentences to the class. Comment on effective spelling and use of *and* to join words and sentences.

Curriculum objectives
• To use the prefix 'un-'.
• To spell common exception words.
• To learn the grammar for Year 1 in Appendix 2.

Resources
Seaside flags made from white paper taped to lollipop sticks or plastic straws; sand tray; sand

3: Seaside flags

Introduction
• Recall using words with the 'un-' prefix to describe the Rainbow Fish.
• Revise common exception words (you could use starter activity 11 'Exception to the rule'). Write examples on the board, such as *the, said, friend*.

Whole-class work
• Write on the board adjectives children may have come across in the stories you have read together, such as *happy, kind, selfish, fair, lucky, usual, popular*.
• Invite children to add the prefix 'un-' to each word and write it alongside. Discuss how the meaning changes.
• Invite further suggestions of words that begin with 'un-'.
• Display the common exception words again.

Paired work
• Provide same-ability pairs with blank seaside flags and make two sandcastles in a tray and label *No prefix* and *Prefix*.
• Ask one child to recall a word from the list without the prefix and write it on a flag, while the other writes the same word on a flag with the prefix.
• Ask pairs to stick their flags into the correct castles.

Independent work
• Ask children to write sentences to include words with prefixes. Suggest they try to include some of the displayed common exception words.

Review
• Gather the class to check the castle flags and read their sentences.

Curriculum objectives
● To use a capital letter for names of people, places, the days of the week, and the personal pronoun *I*.
● To begin to punctuate sentences using a capital letter and full stop, question mark or exclamation mark.
● To leave spaces between words.
● To re-read what they have written to check that it makes sense.

Resources
Resources as for lesson 1; children's written recounts of a seaside visit

4: A seaside adventure

Introduction
● Recall lesson 1, when children wrote a recount about a seaside visit.
● Define the difference between a recount and a story. Talk about how authors often set their stories in places that are really familiar to them to make the writing of detail easier.
● Suggest that children write an adventure story set at the seaside, with some ideas based on their own experiences.

Whole-class work
● Revise how a good story has strong characters, an interesting setting, and sequenced events with a definite beginning, middle and end.
● Write these on the board for reference.
● Ask children to recall rules for punctuation, word spacing and use of capitals. Add their responses to the key points on the board.

Paired work
● Suggest that children discuss their initial ideas in pairs, and support one another in the creation of their plans.
● Ask them to write separate stories but to remain in pairs so that they can re-read their sentences to each other to check that they make sense.

> **Differentiation**
> ● Support less confident learners by asking them to tell you their story idea orally before helping them to compose three sequenced sentences.

Review
● Bring the class together to read their stories and comment on the most exciting adventure.

Curriculum objectives
● To spell the days of the week.
● To use a capital letter for names of people, places, the days of the week, and the personal pronoun *I*.
● To spell common exception words.

Resources
Photocopiable page 205 'Holiday calendar'

5: My ideal holiday week

Introduction
● As the school year ends, discuss what children plan to do in the summer.
● Suggest that they write about one holiday week, for example, enjoying a family holiday, days out or playing with friends.

Whole-class work
● Recall the weekly lunch menu that children wrote (week 2).
● Display photocopiable page 205 'Holiday calendar' and explain that you would like children to write a sentence each day about something they would like to do. Explain where to write the days and where to write their sentences.
● Revise spelling of common exception words children might use, such as *like, house, friend, our, there, come, have*.
● Explain that the week will take place in the future and so children should write about where they *will go*, rather than where they *are going* or *have been*.
● Suggest making notes before writing the final holiday outline.

Paired work
● Ask children to work in pairs so that they can re-read their sentences to each other before writing them on the prepared page.

Review
● Bring the class together to share their ideal holiday weeks. Praise good spelling attempts.

Curriculum objectives
● To begin to punctuate sentences using a capital letter and a full stop, question mark or exclamation mark.
● To write from memory simple sentences dictated by the teacher that include words using the GPCs and common exception words taught so far.

Resources
Three suitable sentences for dictation (include a statement, a question and a sentence requiring an exclamation mark; ensure there are opportunities to write capitals other than to start the sentence, for example, names of people, places and days of the week)

Grammar and punctuation: Punctuate the sentences

Revise

● Recall previous lessons involving writing sentences dictated by the teacher. Discuss things to remember about punctuation and spelling.
● Invite examples of sentences that end in a question mark and write one on the board. Talk about when an exclamation mark is usually used, for example, to highlight a strong statement or something exciting. Invite suggestions and write down an example of this.
● Revise when capital letters are needed, for example, to start sentences, for names, places and days of the week, and the personal pronoun *I*.

Assess

● Ask children to write their names at the top of a sheet of paper and number the sentences as they write them.
● Read your first sentence clearly and slowly and ask children to write it down. Repeat with the remaining sentences.

Further practice

● Differentiate by simplifying or extending sentences and text length according to the reading levels of those involved.
● Challenge very confident learners to write a short poem from memory to demonstrate their understanding of taught punctuation marks and application of spelling rules.

Curriculum objectives
● To respond speedily with the correct sound for all 40+ phonemes, including, where applicable, alternative sounds for graphemes.
● To read accurately by blending sounds in unfamiliar words containing GPCs that have been taught.
● To use letter names to distinguish between alternative spellings of the same sound.

Resources
Photocopiable page 206 'Compound words'; individual whiteboards

Spelling: Join together

Revise

● Recall previous activities involving reading longer words by splitting them into shorter ones, for example, *seashore, lighthouse.*
● Use starter activity 5 'Join together' and play the game.
● After playing, ask some of the pairs to hold their words up separately and 'sound talk' through each one. Write the words on the board and use letter names to describe the phonemes. Compare alternative graphemes, for example, *board, shore.* Link the two words by holding them next to each other and 'sound talk' the new word.
● Display photocopiable page 206 'Compound words' and read the instructions.

Assess

● Provide children with the photocopiable sheet and ask them to cut out the words.
● Allow time for them to pair the words, and observe strategies they employ to read them. Note individual difficulties children have.
● Once their words are complete, suggest that they write them on individual whiteboards.
● Bring the children together so that individuals can read their words to the class.

Further practice

● Provide less confident learners with a selection of words to link by association, *hot dog, rock pool, sun hat,* rather than link to form a new word.
● Challenge more confident learners to read more complex compound words, such as, *anywhere* and *briefcase,* focusing on correct spelling of phonemes.
● Use starter activity 10 'Join us together'.

Curriculum objectives

● To apply phonic knowledge and skills as the route to decode words.
● To read words containing taught GPCs and '-s', '-es', '-ing', '-ed', '-er' and '-est' endings.
● To read common exception words.
● To check that the text makes sense to them as they read and correct inaccurate reading.
● To explain clearly their understanding of what is read to them.

Resources

Photocopiable page 'Extract from *The Troll*' from the CD-ROM; differentiated text chosen by teacher

Reading: Expressive reading

Revise

● Recall stories you have read together involving the theme of water, such as *The Lighthouse Keeper's Lunch* and *The Rainbow Fish*. Discuss key features children enjoyed as they read aloud, for example, modifying voices to suit characters and expressing dramatic words by altering the volume of their voices.
● Choose a suitable page from a favourite book associated with water, such as *The Snail and the Whale* by Julia Donaldson, making sure that it contains an element of speech with questions, exclamation marks and other features (such as large letters designed for effect). A good example from *The Snail and the Whale* is the page where the whale lies beached in a bay.
● Display this on the whiteboard and read it to the children with no variation in your voice. Say to them: *Do you think that I read that with enough expression? Do you think that is how the author intended it to be read?*
● Ask children for clues in the text to indicate how words should be read, for example, when asking a question, using an exclamation mark or reading a highlighted word more loudly.
● Repeat your reading, this time with lots of expression and variation in tone. Invite children to comment on what they noticed about your reading.
● Before asking children to read a passage themselves, spend time revising their phonic knowledge and skills, for example, identifying familiar GPCs, including those with alternative sounds for graphemes, breaking longer words down into separate words, and identifying exception words and plurals. Invite children to find examples of words with '-est', '-ing', and '-er' endings, and plurals ending in '-s' or '-es'. Circle these words and read them aloud.
● Discuss how sentences are punctuated, pointing out the use of full stops and capital letters, question marks and exclamation marks. Emphasise that exploring punctuation improves their reading ability and their understanding of how to read words aloud and interpret them. Include examples of any words written in capitals, different fonts or italics
● Explain that children are going to read a passage from a Julia Donaldson book involving a troll and some pirates and then practise reading this to a partner before reading to a group.
● Remind them to use the approaches they have just worked on as a class to analyse and read the displayed text effectively.

Assess

● Provide each child with photocopiable page 'Extract from *The Troll*' from the CD-ROM to read. Invite the children to read the passage to a partner when they feel ready and then listen while their partner reads it to them.
● Ask them to discuss how to read dramatic words, for example, those written in large bold letters with exclamation marks.
● Observe children as they work, and be ready to support with helpful hints about how to apply their phonic knowledge and skills to decode words they are struggling with. Make note of their successes and difficulties.

Further practice

● Include all children in the discussion and reading of your chosen passage from a Julia Donaldson book, supporting and encouraging their attempts to break down words, identify endings and look for punctuation clues. However, provide any children who are struggling with the reading level of this page with an alternative passage to read aloud from a popular book that presents children with simplified sentences at their own reading level.
● Extend the activity to challenge children's reading skills by asking them to choose one of their favourite passages from a book at their current reading level choices to read to the class. Invite them to choose partners of similar ability to read their chosen passage to initially so that they can correct any inaccuracies and discuss effective ways to read it expressively to the class.

Writing: An underwater adventure

Revise
● Recall stories explored throughout the half-term, and contrast the coastal and coral reef settings.
● Explain that children are going to write stories about an underwater adventure. This could be in a faraway ocean, as in *The Snail and the Whale* or *The Rainbow Fish,* or in a local pond or river.
● Recall how a story follows a sequence of beginning, middle and end.
● Revise work on using connecting words and phrases, such as *At last, Then, After that* to help stories, and events within them, to flow.
● Ask children to consider story language explored previously and call out suitable opening sentences, for example: *Once upon a time, Long, long ago, There was once a ....* Talk about possible story endings.
● Recall sentence writing and remind children about word spaces and correct punctuation. Recall the use of appropriate endings to denote past tense.
● Write the title *An underwater adventure* on the board and invite children to speculate about what this adventure might involve. Talk about the meaning of *adventure*, and discuss how it usually involves excitement and something unknown. With this in mind, consider possible characters that might either live underwater or visit this environment to enter into a great adventure.
● Consider what the main character might look like. Perhaps the children see themselves in this role with imaginary new powers and talents? Alternatively the main character could be purely fantasy, an underwater creation that has never been heard of. Encourage them to be adventurous, keeping in mind any images they have seen of huge jellyfish and menacing deep sea creatures, perhaps an evil octopus with poisonous tentacles waving to and fro, or a fish that can fly with 'wingfins'?
● Consider the story direction, for example, the main character might dive under the water to be carried off on the back of an enormous starfish. Perhaps they possess a super power that might dictate possible events, for example, living underwater and saving rare species from extinction. Ask children to consider whether there will be a problem to solve, and whether the ending will be happy or thought-provoking.
● Divide into groups so that children can discuss their story ideas. Encourage them to decide on the appearance of main characters and draw pictures of them. Suggest they make notes of interesting suggestions to share.
● Write a list on the board, with the children's help, to remind them of things to include in their story, for example, a title, at least three sentences (beginning, middle and end), capital letters, full stops, word spaces, question marks and exclamation marks, as well as possible dialogue.

Assess
● Provide resources and ask children to write an underwater adventure that has at least three sentences representing the beginning, middle and end.
● Invite children to read their finished stories to partners and discuss features, such as imaginative language, strong sequence and sentence structure.
● Choose stories at random to discuss with the class. Give praise for correct sentence punctuation, and appropriate spelling of word endings and exception words. Encourage children to include any missing aspects next time.

Further practice
● Support those who have difficulty by encouraging them to create a picture of their underwater setting and main character. Ask them to make up voices for the characters and tell you the story. Help the children to compose and write three simple sentences as the story emerges. Use correct terminology relating to sentence structure as you draw attention to their completed writing.
● Challenge more confident learners to write complex stories set in a 'water' setting of their choice, such as a voyage to capture a fearsome pirate ship.

New words

■ Select two words from the lists and make up a sentence for each word.

Adjectives	Meaning
accomplished	Someone who has a talent or is very skilled.
brazen	Someone who does not care what others think.
industrious	Someone who works really hard.
ingenious	Someone who is very intelligent or clever.
jubilant	Someone who is very pleased and full of joy.
scrumptious	Something that tastes really good.

Verbs	Meaning
baffle	To confuse someone.
concoct	To mix ingredients together.
console	To comfort someone.
devour	To eat something greedily.
muse	To think silently about something.
scavenge	To look through rubbish for food.
survey	To look carefully at someone or something.
tend	To look after something or someone.

I can write sentences using new words.

How did you do?

Name: _____   Date: _____

Tell the story

- Read the sentences.
- Write a sentence of your own in the empty box to say what you think happened on Sunday.
- Cut the sentences out and put them in the correct order to tell the story.

✂ - - - - - -

Mrs Grinling put some mustard sandwiches in the basket.
Three seagulls took Mr Grinling's lunch for the first time.
Hamish was put in the basket to guard the lunch.
The seagulls ate a fisherman's lunch instead.
Mrs Grinling put the mustard mixture in the sandwiches again.
Mrs Grinling tied a napkin to the basket to baffle the seagulls.

Name: _____   Date: _____

Mr Grinling's diary

- Write the days of the week in order in the small boxes.
- Write Mr Grinling's words about what was in his basket each day.
- Use the words below to help you.

mixed seafood salad	Hamish	drinks
sausages and crisps	assorted fruit	mustard sandwiches
scrumptious lunch	cold chicken garni	napkin
peach surprise	lighthouse sandwich	iced sea biscuits

The day	What was in the basket?

I can write the days of the week in order.

How did you do?

PHOTOCOPIABLE    SCHOLASTIC
www.scholastic.co.uk

A lighthouse sandwich recipe

■ Write the name of each ingredient in a box and draw a picture in the box beside it.

Ingredient	Picture	Ingredient	Picture

■ Write instructions to make your lighthouse sandwich.
■ Number your sentences.

_____

_____

_____

I can write and number sentences in order.

How did you do?

Name: _____ Date: _____

Revising punctuation

■ Read each sentence. Write the sentence on the lines below, adding the correct punctuation and capital letters.

get away from me

_____

_____

_____

the rainbow fish did not want to give away one of his scales

_____

_____

_____

how could I ever be happy without my scales

_____

_____

_____

it was not long before the rainbow fish was surrounded by other fish

_____

_____

_____

I can write sentences with the correct punctuation, including question marks and exclamation marks.
How did you do?

204 ■ 100 ENGLISH LESSONS   PHOTOCOPIABLE   SCHOLASTIC www.scholastic.co.uk

Holiday calendar

- Write the days of the week in the boxes on the left.
- Write a sentence for each day about what you would like to do.

Day	What I would like to do

I can write sentences about what I would
like to do on holiday.

How did you do?

Compound words

■ Cut out the words. Link pairs of words to make longer words.

✂

farm	board
ball	cake
yard	bow
bed	shore
sun	foot
sea	butter
pan	room
rain	fly
skate	shine

Name: _____   Date: _____

Puddle Play

Puddle Play

The rain comes down

And under my feet

Are trees and clouds

All over the street

I splash through the clouds

And I climb through the trees

I feel like a giant

With boots to my knees.

Anonymous